TRULY BLESSED

TRULY
BLESSED

TEDDY
PENDERGRASS

and Patricia Romanowski

G. P. PUTNAM'S SONS
New York

G. P. Putnam's Sons
Publishers Since 1838
a member of
Penguin Putnam Inc.
375 Hudson Street
New York, NY 10014

"Truly Blessed" by Gabriel Hardeman and Teddy Pendergrass,
Copyright © 1990 Ted-On-Music/Gabeson Music, BMI.
Used by permission.

"The Love I Lost" by Kenny Gamble and Leon Huff, Copyright © 1973
Warner-Tamarlane Publishing Co.

"Speedoo" by Esther Navarro, Copyright © 1955 Windswept Pacific Songs.

"Vacancy: In Search of the New Pendergrass," Dennis Hunt,
Philadelphia Inquirer, August 17, 1982.

"Teddy Loves Teddy," David Hirshey, *Sunday News* magazine, June 24, 1979.

Frontispiece photo copyright Ebet Roberts, 1998.

Library of Congress Cataloging-in-Publication Data

Pendergrass, Teddy.
Truly blessed / by Teddy Pendergrass and Patricia Romanowski.
p.   cm.
ISBN 0-399-14420-X
1. Pendergrass, Teddy.   2. Singers—United States—Biography.
3. Soul musicians—United States—Biography.   I. Romanowski, Patricia.
II. Title.
ML420.P44A3   1998   98-28962 CIP MN
782.42164'092—dc21
[B]

Printed in the United States of America
1   3   5   7   9   10   8   6   4   2

This book is printed on acid-free paper. ∞

BOOK DESIGN BY JENNIFER ANN DADDIO

To my loving, devoted mother, Mrs. Ida G. Pendergrass.
Her prayer to God gave me life. Her unwavering faith will always
be my guiding star, and her unconditional love my shelter.
She has always lived, and will always live, in my heart.

ACKNOWLEDGMENTS

Writing this book set me on a journey through my life, a journey I never thought I would take. There were moments of pure joy and moments of pain. I went everywhere I expected to go and some other places I didn't know existed. It wasn't easy, but in the end, it was all worth it. I learned that I could do what I've always said I'd never do, and that's to open up my life to the world. There are many people who helped me on my way.

First, to all my fans throughout the world, who have supported me from the beginning and made this story possible. I am eternally grateful.

My deepest appreciation to my collaborator, Patty Romanowski. She was the driving force who helped me find the courage to open up and express myself honestly and truthfully. Her sweet spirit, her understanding, and her guidance brought me to the place where my story could be told.

For their support and guidance, I wish to thank my agents Jonny Podell and Suzanne Gluck. Phyllis Grann and the team at Putnam stood out among publishers, because in the story I wanted to tell, they saw the heart of it, not just the headlines. My editor, David Highfill, gave us the benefit of his experience, enthusiasm, and insight. Attorney Jessica R. Friedman worked tirelessly on the finer points of the final draft. From the moment I met her, Marilyn Ducksworth impressed me as a woman of class and finesse, not to mention having an unparalleled knowledge of publishing. I didn't just find a great publicist, I made a new friend.

Closer to home, I am grateful to all of my family, friends, and associates, whose love and support make my life better in more ways than they could imagine. I am proud to say that there are more of them than I can acknowledge by name here. But you know who you are, and I thank you every day from the bottom of my heart.

Several special people make it possible for me to accomplish things in my daily life that I otherwise could not. Henry Evans is my lifelong friend on whom I can always depend. You and me, buddy, you and me. In my business life, Caryle Blackwell is the glue that holds it all together. I thank her for helping me make sense of my life and for putting up with me.

I'd also like to thank those people whose medical expertise and care allow me to live life to the fullest: my always dependable nursing agency and the nurses who provide the care I could not function without; the many doctors who over the years have met the challenges so that I could keep meeting the challenges. And, finally, thank you, Claudia.

I thank my managers Shep Gordon, Daniel Markus, and Ed Gerrard for coming into my life and staying there. They never gave up on me, and they stood by me when others would have walked away. They have helped me reach my goals, and, most important, they have believed in me.

To my children, Tisha, LaDonna, and Teddy. I love you all very, very much. You all should know just how very much you mean to me. Joyce, Keya: I love you, too. And, of course, my beautiful grandchildren.

And a very special thank-you to Karen, for so many things. Thank you so very, very much for coming into my life and for giving me your dedication and your unselfish and unconditional love, which I will never, ever forget. I thank you from the bottom of my heart.

And for the Spirit that has been with me from birth and will be with me forever, I give praise to Jesus Christ, the Son of God.

—TEDDY

TRULY BLESSED

INTRODUCTION

❧

Outside my hotel suite window, New York City's lights glimmered like diamonds. Across the street, headlights cut through the shadows of Central Park and scattered into the night. Somewhere to the southwest—beyond the park and Broadway, across the Hudson River—stood my old North Philadelphia neighborhood, with its run-down row houses and treeless streets, not so far in physical distance, yet a world away.

It was March of 1980. Don't ask me the exact date; I never kept a diary. I was in town alone for my thirtieth-birthday party. Turning thirty is, I'd heard, one of those milestones you approach with trep-idation, but it didn't bother me, because at that moment, my life was great. I had no regrets, and I never looked back. What was the point? I welcomed the future, and I believed in myself. And how could I not? I don't mean to brag, but my star just seemed to be glowing brighter all the time. Just ten years earlier, with a singing group called the Blue Notes, I was crooning "Raindrops Keep Fallin' on My Head" to a Miami hotel lounge full of blue-haired ladies, then driv-ing all night to open in a smoky little joint where the audience con-sisted of pimps and prostitutes who demanded a repertoire a lot funkier. No "Raindrops" for them.

Five years before, I left that group for a solo career, and less than two years later my debut album, *Teddy Pendergrass,* went platinum. Now, in 1980, gold and platinum discs hung inside my thirty-four-room mansion, and a crowd of friends, record company executives, assorted VIPs, and other guests were waiting at an exclusive disco to wish me a happy birthday.

Some folks would have been struck by these contrasts, used the occasion to do a few minutes' philosophizing, but not me. At least not then. It would be years before I had any perspective on this time of my life. In March 1980 I was too busy living it to stop and ponder what it meant. I probably thought I'd have plenty of time for that later, if I even thought about it at all. My career was taking off like a rocket, cruising beyond the bonds of gravity, and I was just enjoying the ride.

In preparation for this fabulous party I'd reserved the biggest suite the Pierre Hotel had available. I'd stocked it with the finest drink, the best cocaine, and some good, good friends. I'd hired a classic mid-1960s white Rolls-Royce for the ride to Magique, the hot new disco. Between the smooth, warm burn of Martel Cordon Bleu and the cool buzz of cocaine, I was on my way.

I sat back on the soft leather seat as the Rolls cruised through the busy streets. From a few blocks away, I could see the crowds outside the club lining up, hundreds, maybe even a thousand people trying to get past the bouncers and the velvet ropes. Many of them turned when my car came into view, and through the tinted glass I could see the same curious, smiling, expectant faces that I saw almost every-where I went. Fans, mostly women, craned to catch a glimpse when the chauffeur opened my door. A few cameras flashed, arms reached out toward me, women called out, *"Teddy! Teddy! Teddy Bear! Teddy!"*

I smiled to myself. This had become a familiar scene. I ducked in-side, where even amid the pulsating disco music, I could hear cries of "Happy birthday, Teddy!" from those still out on the sidewalk. In-side, people surged toward me, offering smiles, handshakes, kisses, congratulations. Pleasantly adrift in this ocean of goodwill, I smiled back, nodded, said thank you as men in expensive suits heartily patted me on the back, and fashionably dressed women, with gleaming eyes and glossy lips, slid their smooth arms around mine, leaned near, maybe whispered, maybe kissed. Some were cool, some were eager, all were beautiful. This too was familiar but not routine and, I should add, never, ever boring.

I'd come to know lots of other stars. I knew some who were obsessed with the charts and some who actually read and worried about their reviews. I never understood why, because to my mind, my career was about something much deeper. The money, the hits, the women fans—those just showed me that hard work, perseverance, instinct, and guts had paid off. Someone once asked me if I had been "surprised" by success, and I'd had to answer, in all honesty, no. Don't get me wrong: It's not that I thought I was so great, but I knew how hard I'd worked to get where I was and how much harder I would work to make sure I stayed there. From picking cotton in the dusty South Carolina fields to headlining on Carnegie Hall's hallowed stage, I never stopped trying to improve myself, to do whatever I did better. And the truth was, I hadn't done it entirely alone. Fittingly, one of the gifts I received that night was a beautiful oil portrait of my mother, Ida Pendergrass. So much of what I had achieved was due to her. She raised me to be independent, confident, fearless.

I grew to believe the only reason to conquer one peak was to get a better view of the next one. I embraced every challenge, exploited every opportunity to its fullest. The funny thing is, I don't remember ever really thinking about it back then. Sometimes it's hard to separate what I knew about myself then and what I've come to see looking back. The truth is, while I savored those moments, I also took them for granted. While my brain was telling me that nothing lasts forever, my heart was wondering, Why the hell not?

My comanagers and good friends Shep Gordon and Daniel Markus had thrown a fabulous party. After marveling at the towering birthday cake, being toasted by a contingent of record company executives, and enjoying the troupe of sexy, exotic belly dancers, I made my way through the crowd and the throbbing music to a private lounge upstairs, where I danced with a few beautiful women, had a few more drinks. Then I noticed a gorgeous woman sitting alone. She was tall, with great legs—a knockout—and I remember thinking maybe I wouldn't be going back to the hotel alone. I sat down beside her, and we had a great conversation. She stepped away for a moment, and a man I'd never met before tapped me on the shoulder and said, "You need to know something."

"Yeah?"

"If you take that lady home, you're going to get a big surprise."

At first I couldn't believe my ears—or my eyes—but I took his advice. I discreetly turned my attention elsewhere.

Like so many people then, I did cocaine, but judiciously. When I was working, I never did it until after the show, and I did it only to relax and have a good time. The powdery white lines and little fourteen-karat gold spoons were the chic, glamorous symbols of a new kind of good life. For me, cocaine and cognac were the perfect high. I was up but mellow, relaxed but ready for whatever the night might bring. But something about this night was different. Maybe I overdid it; maybe I was just tired. By 1:00 A.M. the cognac, champagne, and cocaine had worked their wicked spell. I was too damn high to party anymore that night, which I realized while I still had the good sense to return to the Pierre. By 2:00 in the morning, while my guests were laughing and dancing the night away, I was back in my dark, quiet suite, facedown, alone in a big plush bed, dead asleep.

That was my wake-up call, the culmination of many changes in my life. I woke up the next day feeling silly and embarrassed about having to leave my own party. After all, I was a grown man with three children. I had so much going for me, and it bothered me to feel out of control. It was time to finish growing up, I resolved, to slow down.

I arranged my tour schedules with more time between dates and played one show a night instead of two. I became more directly involved in making my records, coproducing tracks on my next album. I spent more time with my children and the people in my life who mattered most to me, including my girlfriend, Karen. Now that the novelty of fame had begun to wear off, I could finally begin to enjoy my blessings. I never stopped looking ahead, but I did stop glancing over my shoulder. I'd made it. Whatever I had was mine; wherever I was, I belonged. I couldn't imagine that anything could change that.

Nearly two years to the day after my thirtieth birthday, I came to another crossroads, but one not of my choosing. It was March 18, 1982, and I was back home in Gladwyne, an affluent Philadelphia suburb, relaxing, gearing up for a magazine photo shoot, a lucrative beer commercial, and an HBO special to be broadcast live from Resorts International in Atlantic City. I arranged to meet my friend Yvette at her house and take her to the Elan, an exclusive downtown Philadelphia club I frequented. We were just friends, and we passed a few pleasant hours listening to music, sipping a little champagne, dancing, and chatting with some other regulars. While I didn't know most of the other patrons well, I certainly knew them by sight, and we exchanged cordial greetings and small talk.

An attractive woman approached our table and reminded me that we had met before, at the Fantasy Lounge, a bar and soul food restaurant across Broad Street from the offices of my record label, Philadelphia International. Everyone in town knew the Fantasy Lounge was a popular hangout with all the PIR artists—including the O'Jays, the Intruders, and the musicians of MFSB (Mother, Father, Sister, Brother), to name just a few—studio musicians, songwriters, and producers. I'd probably met hundreds of people at the Fantasy Lounge, and I did vaguely recall meeting this woman. I invited her to sit with us, and we passed the time in lighthearted conversation and laughs—just having a great time.

It was getting late, and Yvette reminded me that she had to get up early for work the next day. It seemed rude to leave so abruptly, so I said to the other woman, "Come on, you can ride with us. I promise I'll bring you back here after I drop off Yvette."

"All right," she replied. A few minutes later, the three of us were driving through Philadelphia in my 1980 green Rolls-Royce Silver Spirit, laughing and talking about nothing in particular.

We had said good night to Yvette at her house and were heading back to downtown Philadelphia along Lincoln Drive, a notoriously winding road that runs almost the length of the city. I'd driven it a hundred times before and knew well its dangerous twists and turns.

As we were approaching the curve after crossing Wissahickon Avenue, something happened. I braked to slow the car, but it didn't respond. I instinctively gripped the wheel and hit the brake again. Nothing. Then I heard a loud crash as we hit the metal guardrail. After that, I remember my head hitting the ceiling of the car, then a terrifying blur before the car came to a sudden, violent stop. (Only much later did I learn that after striking the guardrail, the car crossed the oncoming northbound lanes, and then sideswiped one tree before plowing into a second.)

I was still sitting in the driver's seat, and my head was bent down in an odd position. I didn't know exactly what had happened, where I was, where the car was, or how it had stopped. When I tried to move, nothing happened, and I was instantly overwhelmed by the wrenching fear that something was terribly wrong. When I tried to speak, my voice was so soft it was barely audible. No matter how hard I tried to speak louder, I simply couldn't. The early-spring night was cool and strangely quiet. I could hear my heart pounding in my chest. This is all I can remember and all there is to say about the moment my life changed forever.

Slipping in and out of consciousness, I heard someone say, "Don't worry, Teddy, we'll get you out."

I don't recall whether I answered. And then I closed my eyes.

ONE

❧

"Teddy!"

I felt an insistent *tap-tap-tap* on my head and opened my eyes. My chin was still resting in my hand.

"Teddy!" In a whisper so soft that no one else in the tiny church heard but me, my mother, Ida Pendergrass, let me know she'd better not catch me dozing off in church again.

I straightened up in the bench and took in the familiar sights and sounds of my second home, the Glad Tidings Tabernacle Church. The congregants' joyous voices rose and fell like waves against a mighty rock as they testified to the faith that bound them to this little church and lifted them above the toil and trouble of their daily lives.

I awoke during the testimony service. Church members were raising their hands, and when acknowledged by the pastor, they each took their turn to stand up to testify: "Praise the Lord, giving honor to God, to Reverend Drayton, all the saints of the church. I just want to say that God is good. And I want to express how God has helped me . . ."

A church member was telling everyone how, through prayer and faith, the Lord had affected her life. Every tribute to the Lord was fresh and inspiring, though the details were familiar. You or someone you knew had been miraculously healed or cured, a vexing problem had been solved, a pressing need met. You might implore the rest of the church to join you in praying to help someone in desperate need. Or you might simply testify to the grace of God and describe how believing in Him and living according to the Scriptures could light your way. Testifying proved the living reality of faith time and again. It banished doubts and renewed our spirits. The power of the Lord to work miracles in this world was beyond question.

Outside the church's double wooden doors lay another world of concrete and brick, the "real" world, a cold one: North Philadelphia, Twenty-seventh and Dauphin, a ghetto by anyone's description and a hard place for a black woman to be raising an only son. Back then, it seemed as if my whole world revolved around that two-story building, where my mother and I lived in one of two apartments above the church. Fiercely protective, she always kept me well within her sight, so that when I wasn't *in* the church, you'd usually find me sitting on its front steps or playing with other kids on the sidewalk.

Prayer is powerful, and I'm living proof of that. I've been truly blessed in so many ways, but being born to my mother was the first, and greatest, blessing of my life, for I was a very loved and wanted child. Ida Geraldine Epps, and my father, Jesse Pendergrass, met and married in South Carolina in 1936 but separated about five years later. Sadly, during that time, my mother suffered six miscarriages—all sons. When my parents reconciled in 1947, my mother began to pray with all her heart, asking the Lord to grant her just one thing: a healthy child.

"I heard people say that children keep families together, and I believed that," she says. She promised to serve the Lord for the rest of her life if only He would send her a baby. "I got tired of waiting and I really cried out to the Lord," my mother recalls. "When Teddy was conceived, the spirit of God let me know that he was not going to miscarry. The Spirit said to me, He's going to be strong, he's going to be wonderful, and he's going to be great in everything he does. So

I told people that while everybody's child is a gift from God, Teddy was an extra-special gift." From then on, my mother has always been in my corner, rock solid, never wavering.

My name, Theodore, does mean "gift from God," though my mother didn't know that when she named me. In fact, she had already picked names: Bernard for a boy, Joyce Jeanette for a girl. She was talking on the telephone to my godmother, whom we called Aunt Bea, and had just finished telling her the name she'd chosen for a son when, she says, "the Spirit just took me out of myself. Bea was still talking to me, but I wasn't aware of it. Some people might say it was like a trance state, but it was more like a vision. And He gave me my baby's name. I heard it in the Spirit. Suddenly I was 'back' and my friend was saying, 'Ida, where were you? I was talking to you and you weren't saying nothing.' And I said, 'I couldn't say anything. God took me out in the Spirit and gave me a name: Theodore DeReese.' " When I was born, on March 26, 1950, at Philadelphia's Thomas Jefferson Hospital, the name became mine. My mother kept her promise to God and has served Him every day since.

My mother's immense joy over my birth was tempered by the fact that only a month before, my father had left the marriage, this time for good. For reasons I've never cared to know, he chose not to be part of my life. I never knew my father, although during most of my childhood he lived no more than a trolley ride away.

Years later I learned that my father was one of nine children born to Mackey and Isabelle Pendergrass, sharecroppers who lived in tiny Cades, South Carolina. Out of his eight siblings—brothers Felix, Tresvent, Wallace, and Jeff; sisters Julianne, Lizzie, Martha, and Mary—I met only my aunts Lizzie and Mary when I was very young. Beyond that, I had no contact with my father's people.

My relationship with my mother's family, though, continues to be a source of love and support. My mother's parents, Clarence and Ida Claretha Epps, were sharecroppers in Kingstree, South Carolina. Although I never met my maternal grandparents, the little I learned about them late in my life went a long way in helping me understand my mother and myself. My great-grandfather, David Epps, was known around Kingstree for riding a large, blond palomino, carrying a pearl-handled pistol in his holster, and fearing no man—black or white. He learned to read, a rare and remarkable accomplishment for a black man in that time and place, and taught his son, my grandfather, Clarence. Like his father, Clarence was proud and strong. Even working out in the field, my grandfather always began the day in a clean, starched, and pressed white shirt and dungaree overalls. Because my grandfather could read, his neighbors who could not came from miles around with letters, newspapers, contracts, leases—anything that they needed to have read to them.

My grandfather thought the world of his children, and so when my grandmother passed, he refused to remarry because he feared another woman wouldn't treat his children right. Raising his children alone, my grandfather didn't discriminate between his sons and his daughters; he taught them all what they needed to know to make their way in the world. This explains why my mother and her sisters came to be so fiercely independent, strong, and proud at a time when women were expected to be anything but. Even though I never knew David or Clarence, I understand them.

I grew up secure in the love of my mother's siblings, my aunts (all of whom were affectionately known by family nicknames) Earlthia (Aunt Ting), Ila David (Aunt Dee), Eloise (Aunt Dumpy), and Clarissa Ruth Ann (also known as Aunt Ruth or Aunt Sinky), and my uncles James, Neveland, and Wilmot Leroy. To her family, my mother was known as Coochie. (Hmm, I wonder why.)

My mother and I were a family. Yes, I grew up fatherless, but as a child I never consciously missed what I'd never had. I wasn't one to sit and wonder, "What if," because the truth is, you really never know. From an early age, I recognized and appreciated what I did have: a strong, moral, loving, hardworking mother who provided for me as best she could and who cherished me and the extended family of aunts, uncles, and cousins who stood by us both.

When I was fourteen months old, Mom took me with her to Baltimore to visit my aunt Ting. From there, my aunt took me to South Carolina, to show me off to the rest of the family. Within a few days of leaving my mother, I developed a dangerously high fever and became severely dehydrated. Realizing how seriously ill I'd become, Aunt Ting whisked me back to my mother in Baltimore. Mom immediately rushed me to the hospital, where a doctor examined me, then shook his head solemnly and told her, "Mrs. Pendergrass, you can do the same thing that I do. Take him home, boil water, put a little salt in it, and have him drink that."

To this day, my mother still recalls holding me down and forcing me to drink, then praying over me all night long. Again I was saved. Only when she took me back to the doctor did he tell her, "You did the right thing when you brought him. I didn't want to tell you when you were here, but your baby was almost gone."

"You didn't have to tell me," my mother replied. "The spirit of God let me know that my baby was on his way out, but God didn't intend for him to go. He gave him to me through prayer, and through prayer He saved him and gave him back to me."

As far as I can recall, I felt like a regular kid growing up. Of course, to hear my mother tell it, I was exceptional in every way. (Isn't that what mothers are for?) I sat up in my high chair at three months, crawled at four months, and walked at seven months. When I was about two, Aunt Dee bestowed upon me the nickname "Teddy the Bear." By then I had already begun singing along to everything I heard, which in our home was gospel. I grew up on the Soul Stirrers with Sam Cooke, Professor Alex Bradford, Shirley Caesar, the Swan Silvertones, the Clara Ward Singers, James Cleveland, the Five Blind Boys, and of course Mahalia Jackson.

I grew up seeing my mother sing in church, and there are several very good singers on her side of the family. My aunt Persephone (or Sep, as we call her) is a truly wonderful singer. So my mother wasn't too surprised when she heard me singing "If I Could Write a Letter to Heaven," a song I'd learned from the radio when I was about three. What did strike my mother was how well I sang it, perfectly on key and with true emotion, as if I truly understood the words. As far back as I can remember, my mother always carried herself with a quiet, unassuming dignity, but she also has a warm, beautiful smile. And I remember her coming to me from the kitchen, where she was preparing our meal, and seeing that smile that told me I'd pleased her and she was proud of me.

My mother must have mentioned my singing in church, because one day the pastor asked if I would "render a selection"—come up and sing. As my mother and I approached the front of the church, someone brought up a small bench or stool for me to stand on so that everyone could see me. I remember my mother lifting me onto the bench, and then I started to sing. I expected her to sing with me, and when I realized I couldn't hear her voice, I stopped and implored, "*Sing,* Mother." And she began to sing. Or so I thought. Actually, she just moved her lips to make me *think* she was singing, but that made me feel secure enough to continue on my own. After I finished, the congregation erupted in enthusiastic applause. My mother told me that everyone was amazed to hear such a voice coming from a small boy. And I stood for a moment basking in the wonderful response. I don't consciously remember this, but my mother says that I was absolutely beaming, so somewhere inside I must have known what it meant. Mother lifted me back down, and we returned to our places.

Until I was old enough to attend preschool, my mother stayed home with me. Before I was born she had worked in various domestic jobs, most recently taking care of a white family's baby in their home. She did all that she could to raise me the way she believed was right, and was of the firm conviction that very young children are best raised by their mothers. At home she patiently taught me how to read, write, and do arithmetic. More important, though, she raised me to be polite and respectful. Except for the rare bout of rambunctiousness, I was always a very well mannered child.

My mother's staying home with me meant that she could work only side jobs here and there, nothing steady enough to support the two of us. Although proud and self-sufficient all of her life, my mother put my needs first, which meant that we lived my first few years on government assistance and received government-surplus food. Every couple of weeks my mother would stand in line at the recreation center at Twenty-fifth and Diamond and pick up our allotment of peanut butter, cheese, canned pork, Spam, rice, butter, flour, powdered milk, and other essentials. We didn't take vacations, nor did I have a lot of toys. But I do recall some great outings with my mother. There was a trip to the zoo, where the sight of a peacock unfurling his tail feathers scared me to death (I thought those black spots were eyes!). Mom also took me ice-skating, and I got to be pretty good. I remember once trying to impress a pretty girl with some fancy moves I hadn't quite mastered. There I was, gliding along, when suddenly my feet flew out from under me, and my head hit the ice with a *crack!* It hurt like hell, but I refused to cry because she was watching me.

Even though I was an only child, I never felt lonely. My first real friend was my cat Tippy. I remember the cat's beautiful patchwork coat of tan, black, white, and orange. When I was four, Tippy and I were standing outside on the narrow wooden back porch. The sky suddenly grew dark, and the wind came up so strong that it seemed as if everything that wasn't tied down was blowing away. Of course, my mother knew the whole area was bracing for Hurricane Hazel, so she called, "It's getting stormy out there. You better come in,

Teddy!" I remember opening the screen door and stepping inside and then suddenly hearing a loud *whoosh* followed by a crash as the wind tore down the porch.

"Tippy!" I cried out. But my little cat was gone and I never saw him again. For the first time in my life I really mourned something I loved.

Through it all, though, I never felt that we were poor. Our small, one-bedroom apartment was always spotless; in fact, my mother had me up on a wooden platform washing dishes when I could barely reach into the sink, and on my knees scrubbing the baseboards regularly. I was part of whatever my mother did, and I remember standing on a chair and watching her make her fabulous buttermilk biscuits—which no one in this world makes better. If you ask me, there's not a cookie or a cake that's as good as Mom's biscuits, and whenever I saw her take out the flour, the buttermilk, and whatever else she needed (hey, I'm not giving away this recipe!), my mouth would start to water. In our home, this was—and still is—a special occasion.

In my mother's hands, these biscuits are works of art, and you could taste the love and care she put into them. Young as I was, I could see in my mother's expression that she was doing something she knew she was the best at. I still love watching her make them, because there's a rhythm to every step—the measuring (all done by feel, of course), the mixing, the kneading. Once she kneads the dough to the consistency of pizza dough, she shapes it into one big loaf-shaped mound, squeezes a piece off the top, rolls it into a ball between her palms, then flattens it between her hands into a perfect circle. She gently sets it just so in the pan, then does it again, until rows of identical biscuits fill the pan.

The rich aroma of baking biscuits fills the whole house, and to this day, we still gather around in the kitchen to wait for Mom to pronounce them done. Right out of the oven, they are so smooth and moist, I can eat a whole pan without even a sip of milk. They are the bomb. When I was a kid, I didn't have to share them the way I do now. In fact, Mom still sends out baskets of buttermilk biscuits to my daughters and other special people.

She also made sure we were both smartly dressed, our clothes clean, pressed, and most important, in style. Mom took a lot of pride in my appearance, and in my baby and toddler years she changed my outfit at least twice a day. Little jackets, bow ties, Bermuda short sets—I was clean and sharp, even then. We couldn't afford to shop in the big department stores like Gimbel's, and it's a testament to my mother's ingenuity that she made the most of whatever she could spend. I'll never forget wearing brogans, these clunky, black, thick-soled, ankle-high lace-up boots with huge steel taps on the heels and toes. You didn't wear brogans unless you had to, and I got teased by other kids sometimes. I never took it to heart, though. I knew that those shoes, ugly as they were, sure beat the shoes I'd had before, the ones that wore through the sole so I had to put cardboard inside them to keep my feet dry. Those ugly old brogans saved my mother hours of wages simply by lasting so long, and I was glad to have them.

A couple times a year, a chubby, partially bald white gentleman named Izzy who sold clothes would come to our house to take Mom's order and then let her lay the clothes away and pay them off over time. (I'm not sure this was a courtesy he offered to everyone; I suspect he liked my mom.) Today this probably sounds like an exclusive service, but these were the days when the milkman still delivered to your doorstep, doctors still made house calls, and the insurance man came by to pick up the premiums. No matter where they came from or what they cost, our clothes always hung as though they'd been custom-made, and they looked great. "Just because you've only got a dollar in your pocket doesn't mean you can't look like a million bucks," Mother would say. There's no doubt about it: I inherited Mom's great sense of style. Great-looking clothes have always been one of my passions.

I wouldn't say we always had the best, but we always had the best my mother could provide. Of course, when color TVs were first in-troduced, Mom couldn't afford to buy one, but that didn't stop her from trying to give me the best she could afford. At the store she bought a multicolored sheet of plastic film that stuck onto our TV screen to simulate the experience of watching in color. It tinted everything, so Zorro's horse changed from white to red to green to blue to yellow as he galloped across the screen. It wasn't perfect, but it worked for me.

You stay here on these steps," Mother would say, "and don't move."

I sat down on one of the front steps and settled back to watch the world go by. While words like *ghetto, fatherless,* and *poverty* certainly have their place in my story, they are not the whole story. No ques-tion about it, life was hard, but there was much more to it than what we didn't have. As anyone who's lived in Philadelphia can tell you, it's a city of neighborhoods, more a group of small towns than a large metropolis.

The streets of North Philadelphia pulsed with energy, and from my vantage point on the church steps the world was fascinating, col-orful, and alive with sounds and sights as real to me now as they were then. Old narrow two-story row houses lined the streets, some with tiny—and I mean no bigger than ten by ten feet—concrete back-yards. The street was the center of the universe, the place where life happened, news traveled, and neighbors got to know one another. The few playgrounds there had long been overrun by teenagers and gang members, so the street was our playground, too. I can't imag-ine letting kids run free on a ghetto street the way we did then, but times were different.

The biggest difference was the strong sense of community. Typ-ical of even the poorest neighborhoods back in the 1950s, in ours neighbors watched out for one another. Having a single mother was no big deal; few of the kids I grew up around had dads. The neighborhood moms created their own "surveillance system." Mrs. Fells lived in the second apartment upstairs from the church, in front, overlooking the street. Even as I grew a little older and could take care of myself, I always knew she was there to call on if I ever needed her. If a neighbor caught me doing something I wasn't supposed to—for instance, speaking improperly or behaving disrespectfully to any adult—I caught it from her, then later from my mother, too.

Many upstairs window frames had angled mirrors we kids called newsy or nosy mirrors that reflected what was happening on the street. They were great for moms, because with a single glance, they could see both ways down the street without us kids ever knowing anybody was looking. We hated those damn things, because they made every mom a spy. Looking back today, I think they were an indication of how much adults worried over and cared about us. The children belonged to the community, and the community had a stake in how they grew up. They say it takes a village to raise a child, and we had an entire village on a single block.

Next door to Glad Tidings was Jeff's grocery store, an old-fashioned place with sawdust on the floor. Jeff was probably the only white shopowner in our neighborhood, but he was a good man who fit in and got along with everyone. He kept running tabs, so you could pick up what you needed even when money was tight. It seemed like I was in and out of there all the time, usually picking up something for my mother, groceries or stockings. I committed to memory my mother's favorite style: size 11 seamless mesh samba.

Directly across the street from the church, right in the middle of North Philadelphia, was a horse stable called Red's. Rambling Fairmount Park sat a few blocks west, and you paid to ride the horse based on how far you planned to go. A dime got you up to the corner and back, a quarter took you around the block, and for a dollar or so, you could ride all the way to the park and back. The *clip-clop* of hooves on the pavement and the very sight of horses added a touch of country to a place that was anything but. The smell of the stables added something, too—something you got used to but never forgot. Living among the horses were rats—big, aggressive, mean ones Mom called wharf rats. And I'll never forget walking home with my mother from another church and feeling one of those big, scary things scurry right across my toes.

Next to Red's was a corner tavern, the site of more than a few scenes of interest to a young boy like me: quarreling lovers, stumbling drunks, people just out to grab a few hours of fun after a long work-day. A man sold raw clams from an ice-filled pushcart right outside the bar. Men would come out of the bar, buy an order of clams, split them open with a knife, sprinkle them with thin, red hot sauce, and gulp them down. *How do they eat that stuff?* I wondered as I washed down a Tastykake snack with a gulp of fruit soda. I couldn't imagine anything nastier or more disgusting.

But the street was also filled with pleasures. On a sweltering summer day I'd sit on the step, and from down the street I could hear the song of a poet, the watermelon man. This was the happiest sound I could imagine. I'd jump up and run upstairs, excitedly calling, "Mom! Mom! The watermelon man's comin'! Can we get one?" I was always afraid we wouldn't get back downstairs before he passed by. As he steered his horse-drawn cart through the cars and horses, the melons rocked gently on a big pile of hay, which kept them from bruising. And the best part was, he didn't just sell watermelons, he sang about them: "Wa-ter-mel-on! Wa-ter-mel-on! Green rind, red meat. This watermelon sho is sweet! Wa-ter-mel-on!" The closer he got, the more excited I'd become. At the risk of playing into a stereotype, I'll tell you, when I was growing up in the ghetto, watermelon was a must-have, the perfect dessert. No other melon would do—no cantaloupe, no Crenshaw, no honeydew, only a big, sweet, green watermelon.

Where other kids might have jumped at the chance to run wild, I was content to while away my time on the steps. I studied passing cars so intently that by age four I could tell you the name, make, and model of every one. Those were the days when you could date a Caddy by the height and sweep of its tail fins or tell a Ford from a Chevy from a Mercury by the face of the grille. With their eye-catching two- and three-tone paint jobs, chrome side molding, and distinctive hood ornaments, almost every car was unique. We didn't have our own car until I was in my early teens, but my passion for beautiful cars never died.

Like so many small, independent, inner-city churches, Glad Tidings was more than a house of worship, it was a haven. In its intense, sometimes emotional expressions of faith, the church service offered us a foretaste of the glory we believe awaits. Inside its doors, the members formed a close-knit community where each person was treated with consideration and respect—something not everyone found outside.

Up to six days a week, for two or three hours a day, and some-times most of the day on Sunday, my mother and I took our places there amid the hard wooden benches, the modest furnishings, and the women dressed in immaculate pressed white dresses. Glad Tidings was a Holiness church founded on beliefs that some other Christian sects found a bit extreme; the major difference between it and other Baptist sects is the belief in a second baptism in the Spirit. In the egal-itarian spirit of Holiness, we were *all* "saints," not yet perfect but still striving to live according to the Word. We believed that anyone who felt the calling could preach, including women and children. Rev-erend Drayton, our pastor, was a woman. While many pastors had earned degrees in theology, not every one did. Having received a call from the Spirit of God was all the qualification she needed to preach.

The pastor's sermon might last half an hour, it might last an hour and a half; a favorite hymn could go on for three minutes or fifteen. It all depended on how the Spirit moved us. Let me tell you, when people in a Holiness congregation talk about being "moved by the

Spirit," they're not just using a colorful expression. They're describing a deeply profound and real experience.

Like most inner-city churches, ours was poor. When offering was made in our church, you heard the coins hit the plate, as they say; few if any could afford to give more than change. One Sunday a month we celebrated communion with grape juice and saltine crackers. We had no formal choir, no fancy altar, no stained-glass windows, but we felt the presence of the Lord, as real and as alive inside us as the beat of our hearts. "Be ye in the world but not of it," Jesus commanded, and so we did not go to dances, parties, or movies. We did not smoke, drink, or gamble. And we did not listen to secular music.

My little world began to broaden once I started school at Mac-Intyre Elementary. Learning came so easily to me that the principal urged my mother to let me skip a grade or go to a special school for academically gifted children. My mother thought it best that I stay with my classmates, though. I never found school challenging, and that probably explains why my school days weren't very memorable, except for music classes and being asked to join the Philadelphia All-City Boys' Choir. I remember the pride I took in singing for an audience. "Edelweiss" and "Climb Ev'ry Mountain" are two songs I recall.

What I remember most from school is getting my work done quickly, then amusing myself by tossing spitballs or picking on the girls. Most of my early attempts to get their attention consisted of pulling their hair. I couldn't resist, but it wasn't because I didn't like them. I *loved* girls. My fondest school memory is my first kiss: in the first-grade classroom coat closet with Rachel Bell.

Even at that young age, I walked to school alone. We lived on Twenty-seventh Street, and my school was on Thirty-first. The dividing line between two different gangs' turf was Twenty-ninth. East of Twenty-ninth, where we lived, belonged to the Village. West of Twenty-ninth, where my school sat, was Tenderlines territory, so I risked a beating every single day just walking to and from school. Back in the 1950s and early 1960s gangs weren't as violent as they are today. Most disputes—usually prompted by perceived transgressions involving turf or girls—got settled with fists, maybe sticks, rarely knives, but never guns. Still, I was a young boy with no father or older siblings to stand up for me. And these weren't the kind of conflicts you could run crying to Mommy about.

Neighborhoods you could trace on a map divided the city, but the declared gang borderlines you negotiated every day were invisible. Each gang claimed a "corner," an intersection that marked a perimeter of their turf, and many gangs called themselves by their corners, like Marshall and York. Other North Philly gangs were more imaginative (like the Village or the Tenderlines), and some just plain rude, like the Mighty Motherfuckers. Gang members were known as "corner boys," and you didn't get much beyond your ninth or tenth birthday without being pressured to join a gang.

Lots of kids in my situation joined a gang just for the protection, but becoming a corner boy never was an option for me. First of all, I didn't believe it was right to join a gang. Besides, what sort of protection was this? Join one gang and you're catching hell from all the others! "A good run is always better than a bad stand," my mother told me, and I usually avoided trouble. Navigating the invisible territories, sidestepping potential trouble, minding my own business—these were keys to survival in the ghetto and lessons that have served me well since. Shortly before I started school, my mother returned to work. She raised me to be independent and taught me to cross streets safely, so that she could trust me to walk to and from school alone as early as first grade.

I wasn't a tough kid in the usual sense of the word, but I learned early on to hide my weakness and my fear. And I can remember exactly the day it happened. I was about five or so and Reverend Drayton was babysitting me. Reverend Drayton copastored with Reverend Branch, and when it was about time for Reverend Branch to come home from work, she let me take his dog up to the corner to meet him. The dog was some kind of mixed breed and not that big, but very powerful. I was so proud of myself for keeping the dog in control. Suddenly, the dog took off running, dragging me down the street until I couldn't hold on anymore, and the leash flew from my hands. The dog bounded to the corner, where he stopped, sat, and waited for his master.

My knees were scraped raw, my hands burned, and I was lying on the street crying. "Teddy, get up," Reverend Drayton said firmly. "Big boys don't cry."

I looked up at her and replied, "I'm a big boy!" I stood up, wiped my eyes, and willed myself to forget how badly I hurt. "I don't cry!" A small moment, perhaps, but it would take me decades to learn how to cry again.

Hey, look at those bananas!" I said, pointing to what looked like a bunch of yellow fruit hanging from a pole. Someone—probably one of my cousins or my aunts—corrected me: "Those are tobacco leaves hanging out to dry." I looked again. They sure looked like bananas to me. Another time, I commented on the "handkerchiefs" fluttering from poles, only to be told those were tobacco leaves, too, but further along in the drying stage. A city boy in Kingstree, South Carolina, what did I know?

Before I started spending the summers with my mother's family down South, I'd never seen tobacco curing before, worked in a cotton field, or used an outhouse. Between the ages of four and ten, I spent several summers back in Kingstree, among aunts, uncles, and cousins. You'd be hard-pressed to find two places more different than Philadelphia and Kingstree, a town of a few thousand on the Black River in eastern South Carolina. But I was a curious, hardworking, adaptable kid, and before long I knew a lot about all of those things.

I split my time down South alternating between two of my mother's sisters and their families. Aunt Ruth (affectionately known as Aunt Sinky), Uncle Jeff, their four sons—Danny, Gurney, Pee-

Wee, and Adrian, whom we called Chico—and their daughter, the baby of the family, Sharon, lived in town, across the street from the cotton gin. Aunt Eloise (known lovingly as Aunt Dumpy) and Uncle Taft lived farther out in the country, where they oversaw the Sandy Bay Ranch for a white owner. Aunt Dumpy had several children, most of them much older than I, so I was closest to her son Walter. Most of Aunt Sinky's sons were around my age, all energetic and fun-loving, and we became like brothers.

For the most part, my cousins were wonderful to me, but I guess they couldn't resist teasing the city boy. One night we walked a distance along a little country road, so I could meet my father's sister, my aunt Julianne. I'd heard it said that she had seventeen children, though for some reason I never did meet her, so I never found out for sure. We were in deep, deep country, and without streetlight or moonlight, even dusk fell so heavy and dark it was like walking with your eyes closed. My cousins snuck away, out of sight, pretending to desert me.

Not knowing where I was or how to get back to my aunt's house, I was scared shitless. I was literally shaking as hoots and howls filled the air. The bushes rustled, branches snapped, and my head was reeling, wondering what—or who—was about to leap from the brush and grab me.

"Okay, fellas, this ain't no joke! Where are you?" I cried out, at first trying to sound as brave and tough as they were. "Come on out, you guys! Come on!" For my cousins, who were hiding from me and could probably hear me choking back the tears, this must have been the funniest scene in the world.

Strange and new as it was, country living gave me a type of freedom I'd never experienced in Philadelphia. The notion of a kid like me running free, out of earshot of my mother, was unthinkable at home, but South Carolina was different. Our family down South didn't have much money, and their homes were simple wooden structures built on raised foundations and heated by potbellied stoves.

To use the bathroom, you had to go out back to the outhouse. Even a run-down Philadelphia row house seemed "luxurious" by comparison.

Despite all that, my cousins didn't seem to be missing anything. They had fun doing whatever it was they could find to amuse themselves. Some of my happiest times were spent learning to do things my cousins did—dangerous, exciting things. For a boy who spent a lot of time sitting on the church steps, jumping off the roof of a cotton gin and landing twenty feet below in the back of a truck piled high with cotton was a *thrill*. So was hurtling downhill curled up inside a truck tire, and searching for snakes among the dust and cobwebs under the house. And I don't think I ever tasted watermelon as good as the ones my cousins and I stole from somebody's patch. Half the fun was running through the big, leafy plants—always being careful not to get your feet full of the prickly little thorns that covered the vines—picking your melon, busting it on the ground, then picking out the sweetest part, the dark pink heart.

Going to Kingstree was no vacation, though. Far from it. Everyone in the family was expected to work. At Aunt Ruth's we rose before dawn every morning and rode to the tobacco house, a warehouse where we strung tobacco leaves on poles to cure. After we'd worked awhile, Aunt Ruth brought us breakfast. Other times we would pick cotton, which is exhausting, backbreaking work, no matter what your age. What I remember most about it was the sun bearing down and the relentless heat. The pickers walked the dusty, hot unshaded rows, bending and picking the feathery cotton and tossing it into the long brown burlap bags that hung from their shoulders. Think how little cotton weighs. Now imagine how much you'd have to pick to collect a hundred pounds for five bucks. Every bit of cotton had to be dry, too. Wet cotton didn't count. I worked the whole day, all the while watching the older, more experienced pickers go at it, picking several hundred-pound bags a day. It seemed a nearly impossible feat, but even at that young age I already knew a dollar was hard to come by, and that people who worked deserved respect. People everywhere did what they had to do to survive.

For the most part, I was the kind of kid who played by the rules and didn't take too many chances. Every now and then, though, I'd feel compelled to push the limits, just to see how far I could go, what would happen. I guess you could say I had an impulsive streak. At the Sandy Bay Ranch, I helped with ranch work. Once I was riding a pretty brown pony named Dingo when I decided I'd take him beyond his usual boundaries. I was galloping along, feeling like one of my TV cowboy heroes, when the horse abruptly stopped, throwing me to the ground with a thud. I got up, slapped the dust from my pants, and got right back on. In another cowboy moment, I was helping one of Aunt Dumpy's older boys, who was on horseback, rounding up a herd of cattle. One calf had broken away from the herd and gotten tangled in a pile of old rusty pipes. I decided I'd single-handedly rescue it myself. Sure, the calf was bigger than I, but I had a plan: I'd shoo the calf toward my cousin.

I was valiantly charging the pile of rusty pipes, when the stings of a hundred wasps pierced my legs. I let out a scream and ran backward, wildly swatting my winged attackers. I was in pain, embarrassed, angry—the whole bit. I was beside myself, but my family took it in stride. "Come on, Teddy, calm yourself down," someone said. My legs swelled up to cartoon proportions, and my temperature soared until I thought I would melt. I didn't go to a doctor, though, and eventually I recovered. A couple of days later, I was back playing again, as if nothing had happened.

Those were wonderful days for me. The only thing I never developed any affection for was venturing to the outhouse in the pitch-black dark of night. The very idea of it scared me to death, but there was no alternative. Walking to the outhouse, I'd imagine all kinds of creeping, crawling creatures lurking underneath, poised to bite or grab me at a most vulnerable moment, in the most undesirable places. The inside was filled with spiderwebs, buzzing flies, and weird little bug nests you didn't want to know about. And the smell—I shudder just to think of it. Still, I had to go, so there I went. As much as I loved these summer adventures, I looked forward to seeing Mom again and hearing the sweet sound of flushing water.

Traveling back north at the end of summer, from a car window, South Carolina's neatly plowed fields gradually gave way to Philly's narrow paved streets. Living in the inner city, I knew some people had it better than we did, but coming home from down South, I also realized how much harder life could be.

When I was about ten, Mom found us a bigger, second-floor apartment half a block away, at Twenty-seventh and Gordon. All the windows opened onto Gordon, so just looking out any window, I felt a part of the world outside. By then, Mom was working full-time at Sciolla's, a nearby supper club, so I became a latchkey kid before the media had coined a term for it. Inside our more spacious, two-bedroom apartment, I was on my own. My mother never worried about my getting into trouble, though; I just wasn't that kind of kid, and besides, mothers were mothers no matter where you lived, and our new neighbors watched over me, too. I spent a lot of time alone and grew comfortable with my own company. Whether it's because of that, or maybe it's just my personality, I've always been pretty much a loner. Each day after school, I came straight home, did my homework and my chores, made myself a Miracle Whip sandwich on white bread, maybe sat out on the steps awhile, and then waited for Mom to come home and make us dinner.

From a very early age, I liked watching girls out playing and laughing, their braids and ponytails bouncing in time as their jump ropes spun in double Dutch. I'd tease the girls by jumping into their hopscotch or jump rope game, and make them wail, "Teddy! You ruined it!" and then I'd laugh. I *loved* teasing girls. I also loved sitting on my steps and talking to them. Maybe because I spent so much time around my mother, my aunts, and my mother's friends, I never found girls "yucky." Even then they fascinated me.

Looking back, I'm grateful that my mother gave me the greatest gift a parent could give: a sense of independence and responsibility. She did even the smallest things with an eye toward teaching me to care for myself. I took pride in doing for myself, even little things, such as my secret recipe for Frosted Flakes, which was simply Frosted Flakes, sliced bananas, and milk in a bowl, refrigerated until mush. I thought I was cool. These were little things that made me feel independent.

My "company" then was the TV, which I'd turn on the minute I walked in the door. I loved cartoons: Popeye, Road Runner, Bugs Bunny, Yogi Bear, Rocky and Bullwinkle, anything that made me laugh. One local cartoon program was hosted by Sally Starr, a gorgeous blond cowgirl. She was every young would-be cowboy's dream, including mine. I also loved the cowboys: Zorro, the Rifleman, Gene Autry, the Cisco Kid, Roy Rogers, Lash LaRue, the Lone Ranger. The good guys. I also passed many hours drawing whatever came to mind, such as space aliens.

I knew other kids whose parents were not as strict as mine, who let them run wild, but I never felt they had more fun or more freedom than I did. In fact, even as young as I was, I realized that I had it better than they did. To live in a clean, well-kept though modest home, to be very nicely dressed, and to never go hungry . . . I looked around my neighborhood and counted my blessings. I knew of some kids who lived in messy, unsanitary homes crawling with rats and roaches, who had parents who drank or just didn't give a damn what their kids did or how they looked. Like I said, I was blessed.

It was after we moved up to Gordon Street that I began to be more outgoing and really started hanging with the neighborhood kids. These were wonderful, magical days. Young girls hopscotched all up and down the block, while young boys clattered by on rickety wooden scooters they had built from salvaged wooden crates and metal roller-skate parts. In those days, everybody got a pair of those dangerous, shoe-wrecking, metal clamp-on roller skates you had to adjust with a skate key. Sooner or later—after you took a bad fall or ruined your good shoes—Mom would declare, "Those skates are goin' in the trash!" Now they were even more valuable to us. We would remove the wheels and, using two-by-fours and a few nails, hammer together wooden scooters. There were two basic designs. One was two two-by-fours nailed and braced at a ninety-degree angle to form an L with a handle fashioned from another piece of wood. The other was just an upright two-by-four nailed to a wooden soda crate. If you were lucky enough to have paint, you'd paint yours, or you'd nail soda-pop caps or streamers to it—anything to make your scooter unique, give it some style. It might take hours to construct a scooter, and without an arsenal of tools, they were never very sturdy—and probably not very safe, either. Yet somehow knowing that the scooter wasn't going to last, that every bump it hit could be its last, made each ride that much more exciting.

Lots of the games we boys played were about proving who was bigger, stronger, tougher, sharper. If, in the process of knocking another guy's marbles out of the circle with your own, you could bust a few of his, you were a cool dude. In tops—where you used your thumb and forefinger to strategically "shoot" your soda-bottle tops weighted with melted wax to knock out those of your opponent— you tried to hit as hard as you could. It was all about turf. Those were simple but wonderful times. Almost every toy we had or game we played we'd invented ourselves, and I think it forced us to use our imaginations.

Even though we grew up feeling secure, the fact is, North Philadelphia was a place where you had to know how to take care of yourself. You may not believe it, but I was a good kid, and while I wasn't a pushover, I'd walk away from a fight if I could do it and still hold my head up. I never looked for trouble, but when I was around eleven or twelve I was constantly being picked on by an older guy named Michael and his brother, whose name I don't recall (and it doesn't matter anyway). They were both bigger and taller than I was, and every day on the way to and from school, they were always gettin' up in my face, poppin' me upside the head, shoving me around. Finally I couldn't take it. I felt exactly like what I'd heard Popeye say a hundred times: "I had alls I can stands, I can't stands no more!" But I was serious.

The day came when Michael provoked me one time too many, and I snapped. In an uncontrollable rage, I saw my chance. My eye caught a big stick—it might have been an old bat or a two-by-four—lying on the ground, and without thinking, I grabbed it and rushed Michael, pushing him up against the wall.

"I've had enough!" I screamed. "I'm tired of y'all messin' with me!"

Michael was stunned because he definitely did not expect this. I had him good, and I was ready to treat his head like it was a baseball in the park. And I'm talkin' out-of-the-park, home run. I meant to really hurt him. Bad.

I gripped the stick so tightly my knuckles ached, and I'd just raised it and was a heartbeat away from lettin' go and bashing Michael's head in when I heard Mom holler, "Teddy! NO! Don't do it!"

It was as if my mother's voice snapped me out of a trance. I blinked my eyes, stepped back, and dropped the stick. A grateful, relieved Michael hauled his sorry butt home, and neither he nor his brother ever bothered me again. As I look back, it's sobering to realize how that one incident could have changed my life forever. If I had hit Michael and hurt him the way I wanted to, I probably would have spent the rest of my life in jail. But Mom saved me, again. She's always been my guardian angel.

But I suspect I have others, too.

———

Teddy."

Jolted from sleep, I sat up in bed. Someone had called me. The deep male voice seemed at once strange yet familiar. I looked around: still night, still my room. Making my way through the darkness to my mother's room, I asked her, "Did you just call me?" I *knew* the voice wasn't hers, but whose could it have been? Mom opened her eyes, looked up at me, and shook her head. "No, son, I didn't call you."

"But I heard someone calling my name," I insisted.

"You go on back to bed, Teddy," she said in her firm but gentle way.

I slipped back under the covers and soon dropped off to sleep.

"Teddy."

There it was again! I sprang out of bed, hurried back to my mother, and asked her again if she had called me. Again she denied it and sent me back to bed. I lay down and it happened *again*. When I told Mom, a peaceful look came over her face, she rose from her bed, and we knelt together and prayed.

"Something wonderful has occurred," she told me. "You have heard the voice of the Spirit and received your calling."

This wasn't the first time I'd heard that voice. A few months before, at a revival, I heard a voice saying, "You will start shouting and praising me when you are ten years old." From then and throughout my life, I've had many more spiritual revelations. The earliest ones I documented in my New Testament Bible that I carried to church as a child and still cherish today. Specifically what the calling is for, why it came, what it all means—nearly forty years later I still can't say. Although my faith is important to me, I am better at accepting than explaining, but I will try.

There are countless ways to express your spirituality every day through your deeds and efforts. For some people, the purpose of the calling is specific and clear: for instance, to preach or to manifest Christ through other means (to work with the poor, to become a teacher, a doctor, a missionary, or an artist who glorifies the Lord through his work, be it singing, dancing, writing, painting, and so on). Or it may be a calling to serve God in your life, to be an example to others, as my mother does. Whatever you do, however you do it, whether you've received a calling on your life or not, you simply make sure that you include Christ in your daily life.

Initially, both Mom and I took my calling to be one to preach in the traditional sense. However, in time I realized that was not my specific calling. Still, I had been called to minister—to acknowledge and to share with others my belief in and commitment to the existence and power of Jesus Christ—in some way. Now, I know that some people hold very strong opinions about the "right" way to express that commitment, and I'm not about to argue my case. To each his own.

With all my heart, I believe that in my singing, God gave me a precious gift, and that He has allowed me to be heard by millions all over the world. Even in those times when it might appear to the world that my public persona in some way contradicted their conceptions of "faith," I never lost sight of the obligation the Lord bestowed upon me with the gift of my voice. That is why, throughout my career, I made sure that along with my secular music I included songs that brought a message, that inspired listeners, that gave people hope, from "Bad Luck" and "Wake Up Everybody" to "Somebody Told Me" to "Truly Blessed."

As you will read, I've experienced some dark nights of the soul. I've endured painful times when I shut my heart to God, when I feared He had deserted me. But I've come through it, and these early spiritual experiences are one reason why. Although over time I've grown to see the meaning of faith in a different light, I've never lost sight of it. I don't need to know what specifically God is asking of me in order to believe or express my faith.

I believe that God has a plan for each of us, and that we are each given a special purpose in life and gifts to help us achieve that purpose. My faith allows me to accept the work of God without fully understanding it on an intellectual level. After all, faith—and the Spirit—speak to the soul. And that night my soul answered.

That was Saturday night. The next day, May 15, I recorded the experience in my New Testament Bible (which I still possess): "Theodore Pendergrass saved and filled with the Holy Ghost, May 14, 1960." I also wrote of my promise to do my duty to God, and to go through trials and tribulations, even though I had only a ten-year-old's understanding of what those words might mean. Looking back, I can't help but wonder if the trials and tribulations were the ones I've known, or others yet to come.

Receiving my calling had a profound impact on me. The next day was Sunday, and while praying in church, I spoke in tongues and prophesied twice. When people "speak in tongues," their words are of a language divinely given only when the Holy Spirit comes over them. Or, as it is written in Acts 2:4: "And they were filled with the Holy Spirit, and began to speak with other tongues, as the Spirit gave them utterance." Anyone who has accepted the Spirit of Jesus Christ into his or her life can speak in tongues, but only those who have been given the gift to discern tongues can interpret what has been said. Speaking in tongues is not something that you do consciously; the words are not your own. Speaking in tongues is one way that the Holy Spirit expresses itself through you.

At first, because I believed that my calling was a calling to preach, I did deliver a couple of talks in church. I recall one sermon on Ecclesiastes 3: "To every thing there is a season, and a time to every purpose under the heaven . . ." In the Holiness church, seeing a ten-year-old in the pulpit was not typical, but it was not unheard of, either. Years later, when the subject came up with reporters, so much was made of my early preaching that I'm afraid some people got the wrong impression. I addressed the congregation a time or two, but I was never a full-time, Bible-thumping boy preacher.

The experience of being called changed me and has remained

with me to this day. By then my mother and I had joined the congregation at First Pentecostal Baptist, at Thirty-seventh and Aspen, which was headed by another woman, whom everyone lovingly called the Reverend Mother Hunter. I call Reverend Hunter the grandmother I never had; I even called her Grandmother. She often took care of me, and we became very close. She was short, plump, gray-haired, and bowlegged, and she had a wonderful way of teaching the Bible. She didn't scream and holler or try to scare you into believing. Her way was gentle and loving; she would discuss and explain God's word so that you understood it. Of course, when the Spirit moved her, she might get a little carried away, too.

Her church was a corner storefront in a West Philadelphia neighborhood far enough away that my mother and I had to take two or three buses to get there. You entered the church from the front, and to the left, in front of the store window, stood the pulpit. Against the wall, to the right, stood a piano, which was played by a frail-looking older woman named Miss Bitsy. As tiny as Miss Bitsy was, with her small, fragile-looking hands, once she started playing, you couldn't resist being swept up in the joy.

Accompanying Miss Bitsy on a large bass drum resting on the floor between his knees was Minister Seegers, probably one of the greatest natural drummers I've ever seen. I watched in amazement as Minister Seegers made that drum—the kind you'd strap onto your chest to play in a parade—sing every tone imaginable just by tapping out rhythms with his fingers on different parts of it.

What made this all so fascinating and so powerful was how the music changed, not only from service to service but from minute to minute. And it all went back to the living heart of all music: the beat. Miss Bitsy, Minister Seegers, and the entire congregation moved with the feeling, each to his or her own rhythm. The basic rhythm went like this: *Badda-tat! Badda-tat! Badda-badda-badda-tat!* But then every person in the church played it the way they felt it. Clapping your hands, slapping the tambourine with your palm, or beating the rim on the heel of your hand, you made your own music, but it was all part of the congregation's great song. You could slow it down, speed it up, throw in your own beats, switch the accents. This wasn't music you could write down, and these were beats too wild to be captured by a metronome. We talk today about the innovations in rhythm made by great jazz musicians and pioneers like James Brown, but the truth is, they had nothing on a congregation going full force in praise of the Lord.

This was a rock-'em, sock-'em, sanctified, feel-the-Spirit church. This music was a living entity, a ritual, a spiritual experience like nothing else in the world. The rhythm danced, and when the Spirit came over you, there's no way you were sitting it out. Some rocked discreetly; others did what we called a praise dance in the aisle. Ladies fluttered their handheld fans against the heat, while others played tambourines or clapped along.

After seeing my mother in church, I know my natural sense of rhythm came from her. She's a proper, soft-spoken lady but, let me tell you, she plays one mean tambourine! The Spirit in the small church was mighty, and when my mother caught it, she beat that tambourine until she'd punched holes in it. She'd rip out the center part and play the rim until the little metal cymbals fell out. Then she played the rim. A joyful noise indeed. We had, as we say, a Holy Ghost good time.

I loved music and I loved singing, especially the spirituals that were the foundation of our services. Old songs such as "The Old Rugged Cross," "Precious Lord," "Amazing Grace," "At the Cross," and "Just a Closer Walk with Thee" not only were beautiful to hear and inspiring to sing but also told a story, taught a lesson, and proved our faith. In our church, just the act of singing brought us closer to one another and closer to the Lord.

———

When I was around seven or eight, my mother took me aside and explained that I had a godfather—Reverend Branch, the assistant pastor of the Glad Tidings—and a biological father, whom I had never met. She promised that one day I would get to meet my real father. As I've said, I didn't know very much about him, and I wasn't all that curious, either. My respect for my mother is such that I would never ask her any question that would invade her privacy or make her feel uncomfortable. I always figured that what happened between my parents was none of my business. I wasn't the type to ask a lot of questions. I had no father; it was a simple fact of life.

I'm not sure what prompted it, but one day shortly after I turned eleven, my mother announced, "We are going to see your father."

I sat beside her on the trolley up Germantown Avenue. As befitted the occasion, both my mother and I were dressed in our best. We soon arrived at our stop, and I climbed down off the trolley without any hopes or expectations, but I was also apprehensive and anxious. I was meeting one of the most important people in my life, yet he was also someone to whom I had no emotional connection. I didn't know how I should act, or what I should say. I didn't know what to expect. Odd as it may sound, I'd never wondered what my father was like or whether I looked like him or what he would say to me when we finally met. I didn't miss him in the way a kid who's had a dad would miss him. He'd never made himself a place in my heart.

We walked a half block over to the house where he lived. I stood silently as my mother knocked on the door and we waited for someone to answer. A woman, who I later learned was one of my father's sisters, opened the door and said hello.

"I came to see Jesse," my mother announced. "This is his son."

The woman looked at Mom, then me, and politely invited us in. This day was so important in my life, yet my memories of it are vague at points. I remember the small house was bustling with activity, because, someone explained, they were all getting ready to go on a picnic. I'm not sure how many children and adults were there, but it did strike me that this was a busy, crowded home. I was surprised to find that my mother seemed to know everyone there, and I remember my aunt introducing my mother as her "sister-in-law" to my father's girlfriend. Mom cordially embraced the woman. A little while later, when my father still hadn't arrived, his girlfriend left the house to find him.

"Would you like a piece of chicken to eat while you wait?" my aunt asked.

"Yes, thank you," my mother replied. Mom sat at the dining room table, and I sat in the living room, only a few feet away, with my back to the door.

We were eating when my father entered. My mother looked up and said, "Teddy, this is your father."

I looked up at him. My father was tall, imposing, and handsome. *Wow, this is my dad,* I thought to myself, but all I said to him was hello before I cast my gaze down again. If I could go back in time for just a moment and look at him again, I would. Was he pleased to see me? Did he smile? Did I look down so quickly because of something I saw?

I'll never forget my mother saying, "Teddy, take a look at your father's face so that you will know him if you ever see him again."

I looked again, but I don't remember if he said anything to me. What I do remember, very clearly, is something that happened a little bit later.

"So this is my son, huh?" he said, looking at me. The adults were making small talk, and then my father turned to my mother and said, "Give me fifty cents."

Out of kindness, she had already given all the other children coins, and even though she probably didn't have it to spare, she gladly opened her purse and handed him the change, which he put in his pocket. It was a moment I will never forget. How could a man who'd never given me anything in my life dare ask my mother for money, and in front of everybody? I didn't understand it. It seemed so wrong to me.

We stayed a little while longer, then my father walked with Mom and me to the trolley stop. I walked along as the two of them talked, and while I didn't hear what they were saying, they were friendly. A few minutes later, the trolley was approaching and we all said good-bye. I suppose many kids in my position would have felt angry, hurt, or rejected, but those thoughts didn't cross my mind—at least not then. I'd met my father. Nothing had changed.

Looking back at how my parents acted toward each other that day, I've wondered how my life would have turned out if my father hadn't left my mother. At eleven, I didn't fully understand why having a father is so important. Sure, he could help pay the bills, teach me how to play ball, talk to me about these things I couldn't discuss with my mom. But beyond that, I wasn't really sure what it would mean. Over the years, I've wondered what it would have been like if he had come back to us.

But he never got the chance. Those good-byes on Germantown Avenue were the last words we exchanged. Just over a year later, on June 12, 1962, he was murdered during a fight with a drinking buddy. According to newspaper accounts, the two were drinking in my father's apartment on North Thirteenth Street when they exchanged some angry words and the friend plunged an eight-inch butcher knife into my father's chest. I never knew what the argument was about and why, really, my father was killed. But whatever it was, it sure wasn't worth getting killed for. Arrested a few hours later, the friend reportedly confessed to committing the crime and was charged with homicide. What happened after that, I never knew; it didn't matter to me then.

The thought of my father being so brutally and senselessly murdered in his own home by someone he trusted haunts me to this day. Always reserved and cautious by nature, I was even less trusting of others after my father's murder.

Right after the incident, the *Philadelphia Tribune* ran a front-page story. Reading it as a young boy, I didn't give much thought to the fact that another woman was identified as my father's wife, or that a ten-year-old girl who witnessed the killing was identified in the story as his daughter, Betty Ann Pendergrass. My mother told me that she and my father had not divorced. The thought that my father would abandon me, his own flesh and blood, and yet still be a father to another child tore at my heart in ways it would take me years to recognize. His rejection baffled me when I was a child, but once I had my own children and knew what it was like to be a father, it angered me. No matter how long I live, that hurt will never go away.

The newspaper gave a vivid, dramatic account of Betty Ann seeing my father stagger toward her with the knife in his chest and how she had been unable to go into the room where he died ever since. Betty Ann was also known as Peaches, and over the years I met her a couple of times. When I was a few years older, I dropped by to visit my father's sister a few times. I wanted to get to know her and that side of my family better, but we did not become close. In the process, I also ran into Peaches, and even though we talked a little, we never connected, either, even though I wanted to. She might have been my sister, but even if she wasn't, she was still the only link to my father. I suppose that somewhere deep inside, I was hoping for something to happen, but it never did. Looking back, I've wondered why I never heard from someone who knew my father or Peaches, or even Peaches herself. Especially after I became famous, I was certainly easy enough to find. Over time, though, I've come to accept that questions like these that have no answers are best left alone.

Learning of my father's death, I responded like a twelve-year-old, swearing revenge on my father's killer. *I'll get him,* I thought, but that soon gave way to a bitter acceptance of the truth. Jesse Pendergrass passed through this world a virtual stranger to his only son. The second and last time I saw him, he was laid out in a seven-foot coffin, a mystery now beyond my reach. I stood beside my mother as we paid our last respects and prayed for God to deliver his soul to its rightful place. I don't know what my mother was thinking at that moment. But when I saw her crying, I cried, too, though more for her than for myself or my father. She had loved him enough to bring me into the world, but he had not cared enough about me even to acknowledge me. Jesse Pendergrass left me a legacy of loss and distrust that would influence my own life in ways I wouldn't recognize for decades to come.

Two

꙳

"Ladies and gentlemen!"

Through the racket of waitresses calling out orders and the clatter of pots and pans, you could sense the excitement in the showroom. While I stood facing an endless stack of dirty dishes and rows of lipstick-smudged glasses, on the other side of the swinging kitchen doors the house lights dimmed, the orchestra waited for its cue, and five hundred well-dressed patrons fell silent, their faces turned expectantly toward the stage.

I hurriedly scraped another stack of plates, lined them up in the rack, and pushed it to where my mother stood waiting to slide them into the large dishwasher. With a pull of the handle, the metal door clanged shut and the big machine began to hum. When Mom opened the door a few minutes later, rows of sparkling dishes emerged in a cloud of damp, hot steam. I remember the cook, Walter, stirring a pot of marinara sauce that, at the time, I guessed to be about ten feet tall, and Jonsey, my favorite waitress. But most of all, I remember the electricity in the air.

Loading the dishwasher again, I cocked my ear toward the showroom. The band started playing and then came the applause. The star—Al Martino, Connie Francis, Al Alberts and the Four Aces,

Frankie Laine, or any of a hundred others—had taken the stage, and for the next hour or so the room filled with music and applause.

Back in the kitchen, Mom (Angelina) and Pop (Gaetano) Sciolla, the lovely older Italian couple who owned the place, were engaged in familiar debate:

"Hey, Mama! Why'd you do that?"

"What?"

"Why you cut it like this? You don't cut it like that! You cut it thisaway, huh?"

"But I don't want to cut it 'thisaway,' " Mom Sciolla would reply. "I want to cut it thataway."

"Ah!" Pop would gaze heavenward or shrug before he found something else he deemed imperfect. It could have been the way the food was arranged on a plate, the amount of fresh marinara sauce ladled over a mountain of spaghetti, a piece of meat that was too small or too well done. When it came to giving their customers high-quality food, drink, and entertainment, the Sciollas never accepted less than the best. Despite their almost daily arguments, Mom and Pop Sciolla really loved each other. My mother was the only black person in their employ, and for all the years she worked for them— from 1953 to 1971—they treated her like one of the family. We got to know the whole Sciolla family—including their sons Anthony, Frank, and Ralph—and I often played with their grandsons Michael, Anthony Jr., Gregory, and Guy.

I often accompanied my mother to work and helped her, usually on Friday and Saturday nights, which were the busiest, and then on Saturdays to clean up. The Sciollas treated me very well, too. Every once in a while, they would let me sit in their private booth, if it was empty, and watch the show for a bit, even though this violated state liquor laws. But most of the time, whenever the bustle in the kitchen slowed down a little, I'd stand by the door and try to catch a peek while dodging the endless parade of rushing waitresses.

In those days, every major American city boasted at least a few supper clubs with top-name entertainment. In Philadelphia, Sciolla's was one of two legendary places that offered music in a posh, so-phisticated, intimate setting (the other, Palumbo's, was in the pre-dominantly Italian South Philly). Sciolla's was very much like New York's Copacabana, except that it did not have a second floor, and a night out there was really an event. I was fortunate to have been able to witness what would prove to be the end of a golden era in pop-ular music. From the canopied entrance and the glass doors leading to the showroom to the plush crescent-shaped booths and perfectly set tables, Sciolla's radiated class. I dreamed of one day buying the place myself and restoring it. But it was not to be. In another decade or so, most of the small, intimate clubs like Sciolla's would disappear.

Of course, I didn't know any of that then; I was just a kid work-ing in the kitchen. I helped Mom clean up the big room and set up for the next crowd. Together she and I would sweep, mop, and buff the floors. It was one of my favorite chores, because I never failed to find a few dollars in dropped change under the tables and chairs.

Aside from singing in church or in the boys' choir, I didn't think of singing as anything more than an enjoyable hobby, just something I did. Between the church and the neighborhood, it seemed as if everybody sang, and I do mean everybody. Singing didn't make you anything special, and just because you could sing didn't mean you thought of yourself as "a singer." I remember walking down the street singing Joe Hinton's "Funny" and Garnet Mimms and the En-chanters' "Cry Baby" as naturally and unselfconsciously as another kid might whistle or kick a can. I wasn't sitting there scribbling down notes on phrasing, delivery, and staging, but I was learning. And it was at Sciolla's that I met my first big star: Chubby Checker.

Chubby is from Philadelphia, and his big hits—"The Twist," "Pony Time," "Let's Twist Again," to name a few—were recorded for Philly's Cameo-Parkway label. I'd seen him many times on *American Bandstand*. When I found out Chubby was going to play Sciolla's,

Mom arranged with Mom and Pop Sciolla for my cousin Pete and me to see the show. Pete was only five months older than I, and we were as close as brothers.

That Friday night, sitting in Mom and Pop Sciolla's private booth, decked out in my suit, I was sharp as a tack. My pulse quickened as the lights went down, and the emcee announced the star:

"Ladies and gentlemen, please welcome the King of the Twist, Mr. Chubby Checker!"

Chubby emerged in a black tuxedo, wearing the stylish but conservative process that was popular back then. He had a friendly, fun-loving demeanor, and he tore through his biggest hits as if he'd just discovered them the day before. It was the first time I'd seen a live rock-&-roll star, but this was hardly what you'd call a real rock-&-roll show. The predominantly white audience rocked a little at their tables (there was no dance floor), and everybody cheered loudly when Chubby did the twist, but it was an otherwise pretty sedate scene.

Of course, Pete and I were excited just to be there, and after the show Pop Sciolla asked Chubby if we could meet him in his downstairs dressing room. I felt truly privileged and special to shake Chubby's hand and have my picture taken with him. This was my first brush with celebrity, and looking at the picture later, I felt pretty cool. I had that feeling most young kids get when they realize that the voice they've been hearing on the radio, the person they've been watching on TV, really exists. The next day, while I was at Sciolla's helping Mom clean up and get ready for the big Saturday-night crowd, I glimpsed that part of fame that goes under the heading "things money can buy": Chubby's sleek, sparkling new Jaguar convertible. To a kid as car-crazy as I was, this was one of the most beautiful things I'd ever seen, and I remember walking over to the car, gazing at the hood ornament and catching my reflection on the polished hood, and thinking, *Someday . . .*

Sciolla's was also where I discovered another side of my musical talent: drumming. I can't adequately explain the attraction; maybe it was just a matter of opportunity. The drums, along with the piano, were the only instruments that were always there. You can't sit down and start playing real music on a piano, but all you need to start playing drums is a natural sense of rhythm, and I had that. Whenever I took a break from helping clean up (or I thought nobody would notice), I'd climb onto the bandstand and sit down on the drummer's round stool. Man! Just as I'd seen Minister Seegers do in church, I would tap out rhythms on the drums. I tried a little ride beat, like on Ray Charles's "Hit the Road Jack": *ting ting-ting ting, ting-ting ting, ting-ting ting* . . . First just the cymbal. Then I added snare drum on the two and four beat—*thwack! thwack!*—and a cannoning bass drum on the one and three. It came so naturally to me. Whatever I heard in my head, no matter how complex or fast, from the time I was about thirteen, I could sit down and play it. Not long after that, I started asking Mom if I could have my own set, and a couple of years later she gave me my first kit—beautiful, white pearl-finish drums with one cymbal that I played every chance I got.

The rhythms in my head came from songs I heard on the radio. When I was about ten years old, someone gave me a little, shirt-pocket-size six-volt transistor radio that I loved. The back kept dropping off, the battery kept falling out, and it didn't last long, but the music I heard through it made a lifelong impression. After that, I had the radio on whenever I could. We didn't own a record player, and my mother didn't allow me to play "that music" when she was around, but it didn't matter, because in those days, music was everywhere. You heard it coming out of people's open windows, in stores, from passing cars. And I loved it.

While in many ways this new rhythm and blues and rock & roll music seemed a world away from the gospel I'd grown up with, something about the way some of the artists sang was not unfamiliar. From the dozens of black vocal groups' gospel-style configurations and arrangements to the call-and-response exchange between Sam Cooke and Lou Rawls on "Bring It On Home to Me" or Hank Ballard and his Midnighters on the most-unholy "Work with Me, Annie," gospel music left its mark. In fact, Cooke, one of the era's biggest black stars, became a leading gospel star as lead singer of the Soul Stirrers. Solomon Burke, who crooned the immortal "Cry to Me," had been a boy preacher in Philadelphia, while Clyde McPhatter had discovered the future Drifters singing in a Harlem church. Bobby Bland, Brook Benton, Ben E. King, Roy Hamilton, Jerry Butler, Gladys Knight, Marvin Gaye—all had started singing in church. Even the Godfather of Soul, James Brown, with his funky, kinetic rhythms, had performed briefly in a gospel act. Their passion and their artistry came from church.

And then there was *American Bandstand,* broadcast every weekday afternoon from the WFIL-TV studios right across the river, at Market and Forty-sixth. Looking back, it's hard to overstate *Bandstand*'s impact on my generation. Everybody you knew watched it. For young fans like me, Dick Clark's program was the closest thing to a front-row seat at a live rock-&-roll show. And in those days "rock & roll" encompassed everything from the classic pop sounds of Andy Williams and Jack Jones to the raucous, sometimes racy performers like Chuck Berry and the Coasters. It was the only TV program that featured blacks and whites, among both the performers and the audience of dancing teenagers. Other popular local deejays, including Georgie Woods, had their own dance shows, too, but *Bandstand* was the show every kid—including me—wanted to dance on someday. You had to be fourteen to get on the show, and so I was devastated when Dick Clark moved the show to Los Angeles just weeks before my fourteenth birthday.

I loved to dance, and my cousin Pete and I would go to the sock hops run by popular disc jockeys like Jerry Blavat. I clearly recall going to a hop at the Wagner Ballroom up on Old York Road, where Pete and I joined the other kids in the whitest dance I ever saw, the Bristol Stomp (made famous by Philly's own Dovells). But then, it didn't matter what dance you were doing, as long as you were dancing.

Because *American Bandstand* broadcast from Philly, a good percentage of the acts were hometown stars. There were the South Philly teen idols, the Italian-American singers like Fabian, Frankie Avalon, and Bobby Rydell, and white groups (Danny and the Juniors, "At the Hop") and black groups (the Orlons, "South Street") who came to typify the "Sound of Philadelphia."

That term's meaning would be changed forever five years later by my future producers Kenny Gamble, Leon Huff, and Thom Bell—Mighty Three Music—and the legendary Philadelphia International Records. But I'm getting ahead of the story here. Philly is unquestionably one of the great music cities, and it's always boasted many more sounds and styles than most people know. From classical to soul, Philadelphia is a singer's town.

All this music was great, but for me the real bomb, the music that turned me on more than any other, was Motown. You heard it on black radio stations, on white radio stations, on television—everywhere. Motown was a label, a sound, a style, an attitude, a revolution. Motown changed forever the way white America and the rest of the world saw black entertainers and heard black music. This wasn't soul or funk but a sleek new hybrid that merged the best of black music with classic pop conventions. The lyrics were more sophisticated, the beat more insistent, the backing musicians more accomplished and adventurous. It was indescribable and irresistible.

Label founder Berry Gordy Jr. took his artists places few other blacks had gone before—to the top of the pop charts, to prime-time television, to the Copa, to Buckingham Palace, to Vegas—and as a black singer, I know I've walked through many doors Motown artists opened for all of us before me. Of course, that's the historical importance of Motown. What mattered most to me then, and now, is the music.

The Motown sound was infectious, riveting, exciting. And while you can always tell a Motown record by its indescribable, unique sound, when you said "Motown," you were really talking about many sounds: from Marvin Gaye's smooth midtempo hits such as "Pride and Joy" and "How Sweet It Is to Be Loved by You" to Martha Reeves and the Vandellas' blistering "Heat Wave" and "Dancing in the Street," Smokey Robinson's shimmering ballads, and Little Stevie Wonder's amazingly soulful "Fingertips, Part 1." Founded, dominated, and run by songwriters and producers, Motown gave the world not just hits but classics: the Temptations' recording of Smokey Robinson's "My Girl"; Marvin Gaye and Tammi Terrell's perfect Nickolas Ashford–Valerie Simpson duets such as "Ain't No Mountain High Enough"; and Brian Holland, Lamont Dozier, and Eddie Holland's "Reach Out" for the Four Tops, "Nowhere to Run" for Martha and the Vandellas, and "I Hear a Symphony" for the Supremes. And Motown's stars were truly stars. They looked and moved as good as they sang. They were all polished, precise, and clean, but the Temptin' Temptations and the Supremes especially set a new standard for stagecraft and pure theater. I remember being especially excited by the idea that Little Stevie Wonder was a star and exactly my age.

The stars that I heard at Sciolla's were established singers who appealed to more adult tastes. A few, such as Connie Francis and Bobby Darin, may have had hit records, but they weren't considered truly rock-&-roll singers as much as first-rate entertainers. With the boom in record sales of teen-oriented music, suddenly the artists whose sounds I loved were only a few years older than I. Not so different and not so distant.

From my window on the corner of Twenty-seventh and Gordon, I caught a glimpse of homegrown pop stardom. I was about eleven or twelve, gazing out my window one warm night, when I recognized my neighbor Dione LaRue. She lived in an apartment above the church across the street, with her brother Roy and cousin Kenny. Her father or grandfather was the church's pastor. One night I saw her getting out of a car. I looked again, then realized the driver was

Dick Clark. *Dick Clark!* Dione, better known to the world as Dee Dee Sharp, had a series of dance hits in the early 1960s: "Slow Twistin'," "Mashed Potato Time," and "Gravy (For My Mashed Potatoes)." I remember thinking, *Wow!*

I was about thirteen when we moved again, to a house my mother rented on Sydenham, between York and Cumberland. We moved twice during my junior high school years, because Mom firmly believed you should seize every opportunity to better yourself or improve your surroundings. Even though each North Philly neighborhood I lived in would be considered "poor," my mother made sure that each time we moved, it was to something better.

This, it would turn out, would be a fateful location for me, because it put me a few blocks from Philly's great R&B mecca: the Uptown Theater, at North Broad and Dauphin. Originally built in 1929 as one of the grand Art Deco–style movie palaces of its time, the Uptown boasted elaborate ornamental plasterwork and metal grating throughout, sat about 2,200, and was known for its fantastic acoustics. By the early 1960s, when I first set foot inside, it was one of several venues that featured predominantly black entertainers in a loosely affiliated chain known as the chitlin circuit. Like its sister theaters throughout the East—Baltimore's Royal, Chicago's Regal, Detroit's Fox, Washington, D.C.'s Howard, and Harlem's legendary Apollo— the Uptown not only presented virtually every major black star, it also served as a proving ground for up-and-coming talent.

It cost three dollars to get into one of the big Saturday-night shows, with a bill that ran for an entire week and could include more than ten top acts. Better still—and more in keeping with my curfew and my wallet—were the special Friday after-school shows, which cost just fifty cents. Can you imagine? For half a dollar you could see the whole Motown Revue—Little Stevie Wonder, Marvin Gaye, the Temptations, the Four Tops, the Supremes, Martha and the Vandellas, the Contours, Mary Wells, to name just a few—plus whoever else was in town. That could have included Curtis Mayfield and the Impressions, Major Lance, James Brown, Gladys Knight and the Pips, the Shirelles, Jerry Butler, the Chiffons, and any number of other stars.

The Uptown also presented some great, great local acts who were every bit as dynamic and talented. Without meaning any disrespect, we often referred to them as "the local yokels on the vocals." To give credit where it's due, that was actually one of disc jockey and Uptown promoter Georgie Woods's trademark rhymes. Among the less well known groups I saw there were the Magnificent Men (to my surprise, a white act and the only one I remember seeing there), Brenda and the Tabulations, Honey and the Bees, the Intruders, the Mad Lads, the Ambassadors, and the Epsilons. That group included Gene McFadden and John Whitehead, later best known as hit songwriters and for their own 1979 number-one hit "Ain't No Stoppin' Us Now," and Lloyd Parks, a future member of Harold Melvin and the Blue Notes. The Epsilons' choreography was the most acrobatic I'd ever seen, and the audience always went nuts for it. Often the disc jockeys who hosted the shows were as entertaining as the acts. I remember seeing Georgie Woods, Jimmy Bishop, and Joe "Butterball" Tamburro (a white disc jockey we all assumed was black until we actually saw him in person at the Uptown), to name a few.

When it came to the Uptown, it wasn't a question of who played there but who didn't. In those days, you didn't really care who was on the bill, because it was always a great show. Every performer had an *act:* a rare talent, a unique style, or just a great gimmick—such as Screamin' Jay Hawkins growling "I Put a Spell on You" from a coffin—guaranteed to hold an audience. I'll never forget seeing another hometown girl, Patti LaBelle, with the Bluebelles (Sarah Dash, Cindy Birdsong, and Nona Hendryx), singing their hit "Down the Aisle" and the classic "Danny Boy." Or Gladys Knight and the Pips executing the most gorgeous, elegant choreography while singing "Giving

Up." To me, that stagecraft was nothing less than pure magic. Whether it was to see James Brown dramatically throwing off his cape during "Please Please Please" or to sigh over a beautiful girl group sashaying across the stage in their towering beehive wigs, skintight matching sequined dresses, and high-heel shoes, the Uptown was the place to be.

Now, you stay here on the steps or you go in the house," Mom said as she gathered her things to leave for work. "You know you've got a curfew."

"Yes, ma'am."

"And I'll be home the usual time, about two. Good-bye, Teddy."

" 'Bye, Mom." As I watched my mother walk toward the bus stop, I couldn't stop thinking about the Uptown. Now that I was a teenager, even if just barely, I was beginning to feel the magic of nighttime, with its promise of freedom and fun. It was a warm summer night, and I was sitting on the steps when my friend Tyrone came by. Tyrone was my best hanging buddy back then. We shared a love of music, and he was also a fledgling drummer. Like me, he loved the Uptown, and when he said, "You want to go?" I was ready.

I knew I wasn't supposed to leave the house, but damn! When faced with the alternative—hanging outside with Tyrone, talkin' shit, doing nothing—I couldn't resist. How could I, when less than four blocks away, just around a corner, I could be *there?* My impulsive side won out. Again.

"Let's go, Tyrone!" We took off down the street. "But I've got to watch the time. If I don't get back here before my mom, I'm gonna get it!" As usual, there was a crowd outside the Uptown, and being broke, we kind of blended in until we could sneak in. Within minutes we were in our seats and groovin'. I might have checked the time once or twice in the lobby, but as the night wore on, time seemed to slow down. Not that I was thinking about it, of course.

Suddenly, the music came up, the spotlight hit the stage, and out strode the magnificent Jackie Wilson. I'll never forget it: He was so clean in his tailored suit and tie, revealingly tight pants, and a fresh, perfectly sculpted 'do. The Uptown erupted in cheers and screams as he grabbed the microphone and launched into his show. Whatever Jackie sang—it could have been his latest hit, "Baby Workout," or "Night," or "Lonely Teardrops," or "Reet Petite"—he gripped the audience in the palm of his hand. He could croon as beautifully as Sam Cooke, shout as loud as James Brown, and move like nobody else. A former Golden Gloves champion, Jackie demonstrated an athletic grace as he executed a series of seemingly effortless splits, spins, drops, and steps so smooth that he glided across that stage as if it were polished glass. There was only one word for Jackie in his prime, and that's "electric."

Girls and women rushed the stage, screaming and reaching out to him. Security guards manned a barricade that created ten feet of no-man's-land between the front row of seats and the stage, so that no one got close enough to touch Jackie, no matter how close to the edge he danced. Still, his every glance, every note, every move teased the fans into a wilder frenzy. The female reaction was nothing less than pure hysteria, and Jackie reveled in it.

Suddenly Jackie dropped to the floor and slowly rolled off the stage. Of course, this part of his act was staged, but we didn't know that, so when he toppled off the stage and landed hard on the theater floor, everyone gasped and stood up, craning to see. Then we all rushed down the aisle, certain that Jackie had been injured.

Lying on his back, he seemed hurt, but I saw him gesture to a guard to let a girl through the barrier. She fell upon him, wrapped her legs around his hips, and starting rubbing her body against him. He was clearly enjoying it. From where I stood, I could have sworn they were actually making love as a throng of screaming, reaching women surrounded them. To say I couldn't believe my eyes barely begins to describe my reaction, an unfamiliar mix of awe, amazement, and envy. On the one hand, I couldn't believe Jackie was getting away with this: *He's really having sex on the floor of the Uptown!* I thought. *Man, I've gotta find a way to do this!* If I had to name a single event that convinced me to become a singer, this was it.

After several encores, the curtain fell and the house lights came up. Passing through the lobby, I happened to glance up at the clock, expecting it to say eleven or twelve o'clock, maybe even one. My heart just about stopped when I realized it was five minutes to four!

"Let's go!" I called out over my shoulder, and Tyrone and I dashed through the lobby, dodging folks casually ambling out into the night. Once I was out the Uptown's doors, it struck me that I'd never been out this late. Running through the dark, empty streets sent a chill of fear up my back. Pulse pounding, I ran the longest three and half blocks of my life. Tyrone lived a block closer to the Uptown than I did, so when we got to his street, we said our quick, breathless good-byes and split up. Outside my front door, I stopped, drew a deep breath, and fished out my house key. I deserved a whipping, and I knew it. *She's going to kill me!*

The house was dark, a good sign. Maybe my mother was asleep. *Easy does it,* I told myself. *Just stay quiet.* My hands were shaking so hard I could barely put the key in the door. As I managed to ease the key into the lock—*So far, so good*—I turned the key . . . and then a voice:

"Come on in, Teddy."

I pushed the door open and saw her sitting in a comfortable chair, waiting for me. There was nothing for me to say. This was the second time she'd caught me overstaying my curfew, and last time I'd gotten a stern talking-to. I knew I wasn't getting away that easy this time.

My mother said, "Go upstairs and take off all your clothes and come downstairs." Mom wasn't about to ruin the good clothes she'd worked so hard to buy me by whipping them, too.

I trudged up the stairs, certain Mom was going to whip my back with a belt, the punishment she resorted to only after she'd tried everything else. Mom did the best she could raising me alone, without a father. She knew all too well what kind of trouble would find me if I made a habit of running wild at all hours. Mom was putting a stop to my breaking curfew, and if it took a whipping to accomplish that, it was a necessary sacrifice, considering what was at stake.

I went upstairs, undressed, and then, out of respect for me, Mom turned off the lights. I came downstairs and awaited my fate. Years later, Mom recalled that night for me: "You came downstairs, but I couldn't raise a finger. I said, 'Dear God, a young man at his age, so humble, with no father around . . . that he would just listen to his mom and go upstairs and undress and come downstairs to accept a beating.' I couldn't do anything."

Mom sat down beside me and in a firm but weary voice explained how much she worried about me. She described all the things that could have happened to me, being out on the street so late. I was so tired, all I wanted to do was lay my head down. Whatever my punishment was going to be, I wanted it to be over, so I could go to sleep.

"Well, if you want to stay up all hours, here we are," Mom said. "You stand in the middle of this room for the rest of the night. And *not in the corner*—I don't want you leaning on anything."

I took up my position and stood there for what was left of the night, with my mother, so tired from working late, sitting on the couch watching me. I'd probably sound like a mature, sensitive guy if I said getting in such serious trouble changed me, but in fact, it didn't. I was a thirteen-year-old boy who had just discovered his dream. After that, there was no turning back.

My dreams were changed forever that night, but it took my real life a few years to get up to speed. In 1964 I was a basically mild-mannered, well-behaved, fashion-conscious, music-crazy, girl-watching kid. Probably the one thing that distinguished me from lots of other kids my age was that I was not one to run with the crowd. I guess you could say I was a loner. Never the most outgoing person, I never felt I'd connected with my classmates through the three different junior high schools I attended: FitzSimon, Gillespie, and Stetson. Maybe if I had stayed at one school for a couple of years, gotten to know people, and settled in, it might have been different for me. As it was, though, I came through my junior high years without ever really feeling a part of the scene.

What stands out most from those school days is winning a contest for having the best smile, an honor I shared with a girl. Another highlight for me was the special award I received from my music teacher, Mr. Fred Bacon. He's the only teacher whose name I can still remember. Mr. Bacon shares some credit with Jackie Wilson for helping me see that music could be my life. It was at Stetson that I became best buddies with Terry Ellington. We walked to school every day; he was my ace. His family and my mother became friends. And I'll never forget the spaghetti Terry's mom made. It was the best, and to this day I still make my spaghetti exactly the same. (Bet you'd love to know how, but I ain't tellin' you, so don't ask.) Beyond friends and music, school didn't interest me. I did my work and kept up my grades.

As I became a teenager, the effects of not having a father began weighing more heavily on me, though I see that now mostly in retrospect. Wonderful as my mother is, I had questions that only a father could answer, questions I wouldn't even *think* of asking her. I was very fortunate, then, to have been taken under the wing of my cousin Pete's father, my uncle Andy. Uncle Andy was a truck driver, a sturdy guy whose morning breakfast consisted of corned beef hash, salt pork bacon, scrambled eggs with cheese, and grits—all smothered in a thick, dark-brown canned molasses that he had sent to him from down South. Uncle Andy could be tough, but he had a wonderful heart. Whether he was trying to make a first baseman out of me, teaching me how to drink liquor, or helping my mother get me back in line, Uncle Andy was always there to lend an ear or offer advice. He was the most important male influence in my life, and for his love and support, I will always be grateful.

As I grew older, the pressure from the gangs intensified, and their intimidation tactics got more brazen and senseless. It was easy to see why lots of guys capitulated and joined. I learned a few martial arts techniques from a friend and could hold my own in a fight, but it wasn't something I liked to do if I could avoid it. On the other hand, I wasn't going to be running scared all the time, either. When some bullies threatened to get me one day after school, I decided to confront them and get it done with. Usually the other guys would form a circle around you and your opponent, you'd throw a few punches, then you'd make up and be friends again. But between the first threats and the final punch, a rivalry like this was a big, big deal.

News that my tormentor and I would be squaring off after the last bell spread throughout the school, so we had a good crowd for our match.

"All right, 'Grass, it's time to rumble," the kid snarled. "I'm gonna whup your ass!"

Next thing I knew he was running at me. I couldn't move, so I closed my eyes, made a fist, extended my arm out straight, and began to accept that I didn't have a prayer. To my surprise, the fool ran right into my fist! I opened my eyes to see him wiping the blood from his nose and looking at me in astonishment.

"Oh! You bloodied my nose!" he screamed as he came charging again. I hit him again—this time more confidently—and the fight was over.

By the time I was in my teens, the rules of engagement had changed. In the schoolyard, the fights we fought were "fair ones." If you called or agreed to a fair one, it meant that you would fight one-on-one; no dirty tricks, nobody else jumpin' in. Now that we were older, it wasn't kid stuff anymore. Knives and guns were still rare, except in cases of all-out gang war. Still, you could take a pretty bad beating if you got "gorilla-ed," or jumped. Once I got into my teens, I started venturing out into different neighborhoods. I was cautious about where I went and whose turf I crossed, but I also refused to let the gangs limit where I could go and what I could do. I just made sure to keep my eyes open.

One particular night I'd left a dance being held upstairs over a Florsheim shoe store, on the northwest corner of Broad and Erie. The stop for the trolley I wanted to catch home, the 23, was on the pedestrian island where Broad, Germantown, and Erie converged. I was waiting for the trolley, casually glancing around, when I happened to look back over toward the shoe store and saw a gang of guys heading my way, and in a hurry. Since I knew the neighborhood, I was sure they were from the gang known as 15V, for their corner— Fifteenth and Venango. *Oh, God,* I thought to myself. My heart was racing, and I could feel the adrenaline starting to surge. I recognized them from the dance, and I knew what they were after: I was set to get my ass beat.

I wasted a couple of seconds wondering why—*Did they see me leave the dance alone? Had I stepped on somebody's toes? Talked to somebody's girl?*—but, bottom line, these guys didn't need a reason. I was from someplace else, and I was alone, and they felt like getting somebody. There was nothing else to know.

What the hell am I gonna do now? A block or so up the street, the trolley stopped. My eyes darted between the approaching gang and the trolley. *Should I run for the trolley and risk getting caught somewhere between stops? Stay here and pray? Run? Where? Into some other gang's territory? Out into traffic, just to get away?* I never felt so alone in my life. Just as I was about to sprint back, the light changed and the trolley began rolling.

Hurry, hurry, hurry, I prayed. The trolley glided toward me in slow motion, while the gang got louder, meaner, and closer by the second. Who was going to get there first? I heard the guys whooping and shouting. In a lightning-quick move, they snatched the belts from their waists and started wrapping them around their hands. I knew what that meant: I was going to get hurt, and bad.

Come on, come on, come on! When the driver stopped and opened the door, the gang was close enough to touch me. I jumped aboard the trolley and felt a sharp *bam!* on the top of my head as a belt buckle ripped my scalp. Seeing the gang and sizing up the situation, the driver quickly shut the doors and took off.

"Son, your head is bleeding," he said kindly.

I put my hand to my head and felt the warm blood running through my fingers. It hurt so bad, and I was so shaken thinking of what might have happened, that all I could think was, *Thank You, Jesus. Thank You.*

There were other incidents over the years, each one unexpected, terrifying, and senseless. The gang mentality made no sense to me, so working out of town in the summer was a pleasant respite from all that crap.

Two blueberry, one banana, three cherry," the waitress said as she handed me the little green order slip.

"Comin' up!" I replied, wiping the sweat from my forehead as I eyed the dozen steaming waffle irons, the big bowls of batter and toppings. This summer, I was thirteen or fourteen and had lied my way into a job as a short-order cook on the boardwalk in Wildwood, New Jersey. Wildwood was a south Jersey shore town whose tourist attraction was a large, carny-style amusement park built on the boardwalk. My aunt Dee accompanied me and a couple of cousins, and we stayed with people who rented us rooms. It wasn't as though we were out running wild for the summer; we were there to work, and we stayed out of trouble.

"Three strawberry and change that banana to a walnut!"

"Got it!" I quickly ladled the batter into the empty iron, gently dropped the lid, and heard it hiss as the extra batter bubbled out the sides. Then I did it again. Then again, and again, and again. Another slip landed on the counter.

"Excuse me, does this say blueberry?" I asked.

"Blackberry! Can't you read?" the waitress snapped.

Can't you write? I thought to myself, but I said, "Okay, one black-berry comin' up!" On the other side of a plate-glass window stood several curious customers who, for some unfathomable reason, found watching the waffle maker so . . . interesting. *What are they looking at? I'm not putting on a show here!* I'd think as I checked the fires under the irons and whipped up more batter. It's hard to say which part of the job bothered me more: trying to keep track of all the orders or being gawked at all day. Whatever it was, I couldn't wait for my break.

When I got my few minutes' break, I walked down the ramp from the boardwalk to the street below, where there was a bus station with a jukebox. I still had my apron on as I fingered a handful of change, peered through the jukebox glass, and read the selections: James Brown's "Out of Sight," the Impressions' "Keep On Pushing," the Supremes' "Where Did Our Love Go?" the Drifters' "Under the Boardwalk." I was minding my own business, when suddenly three or four white boys approached. Like a bolt from the blue, without provocation or warning, one of them slapped the hell out of me, right across the face.

What the—?! I staggered back and instinctively raised my hands to protect myself.

The guy who hit me sneered, "What the fuck you gonna do about it, *Nigger?*"

I glanced around the bus station. Everybody was looking at us, but nobody made a move to help me. One of my cousins worked with me at the waffle place, and for a second I thought that if he'd gotten his break when I did, he'd be here with me right now. The waffle place was close enough that I could have run and called for help. But *"Nigger"*? No way anybody was going to call me that and make me run. I'd rather get my ass kicked fighting for my honor and respect than to escape to safety.

"We don't want Niggers like you around here, you understand?" he hissed, striding toward me.

Scared as I was, no racist white boy was gonna make a punk out of me. "I'll fight *you*," I said, barely able to hear my own voice over the pounding of my heart. "But I'm not going to fight all your friends."

The guy stopped, and within seconds a policeman was ordering us to "break it up." My blood boiled with rage. *Nigger.* I knew that word, knew what it meant, and even more important, knew what white folks meant when they said it. Nearly four centuries of hatred, violence, murder, and pain. One word. This was the first time anyone had ever called me that, and the idea that someone who didn't even know me could see me as nothing more than something to hate, even hurt—it tore through my soul in a way that still pains me to remember today.

Back home in Philadelphia, the police might harass you and treat you like they thought you were a nigger, but they'd never actually utter the word. But that day in Wildwood was the first time I'd ever heard a white person say that word to me in anger. Maybe one reason I hadn't been called that before was that in my younger years, I had few occasions to venture outside my community, or because the whites I did come into contact with, like the Sciollas, were decent folks.

Of course, there was racism, but for the most part it was an oblique, unspoken thing. The last time my mother and I moved into a good "mixed" neighborhood, I made friends with black and white kids. In fact, I used to hang on the corner with some white guys eager to learn those elements of cool we black kids assumed as a birthright. I remember teaching them slang and showing them how to wrap their heads in doo-rags, like black guys wore after they'd had a process. When they found out I played drums, these guys asked me if I knew how to play "Wipe Out." "Wipe Out"? Please. I'm proud to say I have never played "Wipe Out."

We all played stickball, Philadelphia style, using a broomstick to bat a little ten-cent rubber ball we called a "pimple" ball. Our "field" was the high, windowless side of a candy factory on Eighth Street. The pitcher stood across the street from the batter, who "scored" by hitting the ball against parts of the wall we designated "single," "double," "triple," "home run," and so on. We cut the pimple balls in half, so they couldn't travel too far and bust a window, because tearing up the neighborhood like that was something we knew better than to even think about.

We had some great times together. I remember once winning a five-dollar bet that I could guzzle a whole quart of Coca-Cola without stopping. Of course, I tricked them by swallowing very slowly and pretending I was drinking when I really wasn't. But what the heck. We were just kids bein' kids. Color didn't matter.

We all came from different places, but the point is, we got along fine. The only real difference between the white kids and the black kids in my new neighborhood was that over the winter, the white kids' parents usually packed up and moved away. With every spring came new neighbors, most of them black and Puerto Rican, which was cool. I guess it wasn't the fact that people moved away that bothered me: It was why. You could see prejudice in how people described our neighborhood. Throughout Philadelphia there were areas of white working-class people every bit as poor as we were, but only black neighborhoods were called ghettos. The only trouble I had in North Philly was with gangs, and that had nothing to do with color. That all changed that day in Wildwood.

Looking back, I can better understand why my mother was so upset the night I came home late from the Uptown. To be a black teenager was to be vulnerable to violence, to trouble, to suspicion. I learned this the hard way one winter day when I was almost fifteen.

I had just come out of my house on Eighth Street and was on my way to visit some friends over on Fifth. I immediately noticed up the street two young black guys going through the pockets of a white neighbor. He was drunk enough to be unsteady on his feet, and the two guys had him against a wall and were picking his pockets. I knew they weren't hurting him and I didn't want to get involved, so I put on my blinders, crossed Eighth Street, turned the corner, and kept walking.

A few minutes later, a police car slowed down beside me and pulled over to the curb. "Where are you going?" one of the cops demanded.

"Going to visit some friends over on Fifth Street," I replied guardedly. "I live on Eighth."

"Well, we just got a report about some black boys about your age robbing a white man," one of them said in a tone that made me realize I was a suspect.

"I didn't rob anybody," I answered. "I live right back around the corner—"

"Okay, let's go," he said, motioning toward the police car. From the backseat of the police car, I watched the familiar streets of my neighborhood pass by and wondered, *Why me?* I tried to be cool and polite. I knew that anything could happen to me. No one knew where I was.

As the two white cops escorted me into the police station, I spotted the two guys who had done the robbery. Some other cops must have worked them over but good: Blood was dripping from fresh gashes on their heads and faces, and I remember thinking, *Is that going to happen to me?* Suddenly a cop grabbed my arm and led me into a room. There sat the man who'd been robbed, still so drunk he couldn't have found his butt with two hands and a flashlight. He took one look at me, waved his hand about, and said in a slurred voice, "It was all of them. All of them."

"I wasn't there!" I protested. "I didn't do a thing!" But nobody listened. The next thing I knew I was being hustled into another room.

The door closed behind me and I found myself trapped with a short, stocky, hostile white cop with a real bad attitude. His sleeves were neatly rolled up, and he looked as if he'd just kicked some ass and was ready to kick some more. *Is this what I'm in for?* I stood against the wall, scared to death, while he angrily paced back and forth like a boxer wound up for the opening bell, the whole time glaring at me. I tried not to meet his eyes. I knew I couldn't scream for help and hope to get it. I knew I couldn't escape. This was it: He had a license to get my ass, and we both knew it.

"So, you like to rob old white men, huh?"

I was smart enough not to answer. He cocked a muscle-bound arm and clocked me square in the face with such force that it knocked me to the floor. I stayed down, pretending to be unconscious, because if I got up again, he'd just keep decking me until I couldn't get up anymore.

Later that night my mother came to the police station, and I was released. She knew I was innocent, and I will never forget the fear and pain in her eyes. But my mother is nothing if not determined, and our church came together and helped her find a highly recommended lawyer to defend me, Mr. Joseph McNeal. Being young and somewhat naive, I believed that I couldn't be punished. Hell, I was innocent! If the neighbor would just tell the police and the judge the truth, this would all be over with.

So I decided to pay a visit to my neighbor. When I knocked on his door, he greeted me cordially. I explained the whole situation to him and a look of concern came over his face.

"I know you didn't do it," he said. "You're that Pendergrass kid from up the block. You didn't bother me."

"Yes, sir, I know. But you told the police that I had something to do with your being robbed, and now I'm going to court soon."

He promised that he would straighten it out for me, and he did call the police department to explain his mistake. Later, in court, he tried to officially retract his accusation against me, but the judge wouldn't hear it. Because this was juvenile court, I didn't have the legal protections I would have had as an adult, and the judge had greater leeway in deciding which evidence and testimony could be considered. The judge believed me to be guilty as charged, with highway robbery. My heart dropped when I heard him say, "I am not allowing this retraction to come in at this point, because it's very likely that he may have changed his testimony because the defendant threatened him."

It didn't matter that my neighbor had been drunk at the time, or that the other two guys didn't even know that I'd seen them. I was presumed guilty and pronounced guilty. What's always bothered me is that the judge sentenced the other two guys to an indefinite sentence to be served in a much tougher institution than the one I was sent to. Why would he have done that if he didn't have some reservations about the matter of my guilt? And if he did have those reservations, he should have let me go with a warning or perhaps probation. Instead I was given four months at the Youth Study Center in Philadelphia, my punishment for being in the wrong place at the wrong time. And being the wrong color.

The Youth Study Center, where I served my sentence, was a big plain building located at the corner of Second and Luzerne. It wasn't really a jail or even a detention center, but a temporary home for kids accused of minor, nonviolent crimes and kids who had problems at home. In fact, it operated under the auspices of the Philadelphia school system.

The building was divided into sections they called blocks, and you were assigned to one: A block, B block, C block, and so on. On one side of each block was an aisle, and on the other were cubicles, doorless compartments, each with four sets of bunk beds. Every block had a supervisor, who sat near the front and was ostensibly supposed to keep order. To the back of the block was an area where we would gather, play cards, and just hang out.

The blocks and the building were locked, but there were no gates or fences outside. I arrived there frightened but determined to get through it, whatever that took. I'd already decided I wasn't going to waste my time there lamenting my bad luck. It was too late for that, anyway.

As I soon learned, the rules of the street applied at the Youth Study Center, too. It was as though you'd already "passed" one test just by getting in there. Now you had to prove that you were strong enough, tough enough, mean enough to be there, or at least tough enough not be made into some other guy's "girlfriend."

Soon after arriving, I had my "initiation": One by one, they each challenged me to box, and I held my own with each one, from a tiny guy named Preston to a big, tall guy we called the Green Giant. Of course, fighting was forbidden, so you had to do it in a way that didn't attract attention, and you better be sure you didn't make any noise, no matter how bad you got hurt. What we'd do is move to the back of the block, away from the supervisor. As I soon learned, the supervisors were hip to what was happening; they just didn't give a damn if we pummeled each other. Nobody was going to come to my rescue. The way we boxed, the two opponents would stand as close to each other as they could and throw closed-fisted punches every-where but to the face and the groin. Every now and then a guy would get "slid"—"accidentally" hit lightly in the face—just so that his opponent could intimidate him and show he meant business. Ba-sically, you'd just punch the hell out of each other until one of you couldn't take any more punishment.

Finally, I just got tired of it. I was totally alone there and just didn't want to box anymore. I didn't know what else to do, and out of des-peration, I shouted, "The next guy who puts his hands on me, I'm gonna beat the hell out of him with this damn chair!" It was a pretty strong statement, and I made it without even thinking first. Luckily for me, they figured either I was crazy or that I really meant it. Either way, they left me alone.

I would hang with some of the guys, and we'd pass the day just talking, smoking, playing cards, and things like that. But I never let anyone get too close, and after I left I never saw any of them again. I knew I didn't belong there, but it wouldn't have been cool to play the snob. I just went along to get along, marking time.

Whatever bitterness I felt was tempered by the fact that my family supported me 100 percent. Unlike some of the guys there, I had a good home waiting for me when I got out. Sunday was the official visiting day, and besides seeing me then, Mom came by nearly every day to drop off a welcome hot lunch from Sciolla's: a meatball hoagie, spaghetti and meatballs, a cheese-steak sandwich. My other family members visited me on Sundays whenever they could, and we would go out on the grounds. I still remember celebrating my fifteenth birthday there, with my mother and some other relatives. We had cake, candles, the whole bit.

I don't think you can ever understand the depths of a parent's pain until you have children of your own, and as a kid, I probably didn't. But I do know that it broke my mother's heart to see me there. Still, she remained a pillar of strength, the epitome of dignity throughout. Many years later, she told me how much better she felt after the counselors at the Center confided that they believed me innocent. They also told her that they'd never seen a boy pass through there who was so obviously loved and cared about. Again, truly blessed.

I emerged from the Youth Study Center eager to get back to school and my budding social life. None of my friends or I had a car, and our parents and neighbors still watched us like hawks. We used to do something we called "strollin'," a cocky way of walking down the street that parents absolutely hated. You would stroll everyplace except your own block, because if a neighbor saw you and dimed on you, you'd be in trouble.

We did a lot of our socializing at house parties. All you needed for a great house party was a basement or living room, a stack of slow-dance 45s, and a blue or red lightbulb—for atmosphere, of course, during the slow dances. House parties had their own traditions, if you will. You didn't just go to slow dancing right away; you had to build up to it, rap to the right girl, and so on. The early part of the party we usually danced to great records like Jr. Walker and the All Stars' "Shotgun," Major Lance's "Um, Um, Um, Um, Um, Um," Martha and the Vandellas' "Dancing in the Street," and the Contours' "Do You Love Me." And we did whatever dances were popular and cool: the shotgun, the hitchhike, the swim, Mickey's monkey, the twine. And, if a girl would let you, the infamous dog.

But those slow dances . . . To be fifteen, slow-dancing with a girl to "Ooh Baby Baby," "The Tracks of My Tears," "My Girl," or—best of all—"You've Really Got a Hold on Me," in the cool blue glow of a pole lamp, holding her as close as you dared and daring to get as close as she'd let you (and I think you know what I'm talking about) . . . mmmmm, paradise. There was something about "You've Really Got a Hold on Me"—the "tighter, tighter"—that worked magic on young girls. And I speak for millions of men when I say thank God for Smokey Robinson. I was crazy about different girls at different times. I didn't have any one particular serious relationship when I was young, but I loved girls, and not just for the reasons you'd think. Hugging and kissing and making out—that was fine. Actually, it was better than fine. But I also liked girls as friends. I loved to just talk to them. I was interested in what they thought and how they felt. I remember hanging with a girl named Delores who lived around the corner. She might have had a crush on me, but at that time I was trying to get close to another girl. I liked Delores, but not that way.

One day after I told Mom that Delores didn't have a date for the junior prom, she said, "Well, Teddy, why don't you take her?"

"Yeah," I answered. "Delores would really like that." Now, not to pat myself on the back or anything, but I really felt that way. Mom bought me a cool new suit, and seeing Delores so happy made me happy. At heart, I really was a nice guy.

I still hung with a group of guys who were more concerned with dressing cool than running with a gang. Sharply creased khaki pants in dark green, tan, or navy; pastel "highboy" shirts; and flawlessly polished Stacy Adams wing-tip shoes made up the basic uniform, with great attention paid to the tiniest details. Our shirts were called "highboys" because the collars stood a little taller. We'd take them to the Chinese laundry and have them starched so stiff they'd practically bruise the back of your neck. We also wore Banlon pullover knit shirts that we called 'lons and bought on sale at the Big Store. When we were dressed just right, we'd say we were yochin'.

Germantown Avenue was the main shopping strip, and I spent hours checking out the clothes at Leo's and the Red Carpet. They had the sharpest stuff I'd ever seen, and I spent hours gazing in the shop windows, promising myself that someday I'd be sporting one of those iridescent suits that seemed to change color in the sunlight or a crisp sharkskin suit, like I'd seen on some of the guys at the Uptown. And the day I finally got my first sharkskin—man, you couldn't tell me I wasn't clean!

Looking back, I see that one reason the street gangs never attracted me was that I had these other outlets, like social clubs. I was attending Thomas Alva Edison High School, an all-boys school at Eighth and Lehigh, and it's telling that even though I lived only half a block away, I never made it to my seat before the first bell. By then my morning ritual—meeting some guys in a storefront alcove on Germantown Avenue, three blocks from my house and two blocks from school, singing for about an hour, and then beginning the walk to school at the last possible minute—had become as important to me as attending school.

"Hey, you know 'Since I Lost My Baby'?" someone might say.

"Nah, how 'bout 'Storm Warning,' by the Volcanoes? One, two, three—"

We'd stand on the corner and sing everything from 1950s doo-wop classics to the latest Motown hit—basically anything you could wrap a lot of harmonies around. I loved singing on the corner so much that in the bitter cold of winter, I'd stand outside in that alcove, wearing nothing but a thin trench coat, and, I swear, never feel the cold. And, of course, we'd watch the girls go by. There must have been some kind of magic in hearing a guy singing about love, because try as she might, no girl could pass without at least glancing our way. And there was my chance. If I could just hold that eye contact long enough to smile, say hello, and strike up a conversation, I had a chance.

There were fine-looking girls everywhere in Philly—and I can still recall a few, like Sheena Johnson, Jerri White, and Sugie, a beautiful girl who wore a leg brace because she'd had polio—but I found myself most attracted to the girls who caught the bus there to go up to Germantown. They had a certain look, a certain style, and they carried themselves with an aloof air. Most of the time, they acted as if they couldn't be bothered talking to me. I just wanted to rap to them, get some phone numbers. Of course, knowing I didn't stand a chance only made me want to get over with them that much more. Every time one of them snubbed us, we'd laugh and call out, "Hey, look at you, Miss 500!"—trying to be cool, as though we didn't care. But we were teenagers and naturally status-conscious. Getting some Germantown girls to come to your social club's dance was, as they say, the shit.

Pretty soon I was cutting classes, hanging out, and paying more attention to girls. It was all part of growing up, finding out who you are and what you're about. I often cut school with my friend Charlie Boy, and unless one of our friends had parents who were at work and full run of his house for the day, we'd roam the streets. Charlie and I called each other "Ace," short for "Ace-Koon-Poon-Ski-Boony-Roony." It didn't "mean" anything; it was just jive talk we made up to pass the time, have a laugh. My friends and I would play hooky, pool our pocket change, and convince an older guy to buy us a bottle of Tokay (a red, which I preferred) or the white Thunderbird, those cheap—and I mean rock-bottom, gut-churning, head-searing cheap, as in costing less than a dollar a bottle—nasty wines that got you high but left you with a head-throbbing hangover that made suicide look good. Looking back, it hardly seemed worth it, but really getting high wasn't the point. Hanging in an alley, sipping out of a brown paper bag—man, we were bad boys. We were cool.

I was the kind of kid whose early forays into the forbidden often entailed "learning a lesson." My first attempt at "serious" drinking ended in disaster. When I was fifteen, I injured my shoulder while executing a high jump for the school gymnastics team. At the hospital, a doctor popped my shoulder back into place and gave me a sling, along with strict instructions to wear it at all times. A few days later Uncle Andy and Aunt Persephone threw a sixteenth-birthday party for my cousin Pete. Anticipating the romantic possibilities—cute girls, slow dancing, you get the picture?—I decided the sling would cramp my style, not to mention clash with my threads. I left it home.

Pete and I were about inseparable then. We did almost everything together. Uncle Andy, observing a time-honored fatherly tradition, felt it was high time Pete and I learned how to drink. Before the party began, Uncle Andy held up a big bottle of dark amber Inverhouse scotch and declared, "Every time I take a drink, you can have a drink!"

We couldn't believe our luck. It was brown and bitter, and cost more than a dollar a bottle? This was the stuff *men* drank!

The party began. Pete and I would be in the living room, rappin' to the girls and dancing to the music, then Uncle Andy would call us back into the kitchen. He'd put out three glasses and pour a good-size shot in each.

"Okay, fellas, bottoms up!" Uncle Andy said, then knocked it back.

Surprise! That stuff was *nasty* going down, but naturally we didn't let on how nasty. I gulped it down quick, suppressed the urge to gag, and pretended the burning in my throat felt good. Uncle Andy, who obviously had a lot more experience with drinking, sat in the kitchen between sips, while Pete and I were up dancing and sweating and feeling the full effect.

I lost count of how many times we repeated the kitchen ritual, but I doubt I'd have been able to count too high anyway. The room spun one way, my head spun the other, and my stomach lurched around as if it couldn't decide which way to go. I do vaguely recall that by the time I staggered upstairs and collapsed face-first onto a bed, I felt like hell. The sound of the music still playing and people still laughing only made my head throb more.

The next morning I awoke to find myself lying in my own vomit, embarrassed beyond words. And my shoulder hurt like hell. I didn't take another drink of hard liquor again until way later.

I was growing up, and I was drifting away from school. I knew it was important to have a good education; I'd seen firsthand how hard my mother worked. I knew that without an education, my options would be limited. While I had no firm plans to go to college, it was something I thought I'd do someday. I wanted to be somebody, maybe a landscape designer or an architect. Finishing high school had always been pretty much a given. Until I got to Edison.

It's probably not fair to blame the school when the roots of the problems there extended much deeper, to the prevailing attitudes toward kids from the ghetto. I never knew where most of my teachers lived; I knew that one lived around my neighborhood. Still, as a kid, I had the sense that many of them were from someplace else, that they didn't live the kind of life I did and didn't understand what I needed an education to do for me. Most of the teachers at Edison were white, which may have accounted for the cultural gap between them and some of the students. There may have been a few exceptions, but most of the teachers I had seemed to be doing little more than punching the clock until retirement.

For whatever reason, the teachers brought no enthusiasm to the classroom. Most classes consisted of a halfhearted lecture, and teachers rarely encouraged questions or made much effort to help boys who were falling behind. I don't recall there being any tutoring or remedial programs offered. I suppose an extremely motivated student could have wrung a good education out of there, but I never got the sense that any special effort would be acknowledged or rewarded. The guys I went to school with needed someone to reach out to them, someone to spark their curiosity, jump-start their minds. I personally never witnessed that kind of teaching at Edison then, and we all suffered for it.

If I had to pick one word to describe the atmosphere there, it would be *hopeless.* The civil rights movement had shone a spotlight on the inner city's many problems, but nothing really changed for the better. Shortly before we moved into the house Mom bought on Eighth Street, I remember walking from the house she'd rented on Sydenham to the new house with my dog, Bruno, a cocker spaniel–fox terrier mix my aunt Persephone had given me. Something about the new neighborhood made me feel that I could relax. Mom had gone over earlier to get the house ready, and Bruno and I were just walking along when suddenly he started to pull on his leash, and I followed him onto a porch. When we reached the front door, I realized this was the address on the piece of paper Mom had given me, and I found her there. Bruno was my buddy, and a real smart dog, but today I still wonder how he knew this was our new home.

You could see this was a neighborhood where folks cared about their homes. I remember my mother had me out scrubbing the front steps with a brush, sweeping the sidewalk. In the summer, we had block parties, where neighbors brought out food, played records on portable record players, and just had a good, friendly time. Every year the block captain organized "Clean Up, Paint Up, Fix Up Week," and we'd all go out and repaint the house numbers on the curb.

Still, no amount of new paint could hide the fact that the times and the city were changing. For the first time, I was seeing unemployed older guys drunk or nodding off in the street, high on heroin or narcotic cough syrups. And the gang activity started spreading like a cancer. The opportunities people outside the ghetto took for granted simply weren't available to us. If anything, North Philadelphia was as poor as ever, and with gang members more apt to settle disputes with weapons instead of fists, more dangerous, too. It's telling that plenty of guys I went to high school with honestly believed they were more likely to survive a tour of duty in Vietnam than another year on the streets of North Philly.

I didn't see either of those options for myself; it was a mentality that I couldn't understand or accept. There were lots of reasons to join gangs—protection, girls, an excuse to run wild. Looking back now, I can see that many of the guys I knew never mattered to anyone and were never made to feel important until the day they joined a gang. For them, the gang provided the only place in their lives where they felt they were in charge, as though they were somebody.

Another reason gang life never drew me in was that Mom had raised me to be confident, assured, and independent. I never was the type to do something just because someone else said I should. From the day I was born, my mother made me feel special and loved; she taught me not to be a follower, to think for myself. I didn't need to join a gang or intimidate people to feel that I was somebody. I had nothing to prove to anybody but myself.

The example my mother set for me, her teachings and religious beliefs, gave me self-esteem and the ability to know right from wrong. My mother—I thank God for her every day. She always set the perfect example for me. She was honest, sweet, and kind. She lived by her beliefs and her principles. She never smoked, never drank, and never brought men into our home. My mother found all that she needed in Jesus Christ, and she conducted her life accordingly.

Her influence and guidance saved me countless times, but like most kids, I'd reached the point where I wanted to find out some things for myself. This is a journey all kids have to make, but for a young black man, it can be a dangerous one. I knew how easy it was to get into trouble, and I'd also seen so many guys get caught up in the activity of the streets. I was beginning to feel the pull of my buddies' influence, which is how I started cutting classes and my grades began to fall. There wasn't one specific thing that happened, yet I couldn't deny feeling a strange, invisible undertow, like a force drawing me toward things that I knew I shouldn't be doing. I knew playing hooky, drinking in the alley, and racking up detentions weren't the worst things a kid could do, but I also knew this wasn't the kind of life my mother had raised me to lead. Nor was it what I wanted for myself. I believed I deserved better.

I'd worked very hard at catching up in my studies once I got out of the Youth Study Center. For a while there, I was doing okay, but before long I felt myself losing interest. After I received a failing report card and learned I wasn't graduating from the eleventh grade, I decided it was best for me to quit school. I had a long talk with Mom and explained all my reasons for quitting school. Although my mother was very upset over my decision and disappointed that I wouldn't graduate from high school, she wasn't disappointed in *me,* and that's a big difference. If school had offered something positive, I'd have stayed. But that wasn't the case. All I could expect from staying in school was trouble. Mom knew I was making the right decision under the circumstances. I vowed I'd get my high school diploma someday, and I eventually did keep my promise, though many years later.

———

The first morning after I quit school, I was scanning the classified ads for a job. I'd always worked, delivering papers, junkin' (redeeming deposit bottles, collecting and selling newspapers and scrap metal), then working through the summers. If I'd written a résumé covering my first couple of years after high school, it would have included picking peaches and blueberries on farms in New Jersey, driving a cab (I lied about my age), driving a sixteen-foot truck (lied about my age *and* my experience), and delivering and picking up rented outdoor furniture. I'd do anything but stay home and have my mother support me. I learned one thing: There's a job out there for everybody who really wants to work. And when I say I worked, I mean I worked. When I worked on a truck bringing meat and produce to grocery stores, I had to be up at 2:00 A.M., leave the house at around 3:30, and be on the truck by 4:00 A.M. I walked the eight deserted blocks alone. My mother just prayed; so did I.

I was always a quick study. After I accepted the truck-driving job, my only "training" was riding with a driver and teaching myself when to shift gears by watching him. The next day, sitting behind the wheel, I was shaking inside. But I pulled out, and away I went down the street. Clearly, somebody was watching over me, but I wasn't always so lucky. The first summer day I rode the bus down to New Jersey to pick peaches, I came home scratching, which I learned was an allergic reaction to the peach fuzz. Someone advised me to coat my skin with Vaseline, to keep the fuzz off. The next day I tried it. I was up in a tree when I suddenly felt I was burning up. Under the scorching summer sun, the Vaseline was literally cooking my skin. I jumped out of the tree and wiped off as much of the stuff as I could, but then it was back to itching from the peach fuzz. So ended my career as a peach picker.

My point in telling you all this is that I had no problem with hard, honest work. I'll never forget Mom—who accomplished all she did with only a fourth-grade education—saying, "Even if you're a garbage picker, be the best garbage picker," and I applied that philosophy to anything I tried. Music was my love, and if that had never happened for me, I'd have found some other profession and, I'm sure, done well with it. I had too much pride for it to be any other way. But when I look back, the "hardships" of straight work gave me a little extra incentive to roll with the setbacks and disappointments of my early music career.

In addition to a booming local recording industry, Philadelphia was home to countless small clubs. I really wanted to be a singer, but I was practical about it, figuring I'd do anything I had to in order to get my foot in the door. So I took the occasional gig drumming, even if I had to haul my kit on the bus. Artists playing the Uptown sometimes recruited stand-in musicians from outside the stage door, so I'd hang out from time to time, with my sticks in my back pocket. Then one night I got my first lucky break. There was a singer named Herb Ward who had a couple of singles out. Right before he was set to go on, his band up and quit, leaving Ward to hustle up a new band in not much more than an hour.

Someone stuck his head out the stage door of the Uptown and asked, "Any drummers around?"

I volunteered, and with a few other musicians Ward borrowed from other bands (including, I believe, the bass player from the Unifics), we played his show. The Uptown's bandleader, Leon Mitchell, sort of led us through the set. I was up on that stage for only a little while, but it was glorious! I don't even remember whether or not I got paid, but it didn't matter.

I was usually pretty cautious, but I was always ambitious, and so when opportunity knocked, I was eager to answer. Maybe a little bit too eager. My first brush with what I would call *real* show business came in the person of a manager named Gene Lawson, a smooth-talking, impeccably dressed black man who convinced me he would make me a star. "I have connections," he used to say, although never getting more specific than that. And I believed him.

Anxious to make my way in the world, I believed I could handle my budding career myself, so I hastily, foolishly signed a management contract without consulting anyone, not even my own mother. I went with him to a recording studio in Englewood, New Jersey. I recorded two songs for a single (I remember only one: "Angel with Muddy Feet"), then came home and waited to hear my record on the radio. And waited. And waited.

Long story short, I never saw or heard my first record, and I never heard from Lawson again. I never found out what happened. Welcome to showbiz. In fact, though, this was another blessing in disguise. If something good had developed, I'd have been tied to this management deal for quite some time. Of course, this is hindsight talking. In 1966 I was a sixteen-year-old kid singer whose first dreams of stardom had been crushed. To say I was devastated doesn't even begin to describe it.

At the time, Philadelphia's local songwriters, record producers, and managers were concentrated in an office building over the Shubert Theater, down on Broad and Locust. One day I had left Lawson's office and was on my way to the elevator when I heard a piano playing in a room down the hall. Curious, I walked by the open door and peeked in.

There, in a large rehearsal room, four guys were singing around an upright piano, and the piano player was coaching them through the song. The quartet sounded great, with rich, tight harmonies. I listened for a few minutes, but didn't want to interrupt them or risk being told to beat it. I had no way of knowing it then, but looking back years later I realized that the piano player was Kenny Gamble and the group was the Intruders. (Later that year they would begin having a series of hits, peaking with 1968's "Cowboys to Girls," written and produced by Gamble and his partner Leon Huff.) I've often thought to myself, *That's the office* I *should have been in.* I rarely look back and think, *What if?,* but I can't help wondering what might have

been if I'd just nudged that door open and said, "Hi, I'm Teddy Pendergrass. I can sing."

Oddly, my false start with Lawson only strengthened my determination to get into show business. Only one thing threatened to di-
vert me from my path, and that was the draft, which loomed closer
every day. The Vietnam War had begun to really heat up, and every
week it seemed more guys from the neighborhood were packing up
for boot camp, either voluntarily or because they'd been drafted. I
never really checked it out, but I'd heard that an only son would be
exempt from the draft. So I was a little surprised when I received the
notice requesting that I report for my physical. I was determined not
to go to 'Nam. I respected guys who believed in that cause and had
their own reasons for going. But without getting too political about
it, I simply felt that Vietnam was not a place that I should be. I wasn't
in college and didn't have a family of my own, so I couldn't get a de-
ferment on those grounds. I was prime—a healthy young black
man—and I knew there would be no medical exemption. Unless, of
course, I could fake one. Word on the street was that if you ate a cube
of sugar before the physical, your urine sample would show elevated
blood sugar, which indicated diabetes, which meant instant exemption from service. Beautiful.

I completed the physical, confident I'd beat the draft, when a
doctor motioned to me. "Pendergrass!" he barked. "You wait over
here. We'll have to do the urine test again." My heart sank, then I
panicked. Never thinking they'd require two samples, I hadn't brought
along any more sugar. My only hope was to try to talk my way out
of going. Desperate, I pleaded my case.

"I just can't do this," I said firmly. "I'm really afraid to go, and I
don't think I could handle it." I probably said a lot more, but I was
nervous and that's about all I remember.

Now, in those days, who knows how many guys in my position
tried the same thing, got caught, made the same arguments, and still

got shipped out. No one at the draft board seemed in any way moved or impressed by my speech. They'd heard it all before, probably from guys who later came home in flag-draped pine boxes. I trudged home thinking, *Damn. They've got me now.* I started considering whether I should dodge the draft, maybe flee to Canada. I worried about leaving my mother, and what would happen if I refused to go.

A few days later I held in my hand the envelope containing my fate. This was it. I drew a deep breath and tore it open. To my shock, it was a new draft card with a new draft status. I was no longer 1A. I was exempt. I was safe. I closed my eyes and whispered, "Thank you, Lord." I was saved again.

THREE

My determination to make it as a musician grew not only from my love of music but also from the fact that I came up in a time when there was so much great music to love. I know, I know: Every generation thinks the music they grew up listening to was better than whatever came before or after it. But for about a decade beginning in the mid-1960s, black music underwent changes in sound, attitude, and spirit that were inspiring and revolutionary. Its power was so undeniable, its reach so strong, that in 1967 *Time* magazine was moved to give it a cover: It was soul.

Black music *always* had soul, but never before had its essence coalesced in so many different forms, touched so many people, and spoken so honestly and eloquently about what it meant to be black. Soul really spoke to my generation because it was black music on its own terms, free of shrill white backing vocals and polite moon-June-spoon odes to high-school romance, letter sweaters, and first kisses. When white recording artists "covered" (translation: ripped off) the songs of black singers in the 1950s and early 1960s, it wasn't hard to bleach a powerful R&B hit into a hue more pleasing to the white-owned and -operated radio stations playing this new form of music dubbed rock & roll. Just gut the beat and temper any suggestive lyrics, and even Little Richard's ribald, rough-edged "Tutti-

Frutti" could be sanded down into a hit for wholesome Pat Boone. Because soul music addressed universal themes from an unapologetically black point of view, and with a renewed sense of community and pride, it was too damn formidable to be compromised.

In the mid- to late 1960s artists such as James Brown, Aretha Franklin, Otis Redding, Sam and Dave, Jerry Butler, Wilson Pickett, and Sly and the Family Stone followed the crossover trail Motown forged. Their R&B singles were embraced by Top Forty radio and vied with white acts such as the Beatles and Rolling Stones at the top of the Hot 100. I would imagine that by the mid-1970s Top Forty and pop radio programmers would probably reject such glorious records as Aretha's "Respect" and James's "Say It Loud—I'm Black and I'm Proud" on the grounds that they sound "too black." Huh! During that time, it seemed like you couldn't be black enough.

I loved all music, but my drummer's heart beat to James Brown. He was and is Soul Brother Number One, The Hardest Working Man in Show Business, the Original Disco Man. He's got more titles than a library, all of them deserved. He is also the man who literally turned the beat around, the architect of songs built upon a new foundation of rhythm. Before James Brown, virtually every soul and rock song was driven by the crack of the snare drum on beats two and four, the *backbeat* that Chuck Berry sang about in his song "Rock and Roll Music."

James put the beat to work in other ways. His most revolutionary songs—such as "Cold Sweat"—are constructed around a *groove*. Instruments that traditionally provide melody, such as horns and guitars, instead join the drums in punctuating beats in wildly unorthodox and complex patterns. Because James sometimes accented offbeats, playing his songs was the ultimate test of true musicianship. You had to override your brain and let yourself go with the feeling. You didn't *learn* to play James Brown's material, you *felt* it. Down in the little basement of our house on Eighth Street, I felt it and played it for hours on end. My kit was like an extension of me, and sitting behind it, locked into my groove, I got the sense of accomplishment you get when you know you can do something really well. In fact, according to my mother, the trolley that ran by our home used to stop now and then so that the passengers could listen to me play drums.

The summer I was eighteen, I decided to work in Atlantic City. These were the days before the big casinos and hotels moved in, and Atlantic City had definitely lost some of its luster. For black folks all up and down the East Coast, however, Atlantic City in the summer was the place. Several popular clubs—Edgehill's, the Club Harlem, the Mark IV, and the Wondergarden—were on or near Kentucky Avenue, a street that seemed to never shut down. All of these clubs featured live music, and Atlantic City was crawling with musicians, from up-and-coming acts to stars. If there was any place I had a chance of catching another break, Atlantic City was it.

I got a job waiting tables at Reggie Edgehill's supper club, at Baltic Avenue and Illinois Avenue (Reggie also owned the Mark IV across the street). Kenny and Tony, my two buddies from my informal singing group, the Paramounts, worked there, too; Kenny was a waiter, and Tony a dishwasher. Up until then, we were very laid back about our singing. We harmonized as we walked down the street or while we hung at one another's houses. We had an instant, natural chemistry, and over time we developed an extensive repertoire and a unique sound. We were three good-looking but very different-looking guys. Tony was the shortest, a brown-skinned guy who wasn't the greatest vocalist, but he could instinctively float up or down the scale to find the perfect harmony notes. He had a way with words; he was a smooth talker. I was in the middle, I guess you'd say, with my chocolate skin, deep brown eyes, and this baritone voice. Kenny, who was tallest, was very slim. He was a caramel-complected guy with curly brown hair and light brown eyes, who sang in a ten-

der tenor. Man, how the girls dug that! All of Motown's more romantic male singers were tenors: Eddie Kendricks, Smokey Robinson, Marvin Gaye. I handled the harder-edged, rough stuff—the
songs David Ruffin sang with the Temptations, such as "Ain't Too
Proud to Beg"—with a *dangerous,* sexy edge.

We took the jobs at Edgehill's thinking we might get an opportunity to sing in front of an audience. We didn't have any specific
plan; it was just something that we thought might happen. Maybe
we'd even get discovered. It was worth a shot.

Sure enough, one night, it was like a plot right out of Hollywood:
It was show time, and the night's headliners hadn't shown up. The
three of us were just doing our jobs, but you couldn't miss club owner
Reggie Edgehill frantically scurrying through the place and asking
nobody in particular, "Where the hell are they? I got a house full of
people waitin'. Now what am I going to do? What am I going to do?"

Reggie, who had no idea that Kenny, Tony, and I sang together,
stood at the back and stared at a room full of paying and soon-to-be
unhappy customers. I saw my chance and I grabbed it.

"Excuse me, Mr. Edgehill, but Tony, Kenny, and I—we're a group.
We can sing," I said.

"Oh, really?" Edgehill looked more surprised and relieved than
impressed. "Okay, fine, do it."

We whipped off our aprons and bounded up onto the stage. Performing before an audience made me feel . . . different. I knew this
was where I belonged. We performed just one song—a cappella, of
course—the Dells' "Stay in My Corner," one of the year's biggest hits.
It was a real singer's song, climaxed by lead vocalist Marvin Junior's
showstopping sustained note. The climax of the record came when
Junior sang "Baaaaay-bay!" (translation: "baby") holding a single note
for fourteen, fifteen, sixteen—who knows how many?—seconds. It
never failed to bring down the house.

"Stay in My Corner" is a legendary number, and the minute a
crowd recognizes it, you just know they're sitting there thinking, *He*

thinks he can do it? We'll see! It's a gimmick, but it works, because you've got everybody wound up with anticipation from the first note. Of course, the downside is, if you have the audacity to think you can sing "Stay in My Corner" and you punk out on that crucial note, you get your ass booed offstage and out of town. It was a challenge I could not refuse.

When Kenny, Tony, and I reached the end, I was a few seconds into my "Baaaaay . . ." when the crowd started clapping and hollering, and that just spurred me on. I let it rip, holding that long note as if it could last for eternity. With every second, the place got so wild, I didn't cut that note loose until I'd held it longer than even Junior. The applause rang out for a while before I came back to earth. We received a *standing ovation*. Whoa. I will never forget it.

Now, had this really been a movie, some grizzled impresario would have collared us, put down his cigar, and said something like (with a Humphrey Bogart–like inflection), "Hang up that apron, kid. I'm gonna make you fellas stars." Nope! Didn't happen. Reality check! The three of us took our bows and, stepped down off the stage and back to reality. We donned our aprons and got back to work.

The very next night, though, my big break came, in the person of a mysterious soul singer named Little Royal. Let me tell you, Little Royal looked, talked, and dressed like James Brown, sang like James, and copied James's show, right down to every grunt, *Heh!*, split, and spin. But most amazingly, he could do that one-foot slide across the stage exactly like James. I'd seen James Brown live several times, and Little Royal, who commanded a devoted following in little clubs throughout the United States and in Canada, had his act down.

The first night he played Edgehill's I listened closely while I worked the floor. Little Royal definitely had something going on, but his drummer, a guy named Marvin Jolly, totally knocked me out. To this day, I believe he's the absolute best drummer I've ever heard anywhere. Dressed hippie style, with bellbottom hip-hugger pants and boots, Jolly was a show unto himself, as much an attraction as Little Royal. He did things on the drums I'd never seen before or since. For instance, with one hand he could play these funky, accented drumrolls that most other guys couldn't play with two. Then, while he was knocking you out with one of those rolls, he'd be rising off his stool to stand and crash a cymbal set up high, over his head. He was totally amazing.

Word got out around the club that this Jolly was quitting after the engagement, so Little Royal needed a drummer to take on the road. The day Little Royal held auditions, I applied for the job. I introduced myself, walked up onto the stage, sat down behind the drum kit, picked up the sticks, and put everything else out of my mind. I'd never drummed professionally before, and I wasn't fool enough to even dream I was anywhere near the drummer Marvin Jolly was, but here was my chance to leave Edgehill's and become a professional musician.

I auditioned with a song Little Royal was doing in his show, James Brown's "I Got the Feelin'," which I absolutely loved but had never played before. If this didn't win me the gig, nothing would. Have you ever heard the song? It had been a Top Ten hit in the spring. It's got a funky, difficult time signature that simply defies explanation. I'm sure there's some deep, technical, musicologically correct way to explain this, but I don't write about music for a living, I *make* it. All you need to know is it was the funk, pure and not so simple. From the first rimshot to the hi-hat's final *shhhhh-upp!,* I knew I had it in the pocket.

I retired from waiting tables and walked out of Edgehill's as a touring musician with a paying gig and a new name. "Teddy Pendergrass" seemed too long and hard to remember. Back home in Philadelphia, I had a gorgeous girlfriend during my last year of high school named Jerri White. I will never forget her stunning green eyes; she was mesmerizing. She was beautiful enough that for weeks every day after school I made the long walk from my house on Eighth to her house on Thirty-second and Lehigh—that's twenty-five blocks each way—even though her mom watched us like a hawk and I didn't stand a chance of even getting to first base. I guess I wasn't quite over my infatuation, because I changed my name to "Teddy White." I hadn't even told Kenny and Tony I was auditioning for Little Royal, so they were surprised when I said good-bye. Looking back, I can see myself setting a pattern I'd follow the rest of my career: seizing the opportunity and never looking back. This was a chance that might not come again, and I had to take it.

I was eighteen and, technically, I could do what I wanted. But I would never dream of leaving on such a venture without first talking to Mom about it. Little Royal came back with me to Philadelphia. He assured my mother that he ran a clean, legit organization, that he'd look out for me, and so on. You have to understand, this was a little bit of a shock for my mom. I had left a few months before to wait tables and came home with a job playing drums that could take me all over the country. She asked Little Royal a lot of questions, and when she was satisfied, she gave me her blessing. I packed up that drum kit she'd bought for me a few years before and hit the road.

A few days later "Teddy White" was driving north to Halifax, Nova Scotia, with Little Royal and his band, which included a second drummer and saxophonist-bandleader named Andre, who had big, bulging eyes. From there I mailed my first—and only—message from the road: a postcard to Mom.

The road was a whole different world, and my weeks with Little Royal were, um, eye-opening. Lesson number one: Women really dig musicians. A lot. In Montreal, I was chased—and caught—by a pretty white girl, and that was cool. This was something that didn't happen in my neighborhood, and I was game. I started to see that the world was a lot bigger than North Philadelphia. Every situation, every place, every kind of person had his or her own values, culture, and ways of seeing things, and I found my informal, ongoing study of human nature fascinating. (Maybe that explains why I've studied anthropology and how I aced a 4.0 in my last college course.)

Then it was on to the next little club, with its cramped stage and an audience that didn't care much who you were. As long as they could drink and dance, they were happy. This was cheap-ass entertainment, nothing more, nothing less. To me, it was a job, and I approached it the same way I did driving a cab, washing dishes, or picking peaches: I did my work and didn't ask any questions about anybody's business.

That's not to say, however, that I didn't learn a lot. The time I spent with Little Royal was an education. Little Royal wasn't what you'd call a nice, friendly guy. He ran his show with an iron fist, and he had no qualms whatsoever about making sure you—and everybody else in the band—knew when you screwed up. Little Royal could be singing his ass off, pouring his whole heart into a song, but if somebody missed a beat or a note, Royal would shoot the offender a quick, mean glance while at the same time throwing his hand up into the air. Five fingers meant you were getting fined five bucks; five fingers twice meant it was ten. I doubt that anyone in the audience even noticed this, but everyone in the band sure did. We weren't making that much to begin with, so even a five-dollar fine might mean you'd be skipping a couple of meals. Worst of all was being embarrassed like that in public *and then* having to keep right on playing and praying you didn't mess up again.

Every night Little Royal closed the show with "Please Please Please." Like James, Royal did the whole routine: dropping to his knees while the band vamped and the assistant draped the robe over his shoulders, walking off the stage like a man about to die, then suddenly throwing it off and bounding back to the mike to start all over again. "Please, please, please, please . . ." People had seen this bit before, but it never failed to bring down the house.

The other thing I remember about "Please Please Please" is that Little Royal sang it completely differently from show to show, depending on how he felt. If he felt good and wanted to dance some more, he'd take it up-tempo, faster than the original. If he was tired, he'd slow it down. Or he might pick any tempo in between. The challenge for the band was that we never knew which way Little Royal was going until he actually sang the first line. It could be "Please-please-please-please," "Pl-ease, pl-ease, pl-ease, pl-ease," "Puh-leee-eze, puh-leee-eze, puh-leee-eze, puh-leee-eze," or "Pleasepleasepleaseplease"—and you better be ready. If you weren't, you got it: five fingers, ten fingers, and that nasty glare.

I could deal with Little Royal not being the warmest, friendliest guy in the world. After all, he was my boss, and bosses sometimes have to be tyrants. But there was also something else about the situation that made me decide to quit. We were in Quebec City, Quebec, Canada, at the time. Even though our next dates were in Connecticut—a few hours' train ride from Philadelphia—I couldn't wait. Maybe if I'd cooled down and given it some thought, I'd have realized how foolish and dangerous it was to take off on my own, hundreds of miles from home with only twenty-five bucks in my pocket. But I was young, headstrong, impulsive, determined, and, well, *stupid*—you get the picture. Bottom line: I'd made up my mind.

By the time the logistics of my predicament had sunk in, I was on a southbound train to Montreal, which was as close to home as my money would take me. And I still had about four hundred miles to go. Smart, Teddy, real smart. I turned up on the doorstep of the white girl I'd dated before in Montreal, broke, scared, and hoping she might let me stay, maybe lend me money to get home.

When she opened the door, I saw a black guy there and thought, *Uh-oh.* Fortunately, he wasn't upset that I'd come to see his girl. We accepted that she was just the kind of girl who liked being with different guys. No problem. In fact, it turned out that he was driving to New York City the next day, and he invited me along. The two of us hit it off, and I spent a day or two with him at his apartment in Greenwich Village (another new world), hanging out and going to a white rock club. I foolishly let him talk me into dropping some acid. "Try it, man! It'll expand your mind!"

My mind-expanding experience consisted of sitting in the middle of a floor while people stepped around me because I was too damn high to get up. As I recall it, the acid was talking to me, telling me to just sit there, and so I did. And that's all I remember. My new friend was nice enough to lend me a few dollars to get home on. A few days later, I was back home in Philadelphia. Geographically, I hadn't traveled all that far, but psychologically, I'd been around the world.

Mom was thrilled to see me, of course, but to this day I've never told her about the circumstances of my leaving Quebec or much of anything else that happened since I'd left Philadelphia with Little Royal earlier that summer. It wasn't so much that I was trying to "protect" her as it was my being ashamed of my own foolishness. All she knew was that I was home.

Looking back, I can see that this was one time when I really could have used a dad to get in my ass, as they say. I wasn't a bad kid by any stretch of the imagination, but I was naive in the ways of the world and too impulsive sometimes. My foray with Little Royal showed me just how much I had to learn and, more important, how risky it was to try to learn it all on my own.

I know I'm oversimplifying, but moms and dads teach their children different things. Usually, a mother's first instinct is to protect, to teach a child to walk away from danger. If there's something you shouldn't be doing, you just shouldn't do it. On the other hand, dads usually are a little more hip, more likely to teach you how to take care of yourself, even when you're doing the things you probably shouldn't be. I don't mean to sound sexist, but I also feel there are certain things about a young man growing up that fathers can handle better than mothers can. I never could have called Mom from Montreal and told her I was stranded. I was too ashamed, and it would have scared her to death and broken her heart. But, I imagined, if I had a father who'd been out in the world himself and gotten into his own scrapes, I could have called him and said, "Hey, Dad, I fucked up." He'd have wired me some money, and I'd have come straight home and gotten a good talking-to.

Sure, I had a great time in Montreal and Greenwich Village, but I was lucky. Really lucky. Things could have gone much differently. If I'd had a dad, I would have known that. Looking back, I see that I desperately needed an older male role model to give me that Reality 101 course every young man needs.

Instead, I returned to the house on Eighth Street a few months older, but a changed man. A grown man, at least in my mind. My eye-opening foray into the world of show business qualified me to make my own decisions and live my own life, or so I thought. I'd gotten a sweet taste of freedom out there, and I wasn't about to go back to being Mom's good boy all the time. I loved and respected her, but in terms of determination and will, I was every bit my mother's son. And being young and impatient, I tried to buck the rules. After the Uptown incident, Mom had conceded that I was too big for her to whip anymore. I took that to mean she couldn't punish me for, say, coming in too late or having a girl up in my room. Man, was I wrong.

I'd been testing the limits a little bit. Mom and I never had a big confrontation about it, but we both recognized it was time I got my own place. I wanted to find out more about life and myself, and I couldn't do that and respect her rules at the same time. She'd raised me to be independent, but she was always there if I ever needed her.

"My own life" was that of a young musician with a sporadic income (probably not more than fifteen dollars a night when I worked), an elusive dream, and a lot of determination. I briefly played with a band called Signs of the Times and then joined the Soul Messengers, just two of probably a hundred local bands vying to play the local clubs. The money wasn't enough to live on, but whatever I was doing, at least it was music. And a real education. One of the guys I played with told me that he'd learned to play in prison. With so much time on his hands, he'd become *real* good.

One day he asked me if I wanted to go with him on a "job": break into a house, steal some stuff, fence it. I told him I wasn't interested. I heard later that he had done exactly what he said he was going to do, had been caught in the act, and had gone back to jail again. Years later I heard that he was shot dead, up on Erie around Broad, by the police who apprehended him after he stole a lady's purse.

In those days, you just played with whomever you could, whenever you could. Bands didn't so much form, then break up, as much as they kind of evolved as members came and went. I was hired as a drummer to play for a group of guys who called themselves the Cadillacs. I later found out they were fake.

The genuine Cadillacs were a New York quintet best known for their 1956 hit "Speedoo" ("They often call me Speedoo/but my real name is Mr. Earl") and a few more R&B hits after that, such as "Peek-a-Boo." Like so many black vocal groups of the time, the Cadillacs had spawned spin-offs, offshoots, and imitators all over the place. The false appropriation of a famous act's name happened all the time. On any given night, you could probably find a dozen groups of Platters or Drifters in a dozen different cities. This was prior to MTV, so the audiences didn't know what half these guys looked like or what their names were. Nor did they give a damn. As long as you could sing the songs the audiences knew the way they remembered them, you *were* the Cadillacs, or the Coasters, or whoever.

These particular Cadillacs—Bobby, Kenny, Marvin, and Ed—may not have been the real thing, but they were good enough to keep working. We had a long-running engagement at Sid Booker's High Line Club, on Broad and Belmont, in Philadelphia. Once I hauled my drums there on public transportation, no easy feat. Many times I got a ride with somebody, but I do remember once taking two buses each way with my drums. The bus would stop and the driver would wait as I moved my gear, piece by piece, to the sidewalk. I didn't have protective drum cases, so my instruments were taking a beating, onstage and off.

We did five shows a night, forty-minute sets on the hour, with twenty minutes between sets. We started at nine and ended sometime around two, all for fifteen, maybe twenty bucks a night. It was tough, but it was playing *and* paying. That was good enough for me.

One night while we were playing the High Line, a singer, Harold Melvin, came in to see the show. It turned out he was looking for a few singers and a band to take on the road to replace his previous lineup, which had just broken up. By then Harold had been a fixture on the Philadelphia music scene for many years, as a member and later head of the doo-wop harmony group called the Blue Notes. This group had been around in one form or another since the mid-1950s, recording sporadically with varying success. From what I heard, Harold had joined the group in the 1950s, right before they broke up, and he vowed to keep the Blue Notes' name going. Harold was a nice-looking guy with a smooth, confident manner honed through years in the business. You could tell right away that he had clear ideas about what he was looking for and what he expected.

The lineup Harold was now looking to replace included Bernie Wilson, Larry Brown, and John Atkins. Before I met Harold, the Blue Notes had a professional, polished live show that kept them working around the country continuously. Unlike the local bands I'd worked with, the Blue Notes had steady bookings, and best of all, they traveled. This was the real deal.

Because Harold had many commitments, he couldn't take off a couple of months to train a bunch of strangers. The Cadillacs transformed into the Blue Notes, and he hired me to be the drummer in the Blue Notes' band. The other guys in the band were Art, who played saxophone, Rags, whose bass guitar stood almost as tall as he did, and Nate, a tall, slim guitarist and philosopher.

At the time, I remember being happy I got the job and well aware that this was a step up from what I'd been doing. I had no idea how far it would take me.

Joining Harold Melvin was perhaps the single most important event in my career. That's not to say that my situation with Harold was perfect or that I wouldn't have made it without him. Who knows? But I can honestly say that I learned almost everything I needed to know about surviving in show business from Harold.

Harold was a complex guy. He had been leading (not as the sole lead singer, but in the business sense) the Blue Notes in one form or another for many years, had experienced most of what the business had to offer, and had managed to turn the group into an act classy enough to earn monthlong bookings throughout the United States and Canada, in Las Vegas, Miami, Puerto Rico, and the French West Indies. For a local group without a major record deal and a stack of hits, this was an admirable accomplishment. Right after he hired me, I went to see him and his wife, Ovelia, in their apartment on Front and Godfrey. It was expensively decorated and immaculate. But what I really remember is trying to pay attention to what Harold was saying to me without his noticing that I couldn't take my eyes off his wife. Ovelia Melvin was, without a doubt, the most stunningly beautiful woman I'd ever laid eyes on. Mercy! I remember leaving there with the impression that Harold must be doing very well for himself. And I was right.

Even before he top-billed his name over the group, Harold was indisputably the leader. He wasn't the group's only lead singer, but he chose the songs and essentially created the show. While all the group members contributed ideas about staging, choreography, vocal arrangements, and so on, the final decisions were Harold's, and the Blue Notes' tasteful, elegant, yet soulful presentation bore his stamp.

He also was our manager, and so being a Blue Note was like being an employee on a payroll. Whether the salary he paid me in the early days was fair, I can't really say. I had no idea what the group took in; it was none of my business. When I left Philadelphia to hit the road backing the Blue Notes, I was a hired gun. Whatever Harold offered me was more than I could have made staying back in Philly, and it was a great opportunity to travel. It was fine with me.

My first months with Harold were a crash course in show business, in its many and varied forms. For groups like the Blue Notes, without a hit record to their name, your show consisted of the hits of the day, tailored to the audience. While landing a record contract was always the goal, there were hundreds of acts just like the Blue Notes who never recorded yet played the circuit for years and years. For a lot of those guys, being able to travel and sing and "live the life," as they say, was all the incentive they needed to keep going. Compared to most unsigned acts, Harold was doing extremely well. He and the Blue Notes worked almost constantly.

The club circuit was just that: It went around and around and around. It wasn't like a ladder, with each step up leading to a bigger and better date. The Blue Notes could finish a month in the lounge at Miami Beach's Fountainbleu Hotel, then drive a couple of thousand miles to open at a Buffalo, New York, hole-in-the-wall filled with pimps, hustlers, and prostitutes. After that, it might be off for a month at the Flamboyan Hotel in San Juan or to Vegas.

Playing both ends of the spectrum and everything in between required figuring out how to please every kind of audience. For the white-haired retirees at the Fountainbleu, you opened with "Cabaret" and kept your tux buttoned and your tie impeccably knotted, and you smiled a lot; for the crowd at Buffalo's Pine Grill, it was the Temptations' "Get Ready" and gettin' down 'n' funky, undoing your tie, and letting them see you sweat. From behind the drum kit, I made a real study of how crowds responded, and learned that the show, if put together right, could become greater than the sum of its parts.

Of all the places we played, Las Vegas stands out in my memory. These were the days before the city filled up with family-friendly hotels and amusements. Back in the late 1960s and early 1970s, Vegas was the ultimate adult playground, with the Strip's millions of garish lights holding night at bay.

Nothing could be further from the world my mother raised me in than this. Although I wanted to make music my life, I was troubled by the fear that I was doing something wrong by abandoning the church and playing nonreligious, secular music. I remembered the negative, critical reaction in my church—and I'm sure in others across the country—when Sam Cooke left the Soul Stirrers and began having pop hits in the 1950s. In their eyes, he had abandoned the church to sing the Devil's music. I was raised to believe that it just wasn't right to sing secular music or be in places where people drank and smoked and carried on. You could say that being in show business, I was now in the world and of it. I enjoyed doing what I was doing, and I partook of what you might call the fringe benefits: the alcohol, the cocaine, the women. But deep inside, it would be a long time before I stopped worrying about what people in church would think of me. In these early years, Mom never came to see me perform, and I never asked her why. Maybe I knew the answer and couldn't bear to hear her say it.

I could go with the drinking and sniffing a little cocaine, but I never developed a taste for high-stakes gambling. Back then, it was a moot point anyway. We couldn't even afford two pairs of shoes in those days. A Motown fan for so many years, I knew who Berry Gordy Jr. was, of course. One night between shows, I was walking through a casino when I recognized Gordy—a surprisingly compact and sturdy man with the face of a curious little boy—at a table, shooting craps. A small crowd had gathered around the table, and people were whispering about how much he had lost—something like tens of thousands of dollars. It was no secret that Gordy liked to gamble, and over the next couple of days, I'd see him shoot and lose over and over. Finally, he rose from the table and nonchalantly said to no one in particular, "Better luck tomorrow." I remember thinking, *How can you just walk away from all that?* It all seemed so unreal to me. Like I said, this was a whole new world.

On any given night, there were so many performers in Vegas that sooner or later everybody in town saw everybody else's act. Not yet major headliners, the Blue Notes worked the lounges, the smaller rooms, as opposed to the so-called big rooms. In the period before I joined the Blue Notes and while I was drumming for them, I began to make a name for myself on the circuit as a damn good drummer. And I worked very hard at improving my chops.

All the traveling we did to the Caribbean and South America exposed me to rhythms and sounds I'd never heard before. I began combining my basic, straight-ahead, heavy backbeat grooves with the full spectrum of exotic syncopated Caribbean styles. I was always listening, always experimenting, and in the process I developed a sound all my own. It wasn't long before I knew I could make it in the music business as a drummer, if nothing else.

I loved drumming, but my real dream was to be out front singing. I recalled how I felt singing "Stay in My Corner" at Edgehill's, or even singing for girls *on* the corner. I couldn't describe it, but I felt that was where I really belonged. I'll never forget one time at the Flamboyan Hotel in Puerto Rico, something came over me. I'm not a practical joker by nature, but I thought it would be funny if I jumped up from behind my drums and joined the Blue Notes down front for a few seconds. When I did it, the guys were shocked to see me there beside them, but I knew our show forward and backward, so I fell into their dance steps and harmonized with them. The crowd loved it. I turned to get back behind the kit before my next cue, tripped, and fell straight into the kit, sending drums and cymbals toppling and crashing all over the stage! Everyone laughed as I grabbed my sticks, came back right on the beat, and, I should add, died a million deaths. I was so embarrassed.

Life on the road was fraught with adventure, and sometimes danger, too. Once when I was still the group's drummer, we were booked to play the local Playboy Club in Lexington, Kentucky. We were, as always, short on cash, and the places we played never paid you up front. You might be able to take a little draw on the money you were due at the end engagement, but only after you'd worked a few days.

We foresaw our cash-flow problem and so we very honestly told the manager of the hotel where we were staying that we wouldn't be getting paid until after the show on Saturday night. He said he understood and agreed to that. He also told us that our room had been reserved for Saturday morning, and we'd have to be out then, so we came up with a plan: We'd check out Saturday morning, he'd keep our belongings behind the desk for the day, then we'd collect them when we returned after our Saturday-night show and pay him for the room. The manager was holding everything we owned behind the desk, so he knew we had to come back and settle the bill. Problem solved.

In the meantime, with no money to rent another room, we walked around town all day, *then* went to do our show. By the time the show ended and we were leaving the Playboy Club to make good on our bill, we were exhausted. We wearily started out the door only to be met by the local police, who arrested us on the charge of "defrauding an innkeeper." We tried to explain, but it was our word against the racist hotel manager's, and this was the South. A bunch of black guys from out of town didn't stand a chance.

We were taken to jail and held for a while, with a real dilemma. The money we had was just enough to cover the hotel bill and our transportation to our next date. But now we had to pay to get out of jail, so there was no way we could all get to Vegas, too. By the time we got out of jail and paid off the hotel, we couldn't afford to send everyone on ahead. We were stranded at the bus station with an obligation to open in Las Vegas in a few days. Harold decided to take a chance and use the money to send the band ahead. The reasoning was that if he and the rest of the group couldn't make it, at least the band could perform the show and get paid. Later Harold got enough money from Philadelphia to get himself and the group to Las Vegas in time.

We left Kentucky for Las Vegas dead broke. Before we hit the road, I reluctantly called my mother and asked her to wire me some money that I'd pick up Las Vegas, just so I could eat. I had no idea where we'd be staying or where exactly she should send it. There would be a few other times like that, and she never once let me down. Mom worked hard for her money, and I hated asking her, so I never called from the road until I'd gone hungry a couple of days first. I always say you can't be in show business if you're not willing to starve. Literally.

As fate would have it, the trip from Lexington to Las Vegas was my old drum kit's last. These were the same drums Mom gave me, and she couldn't buy me the top of the line, so it's actually pretty amazing that they held up as long as they did. It seemed like every time I played them, something was popping off or snapping. I couldn't take it anymore. When we got to Vegas, it was clear they'd taken their last beating. In a music store I found a beautiful new blue set I wanted, and Harold agreed to cosign on the financing. I brought them back to the Ramada motel off the Strip where we were staying and spent hours just looking at them. They were so damn gorgeous!

Then I looked at my old, sorry white set piled up in the corner. The chipped paint, the tarnished rims, the bent stands—they seemed to be crying to be put out of their misery. I decided to send them on one last "tour." I hauled them out onto the second-floor balcony. "I'm through with you!" I screamed as I sent each piece hurtling over the edge.

As luck would have it, being Harold's drummer provided me plenty of opportunity to sing, though it wasn't planned that way. The truth is, for all Harold's dedication to the act and his show-business savvy, he also enjoyed his fun. It was Harold who first turned me on to drinking the good stuff, like expensive cognac, and snorting a little cocaine, which in those days was a glamorous status drug used only by the elite. I can't speak for anybody else working for Harold, but in the beginning I couldn't afford my own cocaine. Harold often bought a supply and shared it with me and some other guys; I guess you could call it one of our fringe benefits. Even back then, though, I never let it get in the way of my work, because nothing was as important to me as being regarded as a professional.

Unfortunately, that wasn't always the case with everyone else in the organization. There were times when Harold or the group showed up late to the show. The only way for the rest of us to get paid was to go ahead and start the show ourselves. Many a night the band and I sang the first part of the show ourselves, until the group showed up. Singing and drumming are both physically demanding, but singing *while* drumming is really something else. It was hard work, but I loved it.

We were in the French West Indies when Bobby, Kenny, Marvin, and Ed—the ex-Cadillacs—decided to split. By then I'd been with Harold for a while and had sung enough that he knew I had a voice. Between shows one night, I was standing outside the club we were playing, talking to a woman who was a dancer there. I was telling her how badly I wanted to sing and how I was thinking about quitting the Blue Notes to pursue that dream. Harold just happened to step outside about then and overheard me. Later he approached me and asked, "Do you think you'd like to sing instead of playing drums? Because if you would, that's fine with me. I think you'd make a great singer."

Singer? Damn! I couldn't believe my luck. As always, Harold had booked the Blue Notes far in advance, so he had commitments to meet, but he didn't have a whole group at the time. Bobby Cook from the Cadillac Blue Notes stayed on, and so he, Harold, and I did a few shows as a trio.

I remember the three of us playing Vacation Valley Resort, in the Poconos. For various reasons, we did not have our matching stage uniforms, so we performed in our street clothes. I'll never forget our inexpensive knit pants and funky long-fringed suede vests. This is when I first met Henry Evans. He later worked for both Harold Melvin and for me, but then he was just a friend of Harold's and Ovelia's who was doing them a favor by driving us up to the Poconos. It was winter, and some of the band didn't make it. So Harold, Bobby Cook, and I, along with only our guitarist and drummer, rode up together and did the show. I'm not bragging, but even with a stripped-down band, we worked that crowd up until we got a big, loud standing ovation. I'll never forget it.

But this date is memorable for a more important reason, and that's the start of my friendship with Henry. Right away, I could tell he was somebody I could really talk to. He can be serious, but he also has a terrific sense of humor, and we have been close friends ever since. Over the next three decades—through thick and through thin and everything in between—Henry has proven himself time and again to be a kind, trustworthy, dedicated, and honest friend.

It wasn't long before Harold completed the group lineup by enlisting a trio from Boston. Like everyone Harold ever hired to sing, these guys were all tall. Tom was a tall, stocky tenor with a great sense of humor. Big John was large, as you can guess by his name, but very muscular. Not a guy you wanted to mess with, but he had a great baritone. Ray had caramel-brown skin and a rough voice, just like mine. Trading off leads together, Ray and I were thunder and lightning. There wasn't a place we played that we couldn't blow the roof off.

This lineup didn't last too long, either. But ever-resourceful Harold then reenlisted a couple of guys who had been Blue Notes before the Cadillacs became Blue Notes (have I lost you?): Larry

Brown and Bernard (Bernie) Wilson, and a new guy, Lloyd Parks, who was the baby brother of Larry's wife, Pat. (And, you may remember from my Uptown days, a member of the fabulous Epsilons.) We began rehearsing right away in Lloyd's mother's basement. Everybody already knew that I could sing, and I'd been waiting for this chance, so I was ready to go. But once we started rehearsing the choreography, I got taken down a couple of pegs. I was not what you'd call a great natural dancer. There in the basement, trying to pick up the moves the other four guys seemed to do so effortlessly, I felt like a clumpy old slew-footed horse. As time went on, I got better and could hold my own, but it always took a lot of work and practice.

Looking back, one reason the Blue Notes had so much appeal is that we offered a little bit of something for everyone. Not all of the guys were great singers, but each one made a distinct, unique contribution to the Blue Notes image and our act. Wherever we played, we were known for being clean and classy, the kind of guys who could be counted on, who didn't cause trouble.

To the group's credit, we did straddle both worlds: the classier white supper clubs and hotel lounges and the small black clubs and bars frequented by pimps and players. Not only did you have to put on two totally different shows, but offstage as well you had to carry through with a personal style, a public facade that suited your environment. It sounds so simple, but after all these years, I believe that a lot of the stress black performers faced then came from constantly having to fit in, having to alter one's personality in order to be accepted—sometimes in places where they were not exactly wanted. We all knew the stories about Nat "King" Cole headlining a posh supper club only to be told he must enter and leave through the kitchen. We had worked dates where we were made to feel welcome in the hotel lounge—as long as we were singing onstage. Once we came off, no one wanted to see us around. The patent-leather shoes, the tuxedos, the smoothed-down hair, and the clean-shaven faces were all about trying to please—and making sure not to threaten—the white patrons. And as good as we were at it, and as successful as it made us, the truth is, that's not really who we were. The real art was learning how to be a "version" of yourself in every situation without losing your identity. It was a lot harder than it sounds, and there were times that I resented like hell not being able to grow a beard, for instance, because it wouldn't be "acceptable." To be successful, though, that was the price you had to pay.

At the time, I really regarded my job with the Blue Notes as just that. Even after I began singing lead and despite all the time we spent together on the road, my bond with the other guys was mostly about work. Whether it was because I was so much younger and less experienced than Harold, Larry, and Bernie, or because our personalities just didn't click on any deep, profound level, we never became what you'd call close.

At nineteen or twenty, I was one of the two youngest guys in the group. Lloyd, or Baby Lloyd, as we called him, was around my age. Lloyd was a real lady's man, good-looking, with a high tenor voice and a low-key sense of humor. He and I hung together the most.

Harold, Larry, and Bernie were at least ten years older than Lloyd and I, and I looked up to them because they'd been around the business a lot longer than I had. I was still looking for the keys to the universe, and they seemed to know how to handle themselves. Larry was a subtle, soft-spoken guy with a distinctive look and style. Women liked him a lot. He was of medium height, and had a broad, ruggedly handsome face, a radiant smile. Larry had a laid-back personality and did everything with smoothness and finesse. For example, we could all be executing the same dance steps, but Larry always put a different spin on them that made them exciting.

Bernie, on the other hand, was more aggressive. Women liked him, too. He was as tall as I was and good-looking. He lived up to his reputation as a playboy and a jet-setter. He was known for hanging with famous people, a stylish wardrobe, and a love for whatever was new and novel. Bernie was the first person I knew to have a Cadillac El Dorado with automatic doors that you could open by just pushing a button. Bernie would drive along the street, see a woman he liked, pull over, pop open the door, and then close it automatically once she got inside. He loved gadgets. Bernie also possessed the gift of gab, and he did most of the talking onstage. Along with Harold, Bernie created the choreography, and he always exaggerated his movements and his steps. Of the five of us, he was what you would call a dancer's dancer.

Then there was our leader. Behind Harold's back, the four of us referred to him as the Great One and occasionally some things that are unprintable. When you worked for Harold, you knew that the way the world went with Harold was the way that he wanted it and the way it was. He liked to present himself as cool and smooth, but at the smallest provocation, he thought nothing of getting up in your face, jabbing his finger at you, and shouting, "It's my fucking group and I'll do whatever the fuck I want!"

While he could be a pleasant enough guy most of the time, and we had our laughs, Harold took his leadership role *very* seriously. He could be controlling to the point of obsession, and as I later learned, less than honest. Over the years he'd honed that professional image we all copied. Both with the Blue Notes and in my later solo career, I can honestly say I took more than a few pages from Harold's book.

From a creative standpoint, Harold made a tremendous contribution to the Blue Notes' success, both onstage and off. From the day I came up front, Harold really groomed me to be a performer, which is not the same thing as being a singer. Plenty of people are great singers but lousy performers. Harold knew and taught true stagecraft, and I was his most avid student. All through my career, even today, I rely on the knowledge Harold passed on to me. At our best, the Blue Notes were the picture of sophistication. Harold taught us all how to present ourselves with class and finesse: how to glide across the stage, how to move together as if we were one person. Even when we played low-down and funky places where the crowd expected us to really get down, we did it with polish.

Harold had a smooth, velvety tenor-baritone that worked wonderfully on a certain kind of song, especially the ballads and 1950s doo-wop tunes that always closed the show. There, Harold really shone. We did a medley that included "Silhouettes," and we sang "Goodnight, My Love," but only to close the last show of the night.

I know that people speculated about jealousy within the group while I was with Harold, and especially after I left. The truth is, there was none. Each member of the group respected the fact that we each made our individual contributions to the Blue Notes' image and success. Maybe one guy sang better or another guy danced better or the girls liked one guy better than they liked another. It didn't matter. As long as the end result drew more people to the show, we didn't think much about who did what. At least in professional terms, we were all in it together.

The only person whose attitude might have differed a little was Harold. To his way of thinking, none of us was indispensable. I don't think I'm bragging when I say that after we started recording, a few years later, everyone in the group realized that my voice belonged up front, that my new leads on our records brought something fresh and exciting. But whereas I saw my contribution as unique, Harold felt otherwise. In his mind, the fact that he'd discovered me meant that if I ever left, he could simply find somebody else, as he always had in the past.

It was around this time that I met Rose, who would become my son's mother, at the beauty shop—Thee M's—where she worked, on Fifty-third and Spruce. Rose was extremely cute and had a great spirit. I remember having great conversations and laughing a lot with her. We began a serious relationship that lasted several years, and during that time I became acquainted with her two children, Keya and Butchie (whose real name is Gaylord). Because of my feelings about growing up without a father, I believed that if I were in a relationship with a woman who had kids, the kids would be a part of the relationship, too. I never saw somebody else's child as a hindrance or nuisance. If anything, I tried to make them feel the way Mom had made me feel: important and loved. Keya was just six years old when I met her, and even now, thirty years later, we're still extremely close.

Even though I was singing with the Blue Notes, I still wasn't making much money, so I didn't keep an apartment in Philadelphia. Rose and I lived with some friends for a while at Fifty-second and Walnut. Fifty-second Street was a popular strip with lots of bars and a handful of clubs, such as the Coupe de Ville, featuring live entertainment. I spent a lot of time hanging, particularly at Neet and Sonny Viner's bar, Neet's. Rose tolerated this and my being out on the road, but it was clear that I wasn't ready to settle down.

In the early days, the Blue Notes spent most of our time together traveling and hanging out. Although I wouldn't say I was best of friends with any of the other guys, we were all someone the others could lean on. Together, we felt, we could conquer anything, and that was a comfort when you were out on the road, working your ass off doing three or four shows a night, or being hassled in a town where you weren't wanted. I quickly learned that I didn't have to like everybody I worked with as long as I loved what we were all doing. And I did.

As every musician will agree, life on the road is like a parallel reality where the rules of everyday living don't apply. For a group like the Blue Notes back then, money was tight—when we had any. Unless we were leaving the continental United States, we traveled by car, sometimes driving for days and nights on end. We ate where we could and stayed where we could. Some of the biggest fights we had in the group concerned sleeping arrangements. Many times we slept five to a room with one double bed. Here's how: Two guys took the mattress, two guys slept on the box spring, and the fifth made a bed out of pillows. To save money, we often got rooms with kitchenettes, so we could cook our own meals. All those years I spent making my own dinner at home came in handy then. We didn't have the money to eat in restaurants, so we bought a skillet and I learned to make anything and everything that could be made in it, including one huge hamburger that I swore looked and tasted like a meatloaf.

As I said, Harold Melvin and the Blue Notes played every kind of place you can imagine, and some you probably can't. One of our most memorable stomping grounds was Kentucky Avenue in Atlantic City, not far from Edgehill's, where I'd put down my waiter's apron to hit the road with Little Royal a couple of years before. Working there was so convenient, because everything you needed was right there. You could hang out at Sapp's, the local bare-bones barbecue joint, or really dine up the street at the more sophisticated Johnson's Soul Food Restaurant. If you felt like drinking, there was Goldie's right across the street, which was always crowded. The drive home from Atlantic City was only about sixty miles, and sometimes we'd leave after the two A.M. show and come back the next evening. If we didn't feel up to that, since hotel rooms were too expensive, we could sleep on the beach.

Kentucky Avenue was the summer showcase for every pimp, hustler, player, and prostitute on the East Coast, as well as for their "colleagues" from Detroit, Chicago, and elsewhere. It was a part of the city that never slept—and sometimes neither did we. Atlantic City was crawling with singers and musicians, and it was there that I first met such future greats as the Ohio Players and the Commodores (and this was back when Lionel Richie was still the sax player). Before, at Edgehill's, I'd seen Frankie Beverly (later of Maze) and the Butlers.

The Club Harlem, where we played, was a hot nightspot and somewhat unique, because it had two rooms: the front bar, with two stages and continuous music, and the big room, in back, which showcased only the bigger names, acts that had hit records. The front bar featured a jazz trio and a singing group, which alternated sets all evening.

I loved playing the back room of the Club Harlem, but we started in the front bar, which was hell. The stage—which was about four feet high, behind the bar—was the tiniest I've ever played. Picture this: four musicians, with instruments and amplifiers, and five singers crammed on a ten-by-ten-foot stage. Because we worked so many different places, we were pros at adapting our stage routines to suit any stage. We'd been on small stages before, but this was ridiculous. Even though we did smaller steps, I couldn't shake the vision of somebody spinning off the stage and landing in the bank of liquor bottles behind the bar. I hated it.

The Club Harlem had big double glass doors that were always open, so people drifted in and out. They didn't have to pay admission; they just had to drink. We were grateful for the work, but our ultimate goal was that back room. We were good enough to be back there, and we knew it. "We're gonna make it to that back room," Harold promised, and we did. Of course it took a little politicking, making sure Pop, the club's owner, and Huff, the manager, saw how well we could draw and hold a crowd in the front bar.

When we were offered the back room, we were thrilled. This was a real show: People had to pay a separate admission, and there were opening acts, including dancers and a comedian. On Friday and Saturday nights, we did two shows: at 10:00 P.M. and at 2:00 A.M. The downside to the back room was something euphemistically called the breakfast show. Starting on Sunday mornings at 6:00 A.M., the breakfast show was the regular show, with the opening acts and the headliners coming on at 7:30 in the morning. It makes me tired just to think about it.

These crowds were either easy to entertain or very difficult, depending on whether they were still flying high or crashing. And it took a little judicious tinkering with your own biological clock. To make that show, you couldn't drive back to Philly, so you usually had to do a little cocaine after the 2:00 A.M. show, then catch some z's near the boardwalk, in an area called Chicken Bone Beach. The trick was to sleep just enough that you could function for the breakfast crowd but not so much that you couldn't wake back up again. It was an art—the art of survival.

No matter which room you performed in, though, it was always a tough crowd. Every place we played, entertainers were considered something special, and the people who came to see you were usually predisposed to having a good time. Not the pimps and hustlers, though. On Kentucky Avenue, they were the real stars. With creative nicknames like Sugarfoot, Sweet Jesus, and Porky (who used to park his Rolls-Royce on the sidewalk and beat up his girlfriend because she liked me), they strutted the street, flashing diamond rings and ornate walking canes. Turned out in exquisitely tailored suits of every color imaginable and matching handmade shoes, these guys were something else. Cruising up and down the avenue in custom-painted El Dorados fitted with Rolls-Royce grilles, with their elegantly dressed main lady riding shotgun, they made the strip look like a pimp parade.

In their eyes, entertainers were not only less than nothing, they were a threat to their business and their image. Leaning against their cars, comparing notes on whose "hos" made the best money and whose weren't bringing in as much as they used to, they were the kings of this world. If one guy thought he could get more out of a girl, they'd make deals, trading their girls as if they were baseball cards. The whole time, they kept a very suspicious eye on their "merchandise." These guys thought they were the shit, and you'd better not forget it.

This explains why in places like Kentucky Avenue entertainers were hated and despised. We were the only guys who could take their girls away, and that was because a traveling entertainer was often an unhappy prostitute's only safe ticket out of town. And you had to realize that when you, a lowly entertainer, got one of his girls, that pimp was not only losing money but suffering the biggest blow imaginable to his reputation. A singer took his girl? To a pimp this was the ultimate humiliation. That's what made playing anyplace you had pimps—little dives in cities across America to big places like the Apollo, where pimps took up the front row—such a tough crowd. The pimps made it clear they didn't give a damn about you, and any prostitute who showed any interest at all was asking to be yanked back down into her seat, at the very least. And if a guy ever found out that one of his girls liked you, you had to watch your back.

Certain clubs across the country were known for their pimp and prostitute clientele, so we dealt with this situation many times. I passed no moral judgments then or now, and I'm not ashamed to say I became friends with several ladies of the evening. I also incurred more than one pimp's wrath, but I never backed down.

I was spending more and more time on the road, sometimes going a couple months without seeing Mom. I was no mama's boy and glad to be out on my own, but the truth is, I missed her. Mom never came right out and said she didn't want me singing rock & roll and R&B, but I knew full well that she would have preferred that I keep my singing in the church. I also knew there were elements of show-business life it was better she didn't know about. She would not have approved of or understood some of the circles I now traveled in or some of the things I was doing. Although it was hard to admit, the fact that she still hadn't seen me perform weighed heavily on my heart.

One night that I won't forget, we played a very small club in downtown Baltimore, across the street from a bus station. The show had begun, we were singing, and the houselights were down. From the stage, it's impossible to make out anything beyond the first couple of rows of tables and chairs, but your eye is automatically drawn to movement in the crowd. I sensed her presence before I even saw her.

Looking toward the back of the club, I spotted two figures who I instinctively knew were Mom and Aunt Persephone. I knew Mom by the way she was moving across the room. I'd seen it a million times in church: Very politely, very humbly, she would bend slightly at the waist and raise her index finger as if to say, "Excuse me, please" as she made her way across a crowded pew.

When I realized it was Mom, I was thrilled and nervous as hell! Let me tell you, that night I sang my butt off. I had something to prove and a mission to accomplish: I was going to make her like what I was singing. When the show was over, I rushed down to her table, where she was seated with my aunt. "Wow, Mom," I said breathlessly, "what are you doing here?"

And my mother, cool as can be, replied, "Oh, we just decided to come down and see you and see how you were doing."

"This calls for champagne, then," I said, then, without thinking, added, "Mom, would you like some champagne?"

"No, no, I don't drink." I knew that! Where was my head?

"Well, Mom, we'll get you some ginger ale in a champagne glass. That way you can look like you're sipping champagne," I suggested, and she smiled. We toasted, and suddenly it was like everything was okay. I was a grown man out on my own, but knowing that my mother approved of me and what I was doing was the most comforting feeling in the world.

Later, Mom told me she thought to herself as she watched me that night, *Look what I have, look what God gave me.* I could tell that she approved of what I was doing and believed in me, although she didn't say that to me back then. (Actually she told me this while I was writing this book.) But from the look on her face, I knew. Now there was nothing I couldn't do.

FOUR

❧

Throughout the early 1970s, the Blue Notes were out on the road almost constantly, performing a repertoire of current Top Forty hits such as "Close to You," "Raindrops Keep Fallin' on My Head," and "Ball of Confusion"—classics, standards, show tunes, and doo-wop chestnuts. Back home, a new Sound of Philadelphia was being born.

Like Harold, Kenny Gamble, Leon Huff, and Thom Bell were of a different generation, musically speaking. I was too young to have caught Kenny Gamble and the Romeos (which included Bell and guitarist Roland Chambers, later of MFSB—for "Mother, Father, Sister, Brother"—the peerless Philadelphia International Records studio band), or Huff in his groups the Dynaflows and the Lavenders. By the time I started going to the Uptown and taking music seriously, Huff was working as a top session pianist for producer-writer Phil Spector in New York. That's him on the Ronettes' "Be My Baby." He was also a successful songwriter, having penned Len Barry's big 1965 hit "1, 2, 3" and Patty and the Emblems' "Mixed-Up, Shook-Up, Girl" (1964).

Back in Philly, Gamble and Bell (who had been the session pianist on one of my favorite Patti LaBelle and the Bluebelles' hits, "Down the Aisle," and later had led Chubby Checker's band) formed a songwriting partnership that yielded one national hit, 1965's "The 81," a "dance" record by Candy and the Kisses. It was at the session for "The 81" that Gamble and Huff met.

Huff moved back to Philadelphia from New York and began writing and producing with Gamble. In the beginning, like other writer-producers without their own label or distribution, Gamble and Huff leased their finished tapes, or masters, to established labels. This ensured better distribution but also meant a smaller share of the profits. Around 1965, they formed Excel Records—which in 1967 was renamed Gamble Records—and began recording the Intruders. The quartet's first few singles ("United," "Together," and "Baby I'm Lonely") made respectable showings on the R&B chart, but Gamble and Huff were hungry for pop-chart success, too. Gamble and Huff, who consistently cited Motown as their inspiration, finally got it in 1967 with a song they wrote and produced for Atlantic Records, "Expressway to Your Heart," by the Soul Survivors, a white group. And in early 1968, the Intruders broke through with their million-selling "Cowboys to Girls," which would be followed by "Slow Drag," "(Love Is Like a) Baseball Game," and a song I can really relate to, 1973's "I'll Always Love My Mama (Part 1)." (If you listen carefully to its spoken sections, you can hear the Intruders talking about those infamous Philly street gangs.) As independent contractors, Gamble and Huff also wrote and produced a series of hits for other labels: Jerry "The Iceman" Butler's understated, majestic "Only the Strong Survive," Wilson Pickett's "Don't Let the Green Grass Fool You," and records by such artists as Archie Bell and the Drells and Dusty Springfield.

Gamble Records was a hometown venture. Its first offices were on the sixth floor of the Shubert Building, in Philadelphia, where I used to visit my manager Gene Lawson and where I heard the Intruders rehearsing about five years earlier. Eventually they would take over the entire sixth floor (and write a song entitled "The Sixth Floor" about it).

By 1971 Thom Bell had become a writer, arranger, and producer of note himself. His calling card was the lushly orchestrated romantic ballad, like the Delfonics' 1968 hit "La La Means I Love You," which he produced and cowrote. Bell also masterminded the group's second-biggest hit, 1970's "Didn't I (Blow Your Mind This Time)," and several others. When he agreed to join Gamble and Huff as a writer and arranger, they renamed the label Philadelphia International Records and formed its song-publishing arm, Mighty Three Music. Their prescient motto was "You'll Never Forget Our Tunes."

The history of American popular music is filled with talented, ambitious black writers, producers, and performers who tried to start their own record companies and failed. Sam Cooke's SAR label was a rare exception, with a roster that included Cooke himself, the Soul Stirrers, the Valentinos (a.k.a. the Womack Brothers), and Johnnie Taylor. But Cooke was already a star. Other black artists and entrepreneurs quickly learned the hard lesson that no matter how glorious your dream or how great your talent, the music business is about business. I know they like to say the key to success is all in the grooves, but the truth is, that's just the beginning. Without the right promotion, publicity, and distribution, the greatest record in the world is like the proverbial tree that falls in the woods: Nobody hears it. Major labels dominate the charts and the airwaves because they have the financial clout to gain greater access to radio play and record stores, and to churn out records at lower manufacturing and promotion costs. Ironically, a major hit can capsize a small label in a tide of red ink, as the up-front expenses of pressing, promoting, and shipping records exceed the small margin of profit.

Against this backdrop, the spectacular success of Berry Gordy's Motown was nothing short of a miracle, a success story to inspire generations of black entrepreneurs in every field. While Motown was not the first black-owned record label, it was the first to succeed so phenomenally on an international scale. By 1970 the huge white-controlled record labels that had initially dismissed Gordy as no threat were taking notice—and taking notes. Motown's first number-one pop album, *Little Stevie Wonder/The 12-Year-Old Genius,* in 1963, represented a landmark shift in black music. Before that, the only black artists to reach the top position were "adult" singers: Sammy Davis Jr., Harry Belafonte, Nat "King" Cole, Johnny Mathis, and Ray Charles. Between 1963 and 1971, when Isaac Hayes and Sly and the Family Stone had top pop LPs, the only black artists to hit number one were Louis Armstrong, Jimi Hendrix, and Motown's Supremes and Temptations.

But Motown also proved that black and white listeners were ready for albums of provocative, thought-provoking, and ambitious music—LPs that were more than collections of a couple of hits and some throwaway "filler" tracks. On some, the songs were linked by a unifying theme, a trend that began with the Beatles' *Sgt. Pepper's Lonely Hearts Club Band.* The early 1970s brought Marvin Gaye's politically and socially oriented *What's Going On* and the provocative *Trouble Man* soundtrack, Stevie Wonder's *Talking Book* and *Innervisions,* Isaac Hayes's *Shaft* and *Black Moses,* Curtis Mayfield's *Superfly,* Sly and the Family Stone's *There's a Riot Goin' On,* and Aretha's *Amazing Grace.*

Clearly there was a vast audience for black records that were topical, political, and outspoken. For me, as a young black man, this music was a revelation. It spoke to my generation about the contemporary black experience in honest, uncompromising terms. Yet it also spoke to people of all colors. The proof of that lay in the numbers and the charts, because there was no way a black record could vault into the upper reaches of the pop chart unless millions of white people were digging it, too. For the first time, the music industry began to view black artists as "album artists." LP sales are far more lucrative than singles, so with black music representing an ever-increasing share of the market, the major labels began itching for a chance to be dealt into the game.

Yet no matter how much money the big labels threw at black music, they rarely hit upon a sure formula to turn vinyl into gold consistently. The biggest share of black hits was coming from local outposts far removed from the corporate boardrooms of New York: Stax in Memphis, Curtom in Chicago, Motown in Detroit and later Los Angeles.

One of the biggest of the corporate labels was CBS Records (now Sony), home to such hitmakers of the day as Chicago, Paul Simon, Santana, and Bob Dylan. Considering its dominance in rock and pop, CBS commanded a surprisingly small share of the black-music market, aside from Sly and the Family Stone and a handful of other acts. CBS took an appropriately corporate approach to rectifying that problem, one that was unheard of in the music business: The company commissioned Harvard University to study the problem and recommend how CBS might climb aboard the black-music bandwagon. Based on the recommendations of that study, Clive Davis, then the head of CBS Records, sought to strike up distribution deals with self-sufficient producer-writers rather than start from ground zero and develop a roster full of black artists. Gamble and Huff's label, with an ever-growing list of hit records, caught Davis's eye. In 1971, Philadelphia International entered into an historic, lucrative distribution deal with CBS. This arrangement would literally change my life at least a couple of times in the years to come.

You always hear musicians griping about the hardships of life on the road. It *is* hard, but being young, I loved touring. One thing's for sure: Singing in front of an audience night after night after night had built up my confidence to the point where I felt completely at home onstage. The Blue Notes were becoming known as one of the tightest, classiest acts on what the music trade papers called "the Silver Circuit," consisting of the big hotels and clubs.

Of course, we were still playing less refined places, too. I remember one club in particular somewhere in Massachusetts. It had a bar in the front, where prostitutes hung out, a showroom in the back, and a male clientele that appreciated its "one-stop shopping." Rumor had it that the prostitutes could take their customers right upstairs, conduct business, and have them back downstairs in time for the opening number. We played the club several times. During one engagement, I was directly approached by Ron Banks, lead singer of the Dramatics.

"How'd you like to join our group as the lead singer?" he asked. *Whoa,* I thought. The Detroit quintet was going places; they'd just had a Top Ten hit with "Whatcha See Is Whatcha Get" on Volt. It was a great record, and I have to admit, I was very flattered. But after thinking it over, I politely turned down the offer. Given all the time I'd put in already with Harold, it didn't seem right to quit. I didn't think it would be very long before things worked out for the Blue Notes. We kept moving up into bigger and better gigs; people in the business were noticing us. Maybe we would get our own record deal someday.

Sure enough, it happened. We were playing the Apollo Club in Camden, New Jersey, right across the Delaware River from Philadelphia. Onstage we were always hot, but this was one of those magical nights. Kenny Gamble and Leon Huff were in the audience. I later learned that they offered Harold Melvin a recording contract and that he negotiated it on our behalf without ever consulting any of us. All I recall is Harold telling the four of us, "We did it! We've got a deal!" The Blue Notes were the latest additions to the new Philadelphia International Records. To say that I was elated doesn't even begin to touch it. I remember thinking to myself, *Now, here we go!*

The funny thing is, at the time, I didn't know about Gamble and Huff and their impressive achievements. Harold Melvin and the Blue Notes' first single, "I Miss You," would only be PIR's second release (after the Ebonys' "You're the Reason Why"). Our deal with the label was unusual in a couple of ways. First of all, we were signed as five individuals, not as a group. Second, upon signing, Harold decided to let the world know this was *his* group. We were now to be billed as Harold Melvin and the Blue Notes. That didn't bother me, though, because onstage Harold and I shared the lead vocals on most of our songs. Besides, he had started the group. I had no idea that once Gamble and Huff heard us, they would write virtually all of our singles with my voice in mind.

At Philadelphia International Records, making music was serious business. Once you joined the label, you knew that you were part of a winning team, but that's not really the same as being part of a family. Artists, musicians, writers, producers—through hundreds of hours of working together, we all got to know one another and became quite close, even though we rarely socialized much outside of hanging together at the Fantasy Lounge across the street.

Gamble and Huff made a fascinating pair, a study in complementary talents. Kenny Gamble, tall and reserved, is a religious man and a deep thinker. I guess the word that best describes Gamble is *philosopher*. I think that comes through in his lyrics for songs such as the O'Jays' "Love Train" and "Don't Call Me Brother" and my solo songs "You Can't Hide from Yourself" and "Life Is a Circle." He was interested in and in tune with what was really happening in the world around him. And he still is.

One thing about Gamble that always struck me is that no matter how successful he became, he never seemed to care about material possessions; he never even wore a wristwatch. In 1975, when I was proudly driving around in a white Mercedes 450, Gamble still had a '69 Cadillac Fleetwood. I dropped by to visit him and his wife Dee Dee at their home in Wynfield, and Gamble surprised me by asking, "Hey, Ted, can I drive your car?" He took off in it and when he returned a while later, he vowed he'd have his own Mercedes before I got home from my next tour, and he got a blue one just like mine.

Leon Huff was in many ways the opposite of Gamble. He was short and a man of few words, but that didn't mean he wouldn't put his point across if he felt he needed to. Unlike Gamble, who didn't seem to care much about what he wore, Huff was extremely conscientious about his appearance and always sharply dressed. He could be very competitive, even with the artists. I'll never forget the day I drove up in the new Cadillac I'd bought off the royalties from our first hit.

"So you got your own Cadillac," Huff sniffed. "Just remember: For every one you can buy, I can buy ten."

As a songwriter, producer, and musician, Huff was without peer, though. I sometimes felt that whatever it was that he didn't express in words came out through his music.

The third partner, Thom Bell, was a happy-go-lucky guy, always chipper, always whistling, always asking, "Hey, how are you? How you doing?" Because he worked mostly with the Spinners and the Stylistics, and he moved to Seattle, he wasn't a constant presence at PIR the same way Gamble and Huff were. But, of course, he left his mark on the music, through his brilliant original arrangements. I can always tell a Thom Bell arrangement when I hear it by the string section. Beautiful!

Being a singer at PIR was just like being a kid in a candy store. As writers and producers, Gamble, Huff, and Bell were simply the best. They understood all facets of making records, but even more important, they understood how to coax the best performances out of everyone they worked with. Gamble and Huff were singers, Huff and Bell were highly trained musicians and brilliant arrangers, and all three of them believed that hit records could be more than just catchy songs. The company's slogan, "The music is the message," perfectly reflected Gamble and Huff's ambitious commitment to making a difference not only on the charts but in the world.

Gamble and Huff had that rare gift of artistry combined with killer commercial instinct. They put tremendous thought and effort into tailoring songs for each singer's voice. Each office on the third floor was windowless and soundproofed with heavy padding. Walking down the hall, you could hear the muffled sounds of piano and singing, as writers worked out their songs. Gene McFadden and John

Whitehead might be in one room, Linda Creed and Thom Bell in another. Among the other talented composers up at PIR were Victor Carstarphen, Bunny Sigler, Dexter Wansel and Cynthia Biggs, Joe Jefferson, and Charlie Simmons.

No matter how big the company got or how many hits it produced, it would remain an integral part of the neighborhood. Kenny Gamble seemed always to hire people he knew rather than bring in outsiders. Since most of us were from Philly or the surrounding area, we all shared a basic rapport and mutual understanding, which made it that much easier to communicate musically.

For example, I had seen McFadden and Whitehead's group, the Epsilons, at the Uptown, and I also knew John from the neighborhood. We called him Toodles. Songwriter Joe Jefferson, who cowrote the Spinners' "Mighty Love," I met in Montreal when I was drumming with Little Royal, and he was the drummer for the Sweet Inspirations. It was a small world, and a mighty comfortable one.

I had not set foot in a recording studio since my disastrous outing with Gene Lawson five years before, so I was a little nervous when we began recording our first album, *Harold Melvin and the Blue Notes*, at Sigma Sound, on North Twelfth. Since signing with CBS, PIR had moved its offices into a huge old three-story building at 309 South Broad Street, the former home of Cameo-Parkway Records, Chubby Checker's label. Sigma quickly became a "branch office," as Sigma owner and engineer Joe Tarsia, Gamble, Huff, the musicians, and artists huddled in for sessions that ran 'round the clock.

Although I worked hard at perfecting my craft, singing had always come naturally to me. I imagined making a record to be like performing onstage: natural and effortless. One take, maybe two, job done. Well, that bubble got burst quickly.

Now, I knew my singing wasn't always perfect onstage; no one's is. But a live audience, caught up in the excitement of the show, is forgiving. Besides, in a live show, the stray flat note and the missed cue fly by so quickly that most people never even notice them. And singing live, you can always redeem yourself with a head-turning riff or a knockout move. To a singer, a live audience is the perfect lover: thrilled to see you, hot to please you, and willing to overlook your flaws. It's a love affair.

But a recording studio points out your every flaw. She takes what you have to give, then, completely unimpressed, asks, *"Is that it?"* Then she demands that you do it all over again. One more time with feeling.

I will never forget the first time I heard my voice played back over the studio speakers. It was an odd mixture of pride—*Hey, that's me!*—and horror. That's *me?* I'd gone all these years thinking I knew exactly what I sounded like only to discover that I really didn't. I came into the studio brimming with confidence and left with my ego bruised.

The tape never lies, and I remember singing the same part again because one syllable wasn't sharp enough, then again because I'd hit an almost imperceptibly flat note, and again and again and again. Probably the hardest part about singing in the studio is sustaining the illusion that you're singing the song fresh—and perfectly—for the first time when in fact you may be singing it for the twentieth. A completed vocal track can take two hours, and it can take two weeks. And this is for a good singer. Some songs were easier or quicker to do than others, but I don't believe there's ever been a song that I would call easy. Every producer views the process differently. Some want to hear every note sung to absolute perfection. Others, like Kenny Gamble, judge a performance by its full effect. If given a choice between a technically perfect but dull take and a slightly flawed but riveting performance, he'd go with the latter every time. Many an evening I walked into Sigma and emerged to see the sun rising the next day. And Gamble would have me in there singing practically nonstop. There were times Gamble made me sing until I literally could not talk. But I did it. Fortunately, all the sweat paid off. I never recorded anything that I didn't truly feel in my heart was great.

At PIR we usually taped our vocals over prerecorded instrumental tracks, but on a few memorable occasions we sang live along with the incomparable PIR band, MFSB. By the time we came in to cut our tracks, Gamble, Huff, and Bell knew the song inside and out. They were intensely focused and clear about what they wanted, especially Gamble, who, being a singer himself, was a master of phrasing. That said, we were always encouraged to contribute our own ideas, as were the musicians and everyone else who worked there. It all went into the mix, and I remember a couple of occasions where, caught up in the moment, we ad-libbed while Huff kept the band going. You can hear this on "I Miss You." There Harold goes into an extended spoken-word passage, begging his love for forgiveness. On "Be for Real" I deliver what amounts to a sermon on honesty and respect. To show you how amazing the whole PIR machine was, the ad libs on "Be for Real" went down in a single take.

The PIR magic was simple: Gamble, Huff, Bell, all the arrangers, musicians, and singers knew one another so well that in the studio they communicated almost telepathically—or, as we called it, vibing. To me, even the greatest song is nothing more than a script. Singing live—especially years of singing other people's material—teaches you how to interpret and reinvent a song. Standing onstage before a different audience every night forces you to learn how to ad-lib, stretch out a song or cut it short, change your approach to suit the moment.

Following this script, the musicians and arrangers paint the scene, then the singer acts the parts. I always felt that my job really began when the last word of the lyric ended and I was free to dig into the song, interpreting the lyrics as I felt them. It wasn't long before the PIR musicians were able to lay down tracks that anticipated my phrasing and dynamics and those track-closing ad libs.

In March 1972 PIR released our first single, "I Miss You," backed with "I Miss You, Part 2." "I Miss You" had all the elements of a hit: emotional lyrics, beautiful vocal harmonies, and my rough, pleading lead vocals set against a dramatically orchestrated PIR backing. Early that summer, it charted, and while it peaked in the R&B Top Ten, by August it had stalled at number fifty-eight on the pop chart. It wasn't the worst showing, and we knew there would be other records to come. But we had hoped for much better, and our debut single will always remain a bittersweet memory for me.

The key to having a hit, of course, is airplay. Black stations picked right up on "I Miss You," but white stations were not as welcoming. The word that came back to us was that white programmers weren't playing "I Miss You" because it was "too black." Too black? What the hell did that mean? Coming from radio programmers, it seemed contradictory in an era when Isaac Hayes's "Theme from *Shaft,*" the Staple Singers' "I'll Take You There," and the Temptations' "Papa Was a Rollin' Stone" all topped the pop chart. Some artists live and die by the charts, but I learned early on to keep my mind on the job at hand. So some people didn't care for "I Miss You"? We had to move on, thinking, *Better luck next time.*

Besides, the money was in touring, not record sales. Our getting signed to PIR wasn't like having a fairy godmother wave a magic wand over us. We went down to Krass Brothers, a clothing store on South Street that specialized in outfitting performers. The clothes there were stylish but cheap. We invested in some tastefully eye-catching, matching stage uniforms. Over the years, we tried out a few different styles, but we were best known for an elegant look: a finely tailored tux or suit with a little flash in the details, such as velvet or contrasting lapels, ruffled shirts, and many, *many* bow ties. I'd been wearing variations on this style since I was in diapers, so it was cool with me. The only part of our wardrobe I could never get used to were those damn patent-leather show shoes. They were light, smooth, pointy-toed, and shiny as mirrors. But they were so stiff and so hot, it was like your feet were baking. There were times when all we had to wear were our show shoes. Just try walking a good distance to and from the hotel in those damned things or on hot pavement in Vegas or Miami. Not fun. There were many times we probably could have taken a bus, but we enjoyed strolling along, laughing and talking shit. Besides, we were mindful of our professional image, and, truth be told, we were too damn vain to ride the bus.

So as of mid-1972, our recording contract really hadn't changed anything about our lives. We flew when money allowed or our scheduled demanded it. Usually we traveled by car: Harold in his own, sometimes Bernie in his, and the other Blue Notes in one of ours—usually my '69 chocolate brown Cadillac El Dorado with a beige roof and interior. The band, meanwhile, rode either in a station wagon or in a car with their instruments loaded up in a U-Haul. Occasionally we'd rent a van.

I *loved* my El Dorado. That car took us up and down the Eastern Seaboard more times than I can count. In those days, solitude was rare and precious. I fondly remember driving through the night while the other guys slept, watching the white lines disappear under my wheels, Marvin Gaye's *What's Going On* blasting out of the eight-track. I cherished the solitude.

I'll never forget one ride from Buffalo to Miami. We were heading south on I-95 when I dozed off in the front seat, only to be jolted awake. The car was bucking back and forth, back and forth, like a bronco, but going nowhere while the transmission emitted a sickening, grinding sound: *Gnrrrr!*

What the—?

We were stuck, and Bernie was furiously shifting gears, over and over: drive, reverse, drive, reverse. My poor El Dorado. Half awake, I yelled, "What the hell are you doing?"

"Shut up!" he snapped. "I need gas!" I looked around and realized Bernie had tried to cross the median to get to a station on the other side of the highway. Now here we were, stranded in a ditch.

"Need gas? But we're in a *ditch!*"

I could have killed him. Eventually a tractor trailer kindly pulled us out. We were able to get to Miami, but Bernie's maneuver resulted in a five-hundred-dollar repair bill, which was exactly five hundred dollars more than I could afford. I had to leave my precious El Dorado behind.

Shortly after the release of "I Miss You," we hired a gun-toting bodyguard whose name escapes me. I don't recall exactly why we thought we *needed* a bodyguard, but here he was. One night we were in Boston playing the Sugar Shack, a club owned by one Rudy Guarino. Rudy was a great guy, but he looked, talked, and acted like an "I-talian Nightclub Owner" straight from central casting. He spoke in "dese" and "dems" and always had "his guys" around him.

During our sets, our bodyguard usually took up a post near our dressing room, to guard our clothes and other belongings. The Sugar Shack's dressing room was catercorner off to the right of the stage, so we could see him during our show. I never got the full story of what actually went down that night. All I know is that we were in the middle of a number when our guy and one of Rudy's guys got into a heated discussion. The next thing I heard was a gunshot, then someone screaming, "Oh, shit! They're going to shoot up the club!"

Everybody hit the floor. Meanwhile, there *we* were, smack in the middle of the room, on a floor-level stage surrounded by a wrought-iron railing. Panicked patrons frantically crawled for the exits. I remember hugging that cold wood floor, listening for more shots. A few guys came running in, all reaching for their guns, and I thought, *Damn! I've gotta get out of here!*

I crawled outside and kept crawling until I found a car to hide behind. When it looked like the coast was clear, we ran up the street to the Howard Johnson's hotel where we were staying. Amazingly, no one was hurt, but we had to let our bodyguard go. (*"You fire him."* "No, *you* tell him he's fired.")

Though they were fewer and farther between, there were some wonderful moments on tour, too. As you know, Marvin Junior of the Dells was one of my idols. Even though I was just five when their classic "Oh What a Night" first hit the R&B chart, and didn't hear the song until many years later, when they rerecorded it, I *loved* them.

Marvin Junior's romantic, soulful voice was a gift from God. He could sing as smooth as honey one moment, then tear out your heart with an anguished plea. I learned a little something from every artist I saw or heard, but Junior was certainly one of my crucial influences. If I happen to be in a city where the Dells are playing, I'm there. I swear to God, one night in a club in New Jersey, I was standing against a wall, and when Junior hit certain notes, I felt it vibrate, as if the whole place were coming down. And don't forget, the Dells' "Stay in My Corner" got me my first standing ovation when I was waiting tables at Edgehill's. Even though I'd never met the Dells, I felt as though we went way back.

Of course, Harold had been around so long, it seemed he knew just about everybody there was to know. One night we were playing the Burning Spear in Chicago—the Dells' hometown—when Harold spotted them out in the audience and called them up onstage. *Oh, no,* I thought, *they're coming up here to sing with us.* It was one of the few times I've ever felt threatened on a stage. I whispered to Harold, "Are you kidding? They're not going to blow *me* away. I'm gonna go sit over in the corner." I was scared to death.

But the Dells got up and sang with us; I'm pretty sure it was "Stay in My Corner," followed by one of our songs. It was a lot of fun. And instead of being nervous, I found that standing up there with my idol only inspired me. I felt as if I'd died and gone to heaven. That impromptu, old-fashioned jam remains one of the highlights of my life. Best of all, Marvin Junior and I became friends, and to this day I regard him as my musical father. When we talk, it's "Hey, Dad!" "Hey, son!" Just wonderful.

In September 1972, as "I Miss You" was sliding down the charts, PIR released our next single: "If You Don't Know Me by Now," with "Let Me into Your World" on the B-side. Within a few weeks, we had a Grammy-nominated, gold-certified, number-one R&B, number-three pop, across-the-boards smash. As much as any other single, "If You Don't Know Me by Now" was the perfect setting to show off all the facets of Harold Melvin and the Blue Notes and the PIR team. Like most Gamble and Huff songs, this was much more than a simple love song. It overflowed with conflicting emotions ranging from tender devotion and calm acceptance to sorrowful anguish. Bringing to life the story of a faithful man wrongly accused by his longtime lover of cheating was a challenge, but tackling a song this complex and rich is like sitting down to a feast. Arranger Bobby Martin's lush, restrained orchestration and the group's sumptuous harmonies combined to create a classic.

I will never forget the night the Grammy Awards were telecast. We were working in Detroit at the Twenty Grand, and we set up a television onstage. When they were about to present the Grammy for Best R&B Vocal Performance by a Duo, Group, or Chorus, we stopped the show to watch, and everyone held their breath. The competition that year was tough: the Staple Singers, Gladys Knight and the Pips, the Spinners, and the Temptations. Maybe we jinxed ourselves by playing on the Temptations' home turf that night, but the award went to their "Papa Was a Rollin' Stone" instead.

Getting that gold record was one of the finest moments of my life. Growing up, I never had money to even buy 45s; now I had a gold-plated seven-inch disc hanging on my wall. Artistically speaking, it was a wonderful moment, and financially, it wasn't half bad either. The five of us huddled around Kenny Gamble's desk as he presented us with a check for fifty thousand dollars. Unfortunately, this was the first, last, and only time we Blue Notes ever knew the full amount our records earned. After that, we got Harold's accounting based on Harold's say-so. My first royalty check was for a cool, hard, clean, beautiful ten thousand dollars. It was more money than I'd ever held in my hand before. I believed there just had to be plenty more where that came from. Damn, it felt good.

I was on my way. I rented a beautiful one-bedroom apartment in the Gypsy Lane Apartments complex, off Lincoln Drive, hung the gold record on the wall, and bought myself a gold Cadillac Coupe de Ville with a padded top, just like the one I'd seen in the movie *Superfly*. I had an indoor tree and for some crazy reason I decided to hang dollar bills from it and call it my money tree. I was trippin', and it felt great. I was so proud of that place and what it symbolized. Sometimes I'd just look around and think, *Man, I've made it.*

Having that first big hit changed things for all of us, but not in the ways you might think. Sure, it's wonderful to have a hit record, but you can't delude yourself into thinking that having a hit today guarantees you'll have a hit tomorrow. The record business is the closest thing to legalized gambling outside the lottery, and while a gold record can line your wallet nicely, it's a temporary thing. If only I'd realized that then. The success of "If You Don't Know Me by Now" validated our long-standing belief in ourselves, and that alone made it priceless.

I've heard people say that money or success changes people, and I think that's true only to the extent that those things allow you to be more of whoever you were without it. If Harold needed to control things before, now he realized there was more to control. He was tight with money before, and now there was more of it to be tight with. The jet-setter does more jet-setting, the gadget lover buys more gadgets. Whatever your passion—cognac, Cadillacs, cocaine, women—there are more opportunities to indulge it and discover new ones as well. Things you don't know, you'd better learn fast. Now, does that change you? It depends on who you are.

Even with the hit and a little more cash coming in, Harold still held tight to a buck. There were times when I was so short on cash, I'd go over to his apartment, and he or his wife, Ovelia, would slip me a little extra. Even if we were making more money on the road, we were also spending more, because we were each responsible for buying and cleaning our stage clothes in addition to paying for our hotel, food, and travel. My salary just covered my living arrangements on tour. There was never quite enough to put aside for the rent back in Philadelphia.

I'd had my apartment only a few months when I received a hard lesson in the shifting tides of cash flow. Since I'd never had that kind of bread before, I went through it mighty quickly. One night after we'd been away for a while, I invited a woman over to my apartment. She was lovely, and before I'd even parked my gold Cadillac, we both knew a romantic evening was in store. Arm in arm, we strolled to my door, and there I got the shock of my life. It had been padlocked! I'd fallen behind in the rent, the landlord had had enough, and I was out.

It was one of the most humiliating moments of my life. I begged my date, "Please don't tell anyone about this!" She promised she wouldn't. I eventually got all my stuff out and moved back in for a while with Mom, who was very understanding, until I found a cheaper place. But I must say that when I closed the door behind me the last time, it was a heartbreaking moment. I realized for the first time that it hurt more to have something and lose it than to never have had it at all.

From the early to mid-1970s, Gamble and Huff accomplished the unthinkable, unseating Motown as the dominant force in black music. Besides us, Gamble and Huff produced such stars as Jerry Butler, the Intruders, the O'Jays, and Billy Paul (Thom Bell produced the Delfonics, the Spinners, and the Stylistics), spreading the new Sound of Philadelphia around the world. In the process, PIR became one of the largest black-owned corporations in America, with about 150 employees.

That spring we opened, to fabulous reviews, in the main room of Manhattan's Copacabana, the crème de la crème of supper clubs. Although we now had our own songs, the set still included some Top

Forty and classic Broadway show tunes when appropriate. We would open the show with a smooth, up-tempo "Cabaret" (". . . right this way, the Blue Notes are waiting!").

We'd played the Copa before, but in the upstairs lounge. One time crooner Jack Jones was headlining, and night after night we noticed that there were more people coming upstairs to see us than staying downstairs to watch the star. Personally, I thought Jack Jones had a nice voice and a good show. He did a beautiful song entitled "One at a Time" that I thought I might cover one day. But we must have been doing something right upstairs, because even *his wife* was in the audience for Harold Melvin and the Blue Notes.

Because we were entertainers, being chased by women was an occupational hazard (or benefit, depending on your mood). I sure wasn't complaining. But I was about to discover the downside. It was shortly after we signed with PIR, and we were playing the Manhattan Center in New York City. After the show, we hung out with people who came by the basement dressing room. We didn't have any security then, so it wasn't difficult for anyone to just walk right in, but that was cool. We enjoyed meeting new people and seeing acquaintances we'd come to know on the road. In a city like New York, we all wanted to get out and relax, preferably on our own, and one by one the visitors dwindled, and the guys went their separate ways. I was the last one in the room, totally alone, when a woman casually walked in and said, "Hi."

"Hi," I replied, realizing that I'd seen and briefly talked to her earlier in the evening. "How are you?"

"Oh, fine," she replied, glancing around the room. I didn't think anything of it, though I wondered if maybe she'd come to see someone else.

"Look, I'm just on my way out," I said, pulling on my coat.

"Sure, I understand."

We both started for the door, when she suddenly spun around, screaming, "I love you!"

I stopped and looked at her. She was saying she loved me, but the expression on her face was strange and angry, as though I'd done something to her. Then I saw it: *Oh, my God! She's got a knife!*

Clutching the long knife, she took a quick step toward me, then raised it, ready to strike. "And if I can't have you, nobody can!" There was no time to think and really nowhere to run. It was going to be me or her. I instinctively grabbed a chair, swung it, hit her, and then ran for my life. What happened to her after that? I didn't bother to find out. As a young boy watching Jackie Wilson at the Uptown, I couldn't imagine anything finer than driving women crazy. Now I was beginning to see the other side, too.

Right before the Copa debut, we released our third single, "Yesterday I Had the Blues," a moody ballad that sounded like a Philly-sweetened Stax track. When I say they could do anything at PIR, I do mean anything. A departure from "If You Don't Know Me by Now," "Yesterday" slid Lenny Pakula's funky organ and some sassy brass under sweeping strings and Vince Montana's bubbly vibes. While "Yesterday" fell short of the Top Forty, it set the mold for all of our singles to come. In our live shows, several of us shared lead vocals. Our singles, though, were a different story. Gamble and Huff pushed my voice out front, relegating the others to the background.

Go back and listen to songs such as "If You Don't Know Me by Now" and "The Love I Lost," our next and biggest hit, and you'll hear the unorthodox approach we took. Usually the lead singer states the chorus, with the other vocalists harmonizing above and below him. But in Gamble and Huff's arrangement, Harold, Bernie, Larry, and Lloyd sang the full entire chorus in cool, seamless harmony, thus freeing me to growl, shout, and riff around them.

"The love I lost . . ." I would bob and weave like Muhammad Ali in the ring looking for an opening to throw a jab here—"the love, the love, the love I lost"—". . . *was a sweet love . . .*"—"yes, it was!"—and a jab there. *"The love I lost . . . was complete love."* Then a flurry of punches.

"The Love I Lost" topped the R&B chart and went to number seven on the Hot 100. I'm no music historian, but since it came in 1973, I think you can make a good case for its being perhaps the first disco hit. At the time, a full year before George McRae's "Rock Your Baby" and the Hues Corporation's "Rock the Boat," the term "disco" hadn't even been coined yet.

MFSB drummer Earl Young pioneered the pulselike pattern that would become the music's unmistakable (some would say unrelenting) rhythm: bass drum thumping a steady 1, 2, 3, 4, with the telltale hiss of an open hi-hat linking each beat. It seemed to defy listeners not to dance.

Earl's driving rhythm was certainly a major element in the success of "The Love I Lost," along with PIR's trademark "full orchestra" attack. Gamble and Huff were not the first producers to employ a virtual army of musicians on a track; in the 1960s Phil Spector had done that on his "wall of sound" sessions, some of which Huff had played on. And Motown was famous for the lush orchestration its producers added to hits like the Temptations' "My Girl" and "Just My Imagination."

I do believe, however, that Gamble and Huff were the first to consistently record the full range of instrumentation in a way that made it sound natural and fluid instead of tacked onto your basic bass-drums-piano-guitar backing track. Dozens of musicians played on PIR sessions, but the core of the studio band consisted of Earl Young, guitarist Norman Harris, and bass player Ronnie Baker, with Huff on keyboards. But beyond that, a PIR track could have anything and everything else. "The Love I Lost" is a rich blend of polite electric piano, soaring strings, driving organ, and swaggering horns, with some vibes for sweetening and who knows what else thrown in. Miraculously, it all works. Nothing is wasted, nothing gets lost. A singer couldn't ask for anything more.

Interestingly, "The Love I Lost" was presented to us as a ballad in the style of "If You Don't Know Me by Now." But over the course of two days' rehearsal, the faster tempo felt more natural. The group's input was never discouraged, but frankly we gladly deferred to the masters. I've always felt that you get better results when you let people do what they do best.

"The Love I Lost" went gold at Christmas, by which time our album *Black & Blue* had claimed a spot in the Top Sixty. In the coming months, "Satisfaction Guaranteed (Or Take Your Love Back)" would be another R&B hit. The song is special to me because it contains the first lyrics I ever wrote. Unfortunately, I wasn't savvy about claiming credit or the intricacies of music publishing, so the public never knew it.

Nor did most record buyers realize that the predominant voice on our hits belonged to Teddy Pendergrass, not Harold Melvin. There's a long tradition of putting the lead singer's name in front of the group's that goes back to the 1950s, with Clyde McPhatter and the Drifters. Since then there'd been Smokey Robinson and the Miracles, Martha Reeves and the Vandellas, Patti LaBelle and the Bluebelles, and countless others.

Onstage, it wasn't so much of an issue, because I didn't sing all the lead vocals. Even then, though, some people got confused. Henry, our road manager, was besieged by women begging him to introduce them to "Harold." Time after time Henry would bring a woman to Harold; she'd do a double take and say, "That's not Harold! I want to meet the lead singer. You know, Harold." After a while, anytime that Harold saw Henry approaching with an eager-looking lady, he'd sigh and say, "Go ahead. Take her back to see Rug [that was my nickname in the group]. That's who the girls all want to see."

It was one thing to have a few hundred clubgoers—and some beautiful women—think my name was Harold and quite another when suddenly the whole world did. My mom used to hear of people actually placing bets on whether or not the lead singer of Harold Melvin and the Blue Notes was named Harold or Teddy.

One day I was hanging out with my cousin Pete. "You know," he said bluntly, "you're not getting the recognition you deserve."

"It doesn't matter," I replied. "I had to start somewhere." And I truly believed that. All of us in the group were team players. Just as I didn't feel any resentment, at least at the time, Harold and the other guys viewed Gamble and Huff's decision to put me out front on the records as a good career move for all of us. We were all generally reasonable when it came to doing what worked to everyone's benefit.

Yet sometimes when I look back, I try to see where Harold might have been coming from, too. While he did control the group, as always, he did not control our recordings. As good as we were, the honest truth is that Gamble and Huff gave us the push that catapulted us to stardom. Harold, Larry, and Bernie were also of a different generation, in both age and experience. I suppose, though, that for me the seeds of disenchantment were sown around this time. As we enjoyed more success, the difference between me and the rest of the guys became clearer to me. Harold, Larry, and Bernie had been struggling to make it in show business far longer than I had. If I'd played a hundred seamy dives, they'd played a thousand. If I'd logged ten thousand miles sleeping in a crowded backseat, they'd probably done a hundred times that.

Onstage, we were as clean and as tight as ever. When we played the Roxy, a rock club on Hollywood's Sunset Strip, one reviewer raved: "It's hard to imagine a more tasteful exponent of the sleek, showy soul performance than Harold Melvin and the Blue Notes. . . . This sort of act really can't be done any better." We were that good.

So maybe it's not so surprising that where we stood as 1973 ended was as far as some of the guys had ever dreamed of getting. To me, our current success didn't represent the end of the road, it was a bridge to bigger and better things. And I didn't have any problem with working twice as hard as before in order to cross it. Larry and Bernie seemed perfectly content to go on as they had. Sometimes, standing onstage with them, I got the feeling that they were content.

Around this time, we were playing Phelps' Lounge in Detroit when bad weather caused Harold to miss the show. Sharon Paige, who would later be featured on our 1975 single "Hope That We Can Be Together Soon," was opening for us. I remember sitting backstage, feeling frustrated and angry about something that had happened with the group. Looking back, I realize that while there were few memorable blowups, a constant underlying discontent was beginning to color my attitude toward the group. What was it about? Everything: the pay, Harold's dictatorial ways, the other guys' ambivalence. Sometimes I just got tired of it, and this was one of those times.

When I heard that Harold wouldn't be able to make the gig, I saw an opportunity I might never have again.

"The only way I'm doing this show is if I go on by myself," I informed the other guys.

They looked at me like I was crazy (I prefer the word *impulsive*), but nobody objected, because there was nothing for them to object to. It was this simple: They knew that if I didn't go on, there wasn't any show, and if there wasn't any show, nobody would get paid. For them, the money meant more than a few moments' glory in the spotlight, so there wasn't even a discussion. I was going on. Like my decision to quit Little Royal in Montreal, this was another time I went with my gut—partially because I sensed that it was right, and partially because I'm not a believer in "overthinking" a situation.

I went onstage alone that night, and even though the audience was a little surprised at first, they weren't disappointed. I did the same show we always did. Just for fun, I even sang some of the harmony parts for the hell of it, jumped over to the other microphones (set up for the Blue Notes), and, for a couple of bars, did the steps the other guys would have been doing. For the first time in my life, it was really my show, and even though the songs were the same, something about it felt so different to me, so good. There were two shows that night, and I received two or three standing ovations for each. Leaving the group was not on my mind then, but it was reassuring to know that I could do it on my own. Back in the dressing room afterward, I divided the night's take four ways, handed each of the guys his seven hundred dollars, and then pocketed my own.

Our next stop was the world-famous Apollo, in New York City, where we were headlining. The Apollo is, of course, the crown jewel of the chitlin circuit, a Harlem landmark. The name bespeaks elegance and glamour, but that's really the tradition, not the reality. By the early 1970s, the Apollo's better days were long behind it. There are bigger, posher, nicer places to perform, but the Apollo is still *the Apollo,* and most artists would never dream of passing up a chance to command its legendary stage. Well, I did. Harold had done something to piss me off—I have forgotten what—and I decided this time I simply wouldn't show up. Whatever he did must have been serious, because I was known to do anything—and I do mean anything—to avoid missing a show or being late. I would speed hundreds of miles in the pouring rain to arrive minutes before the curtain, even drive on the shoulder of the expressway to catch a plane.

Of course, no me, no show, no pay. Naturally, Henry and everyone else did their best to convince Harold to go on without me. After all these years of hearing about how replaceable we all were, I admit it was heartening to later hear how Harold handled this crisis.

"They don't want to hear me," Harold said angrily. "They want to hear Rug!"

"But, Harold, man, think about it," Henry pleaded, always the voice of reason. "If you don't go on, we don't get paid. Just sing a couple songs, just so we can get some money."

"No! They want to hear that big black Rug. I can't sing his songs. I'm canceling!"

And Harold kept his word, to the financial detriment of all. Tensions between us were rising, I guess you could say. Harold fancied himself something of a jet-setter, and he took a lot of pleasure in hosting parties in his hotel suites and playing the big shot. One night Harold was entertaining some people I'd never met before. They were white folks, and by the way Harold acted around them, you could tell they were important, at least to him. We were hanging out, drinking and snorting a little cocaine. Everything seemed fine.

Exactly what happened, I'll never know, but the upshot is that one of the guys told Harold that I had behaved disrespectfully toward him. Either I didn't answer this guy when he spoke to me or I said something he took the wrong way. Whatever it was, Harold, who had a temper, got furious. Out of the blue, he slapped me.

"Say what?" It took me a few seconds to figure out what was going on. "What the hell—"

Harold said nothing but glared at me with his cold, dark eyes. "What did you say to him? You insulted my friend. Don't you ever insult my friends like that again," he hissed.

Rage surged through my body like a jolt of electricity. The same instincts that kept me alive on the streets of North Philly locked in. My muscles tensed, my heart raced, my jaw clenched—I was ready to whip his ass. Nobody had slapped me since that day on the Wildwood boardwalk, and for a blinding split second, time stood still and I felt the same hatred and power I experienced the day I got that bully Michael up against the wall. Then, as quickly as it came over me, I stopped myself. And not because I thought it through; I wasn't thinking. But I was smart enough to realize that if I'd struck Harold right then, I'd have hurt him and found myself in very serious trouble. My whole life could have changed, and for what? Because Harold was a bigmouthed fool. It wasn't worth it.

I looked Harold straight in the eye and growled, "Don't you ever think about putting your hands on me again! Not ever again!"

Harold, who was at least a head shorter than I, stepped back, and we left it at that. But he'd crossed a line, and we both knew it. I believe Harold knew, without my having to say it, that if he ever tried to touch me again, he would have a major problem.

It seems that no matter how much you plan, the most important things in life come to you when you least expect them. That was certainly the case when my three greatest blessings, my children— Tisha, LaDonna, and Teddy II—were born. Until now, I've been somewhat reluctant to speak of them publicly because the circumstances of their births drew so much attention back in the 1970s. For one thing, all three were born in 1974, to two mothers. For another, neither mother and I chose to marry. But that doesn't tell the whole story of how I became a father.

During this time, I lived most of my life on the road, but when I was in Philadelphia, my home was with Rose. Even though Rose and I had a great relationship and we had been together a long time, I was, I admit, not always faithful on the road. While I was on tour in 1973, I met a beautiful dancer in Baltimore named Brenda. I thought she was wonderful, and even though I saw her only when I was there, I found myself getting more involved with her. I wasn't looking for it; it just happened.

These were both real relationships, not one-night stands. And each of my children was wanted and welcomed, if not exactly planned. All that mattered was that they were mine. When Brenda first told me she was expecting, I was in a state of absolute bliss. The idea of becoming a first-time father gave me a sense of fulfillment and happiness I'd never known before. I've always been like an uncle to my cousin Pete's daughter Stephanie as well as a sort of "adopted father" to a few other children, like Rose's daughter Keya, and Joyce, the daughter of a friend in Detroit. I know it probably didn't square with my emerging public image as a swinging bachelor and sex symbol, but I welcomed fatherhood and the chance to be an important part of a child's life.

I was out of town during much of Brenda's pregnancy and on tour when my first daughter was born. The minute I could, I flew to Baltimore and saw Tisha for the first time, in January 1974, when she was just two weeks old. Brenda and I named her together—the T in Tisha is for Teddy. We were so proud that we had a daughter. There was so much joy, it seemed only natural and appropriate to make love.

To see and hold my daughter—*my daughter!*—was the most incredible experience. And I promised her that she would never grow up not knowing her daddy. In the months before Tisha's birth, I'd thought long and hard about the blessing God was about to bestow upon me. I knew what growing up without a father meant. While I don't think I missed my father while I was growing up, the older I got, the more I realized what I had missed. Years later, long after my children were born, I began to see how being abandoned by my father left a void in my life. No child of mine was ever going to grow up wondering who her father was or believing she wasn't an important part of his life.

Several weeks after I left Brenda in Baltimore to go back to work, she phoned me on the road. From the tone of her voice when she said, "Guess what," I didn't have to guess: We were expecting a *second* child. I was surprised—actually shocked, to be honest—but happy. I was going to be a father again. And they say lightning never strikes twice in the same place. But that's not all: In March, Rose found out that she was expecting, too. What was I feeling then? Euphoric and overwhelmed comes close. As for what was going to happen once all the children were born, I didn't know except that I would love and care for them. Rose didn't know about Brenda, and Brenda didn't know about Rose. And, for the time at least, that was best.

That October—nine months and two weeks after Tisha's birth— Brenda gave birth to LaDonna. Unfortunately, it would be many more weeks before I could get back to Baltimore to see her. During that time, Brenda moved from Baltimore. When I tried to call, the line was disconnected with no forwarding number. I couldn't imagine what had happened, why she didn't leave at least a number and a message for me with my mother or someone else we knew. For a moment I thought, *Well, this is how it begins. This is how fathers lose their children.* Then I thought, *No! This isn't going to happen with my kids. Even their own mother isn't going to keep them away from me.*

So I knew what I wanted—to find my daughters—but, realistically, there wasn't very much I could do. I felt helpless. No matter where I was or what I was doing, a day didn't go by that I didn't think about Tisha and LaDonna and wonder where they were and if I would ever see them again. Somewhere in the world two little angels waited for me to find them. But how? I was determined to be part of their lives, yet there were moments when I secretly feared that I never would.

Meanwhile, back home in Philadelphia, my son, Theodore DeReese II, was born just five days before Christmas, eleven months after Tisha and three after LaDonna. Rose insisted that he not be named "Junior" (though we do call him "JR" here at home so we both don't have to answer every time someone says "Teddy"). I named him after me so that he would grow up to be proud of me. In the years since, I've been very sensitive to the burden of his growing up with a famous name. I'm proud to say, he's handled it beautifully, and though we are alike in many ways, he's very much his own man.

Perhaps because I couldn't see my daughters, I bonded even more strongly with my son. Even before he was born, I would lie close to Rose's stomach and talk to Teddy and sing to him. I was looking forward to being with Rose when he was born, but Teddy II didn't bother to consult my tour itinerary before he made his "debut," so I missed it by a day or two.

I guess somewhere inside, I'd resigned myself to never finding my daughters, because I chose not to tell Rose about them. I fell in love with my son, and the pain I felt over Tisha and LaDonna only made me more determined not to lose him. Like my daughters, he was beautiful, a miracle. Plus, he was a miniature carbon copy of his old man. Some of the happiest moments of my life were spent cuddling little Teddy. I'd sit on our bed and gently "toss" him a few inches up and then catch him in my hands.

The whole time was ripe with paradox and love and longing. The more time I spent with Teddy, the more I missed and worried about my girls. The more I thought about the girls, the more I treasured time with my son. And when I thought of how much joy and happiness he brought, I couldn't help but wonder what kind of man my father must have been to have given up building the same relationship with me. Whenever these thoughts crossed my mind, I'd drop them; it was too painful to think about.

Unfortunately, Teddy's mother and I ended our long relationship shortly after he was born. My mother cared for Teddy for about a year, but once Rose married another man, I lost contact with my son, too.

How could I have been so blessed, three times in a single year, and then have all three children lost to me? I had a very hard time accepting that my children were growing up without me, maybe without even knowing I existed. It was far too easy for me to put myself in their shoes, know their thoughts, feel their hearts breaking with every holiday and birthday spent without Dad. It was ironic that in a world filled with fathers who abandon their kids without a thought, here I was, a father who wanted his children desperately and couldn't find them. The only thing I could imagine worse than my never seeing them again would be their growing up to think I'd chosen to be out of their lives.

Wherever Tisha and LaDonna were, I prayed they were safe and cared for. It was different with Teddy, because I knew where he lived, with his mother and stepfather. For whatever reason, I was not allowed to see him, and many a day I'd drive over in my Rolls-Royce and cruise past the apartment where he lived. I'm not proud to admit that I entertained thoughts of getting Teddy back any way that I could, even if it meant using force. But in the end, all I did was drive on, my heart breaking.

I wouldn't say that having children made me grow up, but it certainly cast my future in a new light. Now I had to think about someone besides myself. Even though I didn't have any of my children then, I was determined to get them and live up to my responsibilities to them.

Harold and I reached an understanding by 1974, and our third album, *To Be True,* was credited to "Harold Melvin and the Blue Notes Featuring Theodore Pendergrass." By the spring of 1975, this gold album had already spun off two hits: "Bad Luck" (number four, R&B; number fifteen, pop) and "Where Are All My Friends" (number eight, R&B). Later in the summer "Hope That We Can Be Together Soon" was a number-one R&B hit. *To Be True* spent more than thirty weeks on the chart and peaked at number twenty-six. Owing to personal reasons, Lloyd had left the group and was replaced by Jerry Cummings, a singer from Baltimore.

For our fourth album, we recorded a song that has always had a special meaning for me, "Wake Up Everybody." Written by Victor Carstarphen, Gene McFadden, John Whitehead, and PIR arranger extraordinaire Bobby Martin (the team responsible for "Bad Luck"), "Wake Up Everybody" perfectly exemplifies Gamble and Huff's commitment to music that inspires. As a general rule, I don't have favorite songs, but if I had to pick one from these days, this would be it. I never tired of singing this (I even performed it in my show when I first went solo), and whenever I did, I knew that this was why God had given me the gift of singing. When I sang it, I felt as if I were singing it to my children. It seemed only right, in a spiritual way, that

Wake Up Everybody become our most successful, highest-charting album. (It also included our original version of "Don't Leave Me This Way," which would be a hit for Thelma Houston, and "Tell the World How I Feel About 'Cha Baby.")

Between the hits, the sold-out shows, and the increasing recognition, there was enough to keep us all together, even if not always happily. Still, we shared some nice moments. I remember one night we opened for Al Green at the Greek Theater in Los Angeles, and we tore the place down. Al came out to do his show, and that stage was still burning. He was great, but rumor has it that our show inspired him to toss roses to the audience for the first time. We stood backstage and lightheartedly joked, "Well, if that's what he's got to do to make them like him . . ." It was good-natured, healthy competitive spirit, but that didn't mean we weren't serious.

Life on the road remained as unpredictable as ever. One of the strangest episodes occurred in 1974 or 1975 when we were driving home from Philadelphia International Airport. As far as dress was concerned, we were always attired tastefully, like hip businessmen. At the time Bernie had a white girlfriend named Patty, who had long brown hair. She was with us that day, when our friend Knuck picked us all up in his Cadillac El Dorado. We were all waiting for him at the curb when Knuck, who had parked up the street, backed up to get us. We jumped in and he sped off. He dropped us off at our places, then went home, where, he later told me, armed FBI agents in bulletproof vests knocked on his door.

"What's this about?" he asked.

"You'd better turn your friends in," an agent warned him.

"But why?"

The agents next went to Bernie's house and picked him up, and then someone phoned us to let us know what was happening. It wasn't long before the FBI agents realized that Bernie's girlfriend was not the kidnapped heiress Patty Hearst and we were not members of Symbionese Liberation Army, the domestic terrorist organization that held her hostage for over a year and a half. Believe me, we busted Bernie's chops over this for a long, long time.

We certainly had our adventures on the road. Each hit record seemed to propel us higher up, where the air was rarer and sweeter, and drugs were everywhere. In the 1970s, I traveled in both worlds. In New York, I could hang with the hustlers and pimps at Small's Paradise in Harlem, or ride downtown and be embraced by the celebrity elite at Studio 54. I was doing my share of cocaine and drinking, of course, but I had it under control. The truth is, being around lots of people doing drugs or lots of drugs always made me very nervous. In the early 1970s, I was in the men's room of a private club in Los Angeles, when the actor Peter Lawford approached and offered me some cocaine. I looked up and there he had it, more cocaine than I'd ever seen in my life—in a small jar! And he wasn't the only seemingly straight celebrity who was doing it. Everybody who was anybody did it. And the unspoken code was that if you wanted to be anybody, you'd better do it, too.

Another time, also in Los Angeles, we were invited to Sly Stone's house for a party. I remember feeling so honored. Sly is a revolutionary figure in popular music, a visionary. I remember Harold and me getting a ride with someone, and thinking how funny it was that Sly Stone lived across the street from the mansion shown in the opening credits of *The Beverly Hillbillies*. As Harold and I walked through the unlocked front door, I could not believe that people really lived like this. Whatever excitement I felt about being at Sly Stone's party was quickly replaced by fear when I saw on a coffee table a mountain of cocaine piled so high you could have literally buried your whole head in it. Everybody was groovin', having a good time, but all I could think was, *The cops are gonna bust in any minute.* After about fifteen minutes, I split. The survival instincts I'd honed on the streets of North Philadelphia wouldn't let me be blinded by the glamorous trappings. No matter how many millions you had or how exclusive your world, there was always danger.

It's funny how the brighter the sun shines, the deeper the shadows. And so it was with Harold and the group. Time and experience had changed us all. For example, when I first joined the group, I used to listen to Larry and Bernie, because they seemed to be men of the world. Now, after I'd let it be known that I wouldn't be pushed around, whenever they had a beef with Harold, they'd ask me to talk to him for them. Since Harold still believed that we were all replaceable, he had little incentive to make us happy. Harold made sure that we never knew how much our records earned or the amount of money we were entitled to. While I'd never seen a full accounting of our earnings from PIR, I'd long suspected that Harold was being less than fair. Way less.

Besides cheating us out of money, Harold began to lose his temper more often, with people we worked for and sometimes even on-stage. In one case, it cost us a gig, which we could not afford to lose. We were in Los Angeles for a weeklong engagement at the Playboy Club. As usual Harold put himself up in a plush suite at the luxurious five-star Beverly Hilton, while Bernie, Larry, Jerry, and I found small studios with kitchenettes at the Beverly Comstock motel. Very early in our engagement—either opening night or the second night—Harold got into a heated disagreement with the Playboy Club management. When the Playboy Club people tried to discuss the matter with Harold, he became belligerent.

"I don't have to take this!" he snarled. "Let's get the hell out of here!" So we did, even though it meant that we would now have to cover a week's living expenses in L.A. and travel to the next date without having any income. Our leader retired to his Beverly Hilton suite, and the guys and I returned to our modest rooms.

I'd managed to put away a few bucks, so while I was unhappy with Harold's impulsive decision, it didn't break me. The other three guys, though, were close to broke.

"Teddy, come on, man!" one of them said. "You know what Harold's done is wrong, and you can talk to him."

"Yeah, man, tell him we need some money. He'll listen to you."

This is ridiculous, I thought, but which part of the situation was most absurd? Our having hit records but needing to beg Harold for money to live? Or our putting up with it in the first place? It was a mess, and I knew we were being ripped off, but instead of feeling that intense anger burning me up inside, I felt just plain sick and tired of it. He and the other guys had long since lost their power to shock or disappoint me. I'd seen too much to feel outraged anymore. I knew I'd leave someday, I just didn't know exactly when.

"Okay," I said. "I'll go to Harold and see what I can do."

Taking a cab would have been an unnecessary extravagance. The long walk from the Beverly Comstock in Hollywood to the Beverly Hilton was hot, smoggy, and miserable. Walking down Wilshire Boulevard, I was pissed enough already. L.A. is not made for walking, and at one point, the sidewalk disappeared and I found myself squeezed between a lush hedge and the signpost bearing the Welcome to Beverly Hills sign, thinking, *Damn you, Harold.* It just rubbed the inequity of the situation in deeper. Every step I took only steeled my resolve to get what we deserved. Past the uniformed doorman, through the immaculate lobby, and down the plushly carpeted hallway to Harold's suite, I couldn't stop thinking, *Why the hell aren't we here? Who the hell does Harold think he is?*

Inside Harold's suite I found the usual scene: a bunch of his well-heeled friends and hangers-on laughing and joking, a white drift of cocaine on the coffee table, and stacks of silver trays and dish covers, telltale signs of a huge room-service tab. And that was probably just a fraction of what he owed the local coke dealer.

Harold, as usual, was playing the gracious host, and he greeted me politely but warily. I could tell he'd been drinking and was high. He must have wondered what I was doing there. The first chance I got, I pulled him aside and told him.

"Harold, here you are up in this suite, and the other guys are sitting down in Hollywood with no money."

Harold stared back blankly, as if to say, "So?"

"You just don't get it, man. We work our asses off and are barely scraping by, and you're up here having a big fuckin' party. It's just not right."

Harold was nothing if not smooth. "Just a minute," he said, giving me a paternal pat on the shoulder. "I'll get you something." Harold went into the bedroom adjoining the main room. Heeding some sixth sense, I followed him. As I peeked around the door frame, Harold, with his back to me, lifted up the mattress of his bed to reveal what looked to be thousands of dollars he'd stashed underneath. Only later did I learn that this was our *royalty* money—thousands of dollars that Gamble and Huff had given to Harold in a check with the understanding that he would cash it and split it equally among the group. That never happened.

Harold came out a minute or two later and handed me a small stack of bills.

"Here," he said. "You take this, for you. But don't tell the rest of 'em about it."

I took the money, put it in my pocket, and left. *This is so damn wrong,* I thought. Back in my room, I sat down to think about my options. Should I stay? Should I go? I wasn't a fool; I knew this deserved serious consideration. But I also knew how I was. Once I made my decision, there would be no turning back, no second thoughts. I did enough cocaine to keep me up and thinking all through the night. It worked, and I admit the little boost in courage it gave me didn't hurt, either. I was high, all right, but my thinking was crystal clear. I'd been singing "Wake Up Everybody." Maybe it was time to take my own advice. Staying with Harold Melvin was going to undermine not only my career but my principles. Strange as it sounds, this wasn't a real emotional decision for me. Whatever emotions the situation had provoked over the years, I'd felt them so many times, I just didn't feel them anymore. Maybe that's why when I finally reached my decision, it wasn't hard to follow it through.

The next morning, Henry knocked on my door. "Come on, Ted. It's time to go."

"Henry, I'm not going. I quit."

Henry laughed uncomfortably. He knew me better than anyone else, and I think he knew I wasn't kidding. "Stop joking around, Ted. We've got to get going. We've got a date."

"Henry," I repeated, *"I'm not going."* By the time Henry left to fetch Harold, he knew I wasn't changing my mind, but our boss was not so easily convinced. He came back to the Beverly Comstock with Henry, thinking he could persuade me to reconsider. The minute I saw Harold, I knew he was quite surprised, to say the least.

"Do you mean it, Rug?" he asked.

"Yeah, I mean it. I'm not going. I'm quittin', Harold. I've had enough."

Once Harold realized I meant it, a strange ambivalence came over him, and I remember thinking, *He really does think he can replace me!* Harold didn't ask if I'd reconsider, or if I'd stay for more money— nothing. After a few minutes of awkward silence, it was clear that there wasn't much to say. Looking back, I've always wondered why Harold didn't stop and think, *Hey, he's the lead singer, and the group is hot, and to keep this going, maybe I'll have to be fairer.* But his steadfast belief in his power to continually reinvent the Blue Notes clouded his judgment. I held no personal animosity toward Harold or the other guys. They were creatures of habit, of a different time and place. In their minds, they'd reached their pinnacle. Mine was still off in the distance. We had to go our separate ways.

I stayed around L.A. a day or so, just thinking. I'd made a sudden decision, but it wasn't rash or impulsive. It was a long time coming, and if it hadn't happened that day in L.A., it was bound to happen sooner or later. Most important, I didn't feel I was running away from a bad situation but running toward a better one.

Not everyone saw it the same way I did. News traveled quickly back to PIR, where Gamble and Huff were quite upset, to put it mildly. Each of us had signed directly, individually, to PIR. They had a contract with me already, so they stood to benefit by my going solo if I was successful. But in the music business, that was a big if. The track record for lead singers who'd left their groups for solo careers was not exactly encouraging.

"C'mon, man, think about this," Kenny Gamble implored. "Go back to the group." I could understand Gamble's reasons for wanting to keep the group together; PIR's hard work was really paying off. But I would not be swayed. I did, however, return for one date. Harold and the Blue Notes had a big one-nighter coming up and asked if I would join them for that. Without a second thought, I replied, "Sure—if you want to pay me ten thousand dollars." How interesting that before I'd quit, he didn't think I deserved an equal share. But things were different now; I was calling my own shots. I did the show and got the ten thousand, but it wasn't enough to make me change my mind.

Back in Philadelphia I lay low and starting making plans. I didn't have a manager, a record deal, a band, a paying date lined up—nothing. Yet I hadn't felt this good in a long, long time.

FIVE

❧

It's funny how things work out sometimes. I left Harold Melvin and the guys in October 1975. My first impulse was to handpick some guys from other vocal groups to create my own. I considered asking tenor Harry Ray of the Moments and Harry, the bass singer of the local group the Futures, and some other guys. Then I realized that being part of another group wasn't what I wanted to do. On the other hand, I knew that going out as a solo artist without name recognition would be tough. But the next thing I knew, I was leading my own group: the Blue Notes.

Back in Philadelphia, I'd set up my own production company, Teddy Bear Productions, at 215 South Broad Street. A local artists' manager named Ernie Pep had a suite of offices there, and I rented a single office from him. Ernie was a big jolly Italian guy whose stomach shook when he laughed. Until I could afford a secretary, I answered my own phones and typed my own letters, using two fingers. At first I rented a single office; over the next year or so, I took over the entire suite.

I was in business, although initially most of my energy was put into getting out the word that I was no longer in the group and that I had my own act. I knew people were still going to see Harold Melvin and the Blue Notes expecting to see me. When I heard they were playing Philadelphia's big arena, the Spectrum, I informed the local newspapers that I'd left the group. It stirred up attention, got my name in the paper, and probably hurt Harold's business somewhat. I also have to admit to feeling a twinge of satisfaction when I found out afterward that the Blue Notes were confronted by people in the audience shouting, "Where's Teddy?!"

I hadn't been gone from the group many weeks before Larry, Bernie, and Jerry called to say that they wanted to leave Harold, too. They proposed that we work together. I could offer a lot of high-minded reasons why we became the Blue Notes Featuring Teddy Pendergrass, but the truth was that I needed to prove to the world that I wasn't Harold, and the Blue Notes needed to work for some-body who wasn't Harold. From every angle, this was the best move for all concerned.

In early 1976 *Billboard* named *To Be True* the number-six R&B album of 1975, and in early 1977 listed "Wake Up Everybody" as the number-eleven R&B single of 1976. Judging from the big play the media gave my splitting and the group's ever-growing popularity, the re-formed Blue Notes made sense. Why shouldn't we reap the re-wards from our years of hard work? If we didn't get our due finan-cially from Harold, at least we could use the name we'd helped make famous to ensure our futures. Now that I'd left to go solo, I fully in-tended to see that plan through. But I wasn't entirely ready just yet.

Along with the Blue Notes came Harold's road manager, Buddy Nolan. Buddy had been around the music business for years and had once worked for James Brown. I believed we were in good hands. From the get-go, it was clear that I was the boss. I had learned a lot from Harold, including what kind of boss *not* to be. I listened to the other guys' input, and I sure paid them a hell of a lot better than Harold ever did. I covered such expenses as travel and hotels, too. I never partied until after the show, and I handled problems diplomat-ically rather than dictatorially. I was a *nicer* captain, but there was never any doubt as to who was steering this ship.

Looking back, I can see that I probably overlooked the guys' occasional lack of drive. I don't think the guys viewed me as a boss, even though everyone understood that I was pulling in the crowds and signing the paychecks. My appreciation of Harold's organizational and musical abilities only grew as our new act set out playing to significantly smaller crowds than we were used to. I hired three background singers from Texas—Diane, Peaches, and Phyllis—to strengthen the guys' vocals onstage. This freed the guys to put their all into executing their routines and looking sharp—in other words, to do what they did best, which did not always include singing.

Within a few months, my good friend Henry quit Harold's group too and asked if he could come to work for me. We were working at a club on Long Island when Henry tracked me down and called to ask for some help with a personal matter. "Of course, no problem," I told him. Soon afterward, Henry came to work for me. "You'd better not be spying for Harold," I teased. But he wasn't, and I was thrilled to have him along. Buddy and Henry possessed a world of experience dealing with booking, transportation, hiring musicians, and the general headaches of life on the road.

One of my headaches was the other guys. The way I saw it, they were getting a new lease on life, a chance to go for it and make it even better. But the group quickly fell into the old pattern, and before long I realized this couldn't last forever.

Anything could happen. For instance, Jerry was a nice enough guy, and he certainly tried hard. But he was young and green. Jerry had a softness about him. Being a tenor, he had a high speaking voice and came across as timid. While we were playing the Total Experience in L.A., Jerry met a white girl who really rocked his world. Whether she turned him on to drugs or great sex or both, I don't know, but Jerry underwent an amazing transformation. He began speaking in a lower voice and suddenly seemed to have all the confidence of Eddie Murphy's Nutty Professor's alter ego, Buddy Love. One night Jerry surprised us by showing up late for the gig.

"Man, you are messed up. You're not going on tonight," I told him firmly. He nodded okay and sat down, and Bernie, Larry, and I went out to start the show.

We were in the middle of a song when out of the corner of my eye, I glimpsed Jerry, dressed in his stage uniform, sauntering onstage, doing an awful imitation of James Brown. Imagine the TV character Urkel trying to make like Mike Tyson, and you'll have an idea how ridiculous he looked. Bernie, Larry, and I shot one another nervous glances. Being pros, though, we went with it, like it was part of the show. The audience thought our little comedy bit was great, but pretty soon we could see Jerry had no intention of leaving the stage.

Now, Buddy had worked for James, so he knew just what to do: "I'm gonna put a cape on that fool and walk him off the stage like James Brown when he does 'Please Please Please'!" Jerry was so high, he went with it, and that's how Buddy and Henry saved the show. Looking back, it's real funny, but at the moment all I wanted was to have a stage to myself, so I could stop worrying about who was going to do what next. After that incident, it wasn't long before Jerry left the group and Lloyd returned.

Going solo was my real goal. Before I left Harold, I'd met a wonderful woman named Ruth Bowen, who gave me a lot of encouragement and support. Ruth is a true legend in the music business, and I was flattered (and greatly relieved) when she started booking some dates for us. Her company, Queen Booking, was the biggest black-owned booking agency, and she persuaded promoters and other booking agents to take a chance on us. Ruth's list of management clients included such greats as Dinah Washington and Aretha Franklin, and she'd been married to Billy Bowen of the legendary Ink Spots. Having managed top stars since the late 1950s, Ruth knew the business inside out and everyone in it worth knowing.

Ruth is a petite, lovely woman, and we became very close friends.

As a manager, Ruth thought big. She believed it would be a good idea for me to open for Elvis Presley in Las Vegas, for instance. She believed that I had a future as a solo artist, and she encouraged me to move to New York City, where she was based.

I lived in the Navarro Hotel on Central Park South, then took a place over on East Forty-fourth Street, near the United Nations. There's a lot to love about New York, but a city that never sleeps is more than even I can handle. You know what eventually drove me back to Philadelphia? Alternate-side-of-the-street parking. I always parked in the wrong place at the wrong time; I shudder to think how much money I lost in parking tickets. And the streets of New York. Within weeks, the craters they call potholes had loosened every nut and bolt in my trusty gold Caddy. Traumatized, I drove back to Philadelphia vowing never to leave home again.

For the most part, my relationships with other performers I worked with were professional and cordial. But performers being performers, with their own attitudes and egos, let's just say the heads could get too big for the room. Sometimes when neither act on the bill could be considered that much more of a draw than the other, you might alternate headlining. Ruth Bowen and promoter Teddy Powell put together some dates where the Blue Notes and I split the bill with Bobby Womack, a respected singer, guitarist, and song-writer best known for "Lookin' for a Love" and "It's All Over Now." The arrangement was that we would alternate opening and closing for each other. Bobby had been around a little while longer than us, and I guess he felt that he should have been the headliner every night. All through the tour, he bitched and moaned until one night he decided to do something about it.

It was our night to close the show, but shortly before show time, we got word that Bobby was sick and wouldn't be able to perform. I was more than a little suspicious, but we went on, did the show, and, convinced Bobby would try to pull something, I announced from the stage that the show was over, good night. The houselights went up, and we headed offstage.

I hadn't even gotten backstage, and what do I see but Bobby and his band haulin' ass for the stage, ready to go. I remember thinking, *Why, that—!* I ran backstage, where I found Bobby in the wings, ready to go on. Funny, he looked perfectly healthy to me.

"You are not going on!" I shouted in his face. "This damn show is over! I just closed it!"

"No, Ted, you just *opened* it," he replied sarcastically. "I'm going on."

He thought he was so damn slick. I couldn't stand it. When the emcee announced that Womack had "recovered" and was going to play, the crowd applauded. I stood backstage, glaring. *He is not getting away with this!*

"Henry!" I shouted. "Unplug that asshole!" We unplugged their amplifiers, the stage went dark and silent, and that was it. You should have seen the look on Bobby's face when he realized he wasn't going to be headlining that night.

The incident didn't end there, however. A member of Womack's road crew threatened to shoot me, forcing me to hide out in my dressing room. I was scared to death but, you know, it was well worth it.

The Blue Notes and I worked through the first half of 1976, despite Harold's suing us for more than half a million dollars over use of the name "Blue Notes." He lost the case because he was unable to produce any proof that he'd ever owned the name anyway. All of this drove Harold to suffer an emotional breakdown that led to hospitalization and a hiatus from performing. He'd been so furious at Henry for leaving that he threatened to shoot the two of us. People close to Harold told me that he finally realized it wasn't so easy to replace this group of Blue Notes, after all. I don't know if he *ever* accepted the fact that we were a team, and that our contributions to the group's success were at least as important as his. Years later I read that he said that as long as he had the mold, he could always bake a new cake (or something to that effect). For some reason, though, he never managed to bake another one as good as ours.

PIR had no immediate plans to record the Blue Notes Featuring Teddy Pendergrass. The label was on too hot a streak with us to let it cool too long, but there was concern about the name business and other legal issues. Anxious to get back in the studio, I began talking seriously to other record labels.

One day Kenny Gamble asked me, "Would you mind if I kept both you and Harold on the label?"

"Hell, yes, I'd mind," I replied, surprised he'd even consider it. "I don't want to be on the same label as Harold, because I never want to have to wonder if there's a conflict of interest. It's either him or me."

That fall Gamble and Huff came through with a deal for me alone. Needless to say, the Blue Notes weren't thrilled to learn that I was leaving the Blue Notes again, but they landed on their feet as the Notes of Blue. (There are only so many permutations you can squeeze out of the name Blue Notes.) Harold, meanwhile, put together a new group of Blue Notes, some guys from Baltimore and a lead singer named David Ebo, whom I knew from the 'hood. Interestingly, Gamble and Huff released Harold from his contract, and he and the group signed with ABC Records. In early 1977, Harold had his last major hit, "Reaching for the World." Like many other black artists who left independent black-run labels for one of the majors, Harold and the new Blue Notes saw their career lose stride. He would lead successive lineups of Blue Notes until shortly before his death in 1997.

At this point, I suppose it would be nice if I could say that Harold and the other Blue Notes and I shared some important moments in the years after I left for the last time. But that would not be completely true. I hoped there would not be any hard feelings. In those first years after I left, I tried to stay in touch. Harold and I socialized now and again, and in more recent years, we appeared together briefly at a few public events, such as the unveiling of my plaque on Philadelphia's Walk of Fame in 1989. You may have seen Harold join me for "If You Don't Know Me by Now" on Arsenio Hall's TV show a few years back. To the outside world, it probably looked warm and cozy, but once the music stopped, we had nothing to say. There were reasons we went our separate ways, and time didn't change them.

Not long after I came back to Philadelphia from New York City, I fell in love with a beautiful, savvy woman named Taaz Lang. Taaz was short for Taazmayia, and she was every bit as unique as her exotic name. Taaz had a face you'd never forget, with beautiful caramel skin, big brown eyes, and a winning smile. She was shapely, petite, and elegant, and her hair was a striking platinum blond. The ex-wife of Philadelphia Eagles fullback Izzy Lang and a well-known business-woman in her own right, Taaz was considered a real catch. We met sometime in 1974 or so, where I don't recall. But one day on a whim, I drove by her beauty shop at Germantown and Broad, and we became reacquainted. She gave me her phone number, and within a couple of days, I'd visited her at her home. From then on, we were inseparable.

We began dating in 1975; around late 1976, I moved into her beautiful Mount Airy home, which she shared with her son, Izzy Jr., and her mother. Taaz's mother also supervised several adults who were considered too mentally unstable to live entirely on their own, and a few of them shared the house as well.

Not only did I love Taaz deeply, but I quickly saw that she had impeccable business sense. Despite my years in showbiz, I knew piti-fully little about the business end of things. All the fine-print details of booking dates had been the secret province of Harold. Whom to call, how much to get paid, and how and when. Even with Buddy Nolan and Henry around, I knew I needed more help, and fortunately Taaz was a quick study and understood the nuts and bolts of running a business, keeping the books, and so on. She'd never worked in the entertainment world before, but she was no stranger to it, either. She'd worked as a model and counted Nancy Wilson and Lola Falana among her friends.

Taaz wasn't my manager as such; she functioned more as a liaison, a buffer between me and the rest of the business. So, for instance, when I was negotiating my solo deal with PIR, I told Taaz what I wanted, and she passed it on to Gamble and Huff. Looking back, I can see we made our share of mistakes, but for the time, Taaz's input, encouragement, and support were invaluable to me.

I have some great memories of living in that house with Taaz. Our next-door neighbor was Grover Washington Jr., and his son Grover and Izzy used to play together all the time. This was also where the Jacksons came to visit while they were in town recording their first album since leaving Motown, *The Jacksons,* with Gamble and Huff. I remember Tito, Randy, Marlon, and Michael all sitting in the living room. We were just hanging out, joking around, except for Michael. I couldn't help but notice how quiet he was and how he was too interested in the trinkets and knickknacks displayed, and how beautifully Taaz had decorated the house, to join the rest of us. I must have looked at him a little funny, because one of his brothers said to me, "It's okay, Teddy, that's just the way Michael is."

The Jacksons had a reputation in show-business circles for knowing their way around a basketball court, and we discussed getting a game together sometime.

"Well, Teddy, you know we're *pretty good,*" one of them warned.

"We're no slouches here in Philadelphia, either," I retorted. "I can play." Truth was, I hadn't shot a basket in years, but to have guys from L.A.—*L.A.!*—suggesting they could beat me and my team on my home turf? Uh-uh.

"You want a game? I'll give you a game. And then we'll see."

"Great. You're on!"

An assistant of Gamble's named Preston got the whole thing to-gether for us. We arranged to play the game at the Bright Hope Baptist Church gymnasium, at Twelfth and Columbia, and set the rules: a best-of-four series, 20 points per game. My team consisted of me, Preston, Randy Jackson, and Sonny Hill. Sonny was the coach of a local youth organization called the Sonny Hill League, which gave inner-city kids the opportunity to play basketball as an alterna-tive to hanging out on the street. Marlon and Tito were joined by George McInnis, a formidable center for the Philadelphia 76ers, and a fourth guy whose name I can't recall.

Everyone on the court took their b-ball seriously. With Sonny and Randy taking most of the shots for our team, Marlon and Tito's crew never won a single game. I think it's safe to say they were sur-prised. As for George McInnis, he was downright pissed. And I was loving every minute of it. I hadn't exactly embarrassed myself, either. I had the ball for the match-ending shot, and I had the guts to call it, too.

"This is gonna win the game!" I announced. Then I shot a three-pointer that barely made a sound as it dropped through the net. Truly a thing of beauty.

The small but enthusiastic crowd whooped and hollered while Sonny cried, "You all heard my man Teddy say he was gonna do it!" We all hugged and high-fived one another—except for McInnis, who stormed off the court. The Jacksons left Philly having learned a very important lesson, one I never fail to remind any of them about whenever I see them.

Between the time I left the Blue Notes and the release of my first album, I started testing the waters as a solo performer. I've never taken a stage without at least a few moments of preshow jitters. I always felt comfortable onstage, but standing out there alone took some getting used to. Honestly, I missed having the other guys there with me, and the realization that the whole show rested on my shoulders was at times a bit overwhelming.

In early 1977 I was acutely aware that my future lay in the eight tracks Gamble and Huff were assembling for my solo debut album. Singing to half-filled theaters with the Blue Notes had been a rude awakening, to say the least. So many talented lead singers had left popular groups and fallen flat on their butts. I didn't plan to be one of them. But I'm sure plenty of other people questioned the sanity of leaving a top act to strike out on my own in a time when black music's ability to consolidate R&B hits into pop success was weakening. Even making the R&B chart was no longer a sure thing. Disco, with its rushing metronomic beats, one-dimensional subject matter, and disposable vocalists, washed over black radio playlists like a tidal wave. By the time it finally swept back out to sea, it had taken with it many established R&B stars.

Listening to the playbacks only deepened my faith in Gamble and Huff and the whole PIR operation. If the tracks they cut on me with Harold and the Blue Notes fit like a glove, these were like a second skin. It was easy to record and believe in the songs, because they wrote them *for* me. It's impossible to describe, but when I sang their songs, they immediately became my songs. I not only sang them, but I could imagine myself speaking the lyrics, even writing them myself. One of my favorites, "Somebody Told Me," another Gamble, McFadden, Whitehead, and Carstarphen creation, is inspirational in the same vein as "Wake Up Everybody." "And If I Had" is a gorgeous, longing ballad (it later turned up in the movie *Choose Me*), while "The More I Get, the More I Want" and "Easy, Easy, Got to Take It Easy" are wonderfully sexy. "The More I Get" is soulfully direct, and "Easy" is just that (ah, the many moods of the Teddy Bear!). And of course the album included one of Gamble and Huff's timely messages—"You Can't Hide from Yourself" ("Everywhere you go, there you are")—hot enough to get crucial disco play. But I refused to do straight disco. As I told *Newsweek* magazine, "You can get some feeling out of good music. The only thing you can get out of disco is smelly underarms."

Gamble and Huff's ability to tap into each artist's psyche and create for each a repertoire that was not just unique but uniquely suited to him was their genius. The albums they wrote and produced for me didn't give me just songs to sing; they gave me a story about myself, told in music. If you listen closely to "Somebody Told Me," I sing about receiving my calling at age ten, for example. As for the sensual, romantic songs, Kenny Gamble once told a reporter that he wrote those for me after seeing the way women related to me. I didn't feel I was that different; I certainly didn't consciously work on being viewed as a sex symbol. To me, it just came naturally, like sitting on the front steps, rappin' to the neighborhood girls. Only now the neighborhood was bigger, and I had a better rap.

Teddy Pendergrass was released in March 1977. By then Taaz and I were no longer romantically involved. Both of us being typical strong-willed Aries, we butted heads too often. We wisely realized that we could share only one relationship successfully, and so she continued as my agent and good friend. She never stopped watching my back. Taaz caught someone who worked for me falsifying receipts for concert grosses and expenses. So, for example, I'd think I came away with a few thousand for a date when in fact it had been significantly more. Taaz's suspicion was first piqued when she noticed that the "receipts" were scrawled on napkins and scrap paper. I was amazed that anybody thought they could get away with something like that. Boy, did I have a lot to learn.

In preparation for the album launch, Taaz coordinated dozens of interviews, photo shoots, and concerts. Of course, many other people, at PIR and CBS, worked hard to make everything fall into place, but Taaz was the closest to me.

The LP's release brought a marathon of interviews, visits to radio

stations, and other promotional activities. CBS Records' campaign—
"Teddy Is Ready"—said it all. In April, with *Teddy Pendergrass* rising
toward number seventeen on the national album chart and the first
single, "I Don't Love You Anymore," moving up to number five
R&B, I did a number of shows on the East Coast. On my days off, I
returned to Philadelphia.

The shows were going well; I had my Teddy Bear Orchestra and
Teddy's Angels, but the stage still felt empty to me. Taaz and I were
in Atlantic City, where we saw a show that included several female
dancers. They were so elegant and graceful, we decided that was just
what I needed. Taaz found out they were dancers from Philadanco,
one of Philadelphia's leading dance troupes. I was scheduled to make
my Carnegie Hall debut in late April, and Taaz approached four of
the women and offered them the job.

Now, here the story takes a funny turn, because one of those
dancers was Karen Still, who later became my wife. You have to
understand that in the world of serious, professional dance, show
business is looked down upon. We do "shows"; dancers give "performances." Our work is "entertainment"; theirs is "art." When the
head of Philadanco learned I wanted to hire some of her dancers, she
was appalled. And to give you an idea how sheltered the dancers
were, when Karen learned that she'd be dancing for Teddy Pendergrass, she asked, "What does he sing?" She had no idea who I was.

On April 14, 1977, I was at the office getting ready to leave that night
for the next date. Our tour bus was loaded and we were set to leave
around ten that night. Taaz was tending to business in New York, but
she got back to Philly in time to say good-bye before we left. We
promised to talk the next day.

We drove through the night and arrived in Buffalo the next
morning. As the rest of the group checked into the hotel, a desk clerk
said, "Mr. Pendergrass, you have a message to call Philadelphia im-

mediately." Concerned, I didn't wait to get up to my room. I spotted a pay phone in the lobby and dialed home, all the while thinking, *Mom*. A shaky voice at the other end told me that Taaz had been murdered. I say "a voice" because I don't remember whom I spoke to. I was in shock.

The night before, Taaz and Jo Jo Tynes, an employee of mine, drove my Mercedes to her home. As I was told, Jo Jo was getting something out of the trunk and Taaz was getting out her keys to open the front door, when someone emerged from the bushes and shot her at close range. The bullet passed through Taaz's arm and pierced her heart; she died almost instantly on her front steps.

Like everyone who knew her, I was devastated by the murder. Why Taaz? From the few details I learned at the time, none of it made sense. More than twenty years later, it still doesn't. Shortly after I returned to Philadelphia, the police asked me to come in for questioning. I cooperated, without an attorney, and after one, maybe two interviews, the police were satisfied that I knew nothing about the murder.

It goes without saying that Taaz's death was most devastating for her son and her family; I've always respected that. I'd also lost a very dear friend in Taaz, whom I was still in love with. And, having lost my father to murder, I understood her family's pain all too well. So it has saddened me that through the years certain people close to Taaz have suggested that her involvement in the music business was in some way connected to her murder. The police department's failure to find Taaz's killer left her case an open book in which people have scrawled their ungrounded theories and suspicions. At least one newspaper article implied that either I or PIR was somehow connected to Taaz's murder. Every few years, it seems, the press exploits the mystery of Taaz's death, dredging it up again, opening old wounds, but never bringing us any closer to the answer.

I can understand how some people around Taaz might have considered show business unsavory: the nightlife, the drinking and drug-

ging, the odd hours, and the travel. And maybe, as the press has speculated in the years since the murder, Taaz was unhappy and planning
to quit. All I know is that she never did or said anything around me
to indicate that she felt that way. The Taaz Lang I knew was thrilled
to share in my success and justifiably proud of her accomplishments
and her reputation in the industry.

I understand how, in the depths of grief, people strike out with
accusations and blame. In such times, it's only human to want the answers, and not knowing who killed Taaz or why makes it even harder
to accept. My father's murder had made it difficult for me to trust
others, and after this it would be years before I felt safe entering a
house that had large shrubs around the front door. Even though I feel
certain the music business had nothing to do with what happened to
Taaz, and this senseless killing has all the markings of a botched robbery, naturally, in the back of my mind, I do wonder. Maybe if she
hadn't been driving my expensive car, maybe if she hadn't been so
well known around town as a successful businesswoman, maybe if her
mother hadn't opened Taaz's home to people who were mentally unstable, maybe if she didn't live in such an affluent neighborhood,
maybe, maybe, maybe.

As I sat with the family in the front row, listening to the Reverend
Jesse Jackson eulogize Taaz at the funeral, it finally struck home that
I would never see her again. I was acutely aware that some people at
the funeral felt Taaz's work with me somehow led to her death. I
could almost handle their sideways glances, but when Reverend Jackson made a reference to drugs as he glanced at me, it felt like a knife
in my heart. (Of course, the reverend knew only what some of Taaz's
family told him, so I can't blame him personally for that.) Twenty
years later I still miss her.

Exactly one week after Taaz's death, I made my solo debut at
Carnegie Hall in New York City. I'd performed there once before

with Harold Melvin and the Blue Notes. As you can imagine, it was a tense time for everyone, and bringing a relatively new show into the media capital of the world turned the pressure up a notch.

I expected to be somewhat anxious, but hours before curtain time I was a nervous wreck. My stomach was churning, and all I could think was, *Oh, God.* I'd done a few solo shows down South to warm up the act and work out the kinks, but what if it wasn't enough? I'd had plenty of time to imagine how it would be: the euphoria, the excitement. But once I got backstage that afternoon, I quickly learned that a date at Carnegie Hall was all that and more. This was *Carnegie Hall!* What happened tonight could make or break me. I was absolutely terrified.

The day did not get off to a promising start: My three background singers' dresses never made it to New York. Luckily, Karen and the other dancers always brought a change of clothing with them, since they often attended receptions after their performances at Philadanco. They lent their dresses to the vocalists.

Further compounding my anxiety, who unexpectedly shows up backstage but my uncle Neveland. Now, I loved my mother's brother, but he did like to drink. I still can see myself pacing the dressing room, practically sucking the tobacco out of one cigarette after another and feeling as if my head were going to explode. And there's Uncle Neveland, a small, half-pint bottle in his pocket, announcing to one and all, "Yeah! This is my nephew!" He'd corner a stagehand, pop his head in someone's dressing room, just making sure everybody he saw knew: "Teddy Pendergrass! That's my nephew!"

He was so proud of me, bless his heart, but he was driving me nuts. I never touch drugs or drink before a show, but I heard "Yeah, I'm Teddy's uncle! That's right, Teddy Pendergrass!" one time too many.

He was in my dressing room and I needed something to calm my nerves. "Uncle Neveland, gimme that bottle." I took a swig.

"I'm so proud of you," my uncle said, before swinging around to holler at someone else, "Hey! I'm Teddy's uncle . . ." I gulped down another swig, and probably a few more for good measure.

Standing in the wings in an immaculate white suit, I heard the band start to vamp. Unlike some other performers, I don't have an elaborate preshow ritual. Just give me five minutes alone, let me take off my glasses, and I'm good to go. Everyone who worked with me then called me "Clark Kent," because once the glasses came off, my whole demeanor changed.

As I burst onto the stage through a giant photo of myself, the crowd went insane, clapping and screaming. I mentioned Taaz's passing and dedicated a song to her. She must have been watching over me, because from that moment on, my doubts and worries evaporated like a mist. I stormed that stage as if I owned it; I grabbed the audience and I never let go. I remember moving through the show and making sure I pulled out every trick in my bag. Although I'd received this kind of reaction before, this was the first time I felt connected to my audience in such an emotionally intense way. From that moment on, I was the Teddy Bear, and the night flew by like a dream.

For my encore, I came onstage wearing a flowing white sequined robe and sang "Somebody Told Me." Not surprisingly, several reviewers mentioned the seeming contradiction that would mark my work forever: the mix of the sensual and the sacred. As the *New York Times* put it: "Mr. Pendergrass seems to want to have his cake and eat his communion wafer too," but it was intended as a compliment, not a put-down. It seemed that the only thing the critics didn't like was the robe. Hey, you win some, you lose some.

From there, we toured the country through most of the summer, arriving to make my Los Angeles solo debut at the Hollywood Bowl in mid-September. We'd worked out all the bugs, *Teddy Pendergrass* had been certified gold, and PIR had just released "The Whole Town's Laughing at Me." There's a joke in there somewhere, but this memory's almost too painful for me to start looking for it. What went wrong? Try everything, everything, and everything.

The Hollywood Bowl is a unique outdoor amphitheater, which makes getting the sound right very tricky. But this wasn't just a misbehaving sound system, as sometimes happens. Thelma Houston, who'd had a big hit with one of my songs, "Don't Leave Me This Way," opened the show and had some problems with the sound. When I came out, though, the sucker attacked me. The overmiked orchestra all but drowned out the opening number, "Wake Up Everybody," then the system began breaking down. Snapping, crackling, popping—yeah, I was singing inside a bowl, all right; a bowl of Rice Krispies. No one could fix it, and I wasn't going to continue making myself look bad, so I cut the show short and left.

The following month, we were playing the Latin Casino, in Cherry Hill, New Jersey, not too far from my hometown. The Latin Casino was another of those fondly remembered, now-extinct places to play: about two thousand seats, intimate supper-club atmosphere. Perfect. By now, word had spread throughout the industry that I was working without a manager, and with the records zipping up the charts, the big-name managers started lining up. Literally. I came offstage that night to find a column of them outside my dressing room and all the way down the hall. It was flattering, but I noticed quickly that every guy's rap was basically the same:

"I'm the best, just the best . . ."

"I've worked miracles for my other clients. Like, just the other day . . ."

"Teddy, I can make you the biggest . . ."

I may have been young, but I wasn't dumb. I'd listen politely while they essentially talked and talked and talked themselves right out the door. When the last one had gone, I thumbed the stack of business cards they'd left behind and tossed them in the trash. What I didn't know that night was that the only manager worth having, a gentleman named Shep Gordon, had taken one look at the line backstage, said a quick hello to me, then split. The fact that he was so laid back intrigued me. After talking to some CBS Records executives who suggested I call Shep, I invited him to my apartment to discuss business.

We talked a little, then Shep came right to the point: "No matter what I say to you, ninety-nine percent of the people who do what I do are complete liars, and they're good at it, too. So there's nothing I can tell you that will help you make a decision."

"Okay . . ."

I liked what I was hearing, but Shep sounded so different, I was starting to suspect he was a little bit nuts. Plus, most of his expertise was in white rock acts—like his clients Alice Cooper and Blondie. He'd never handled an R&B singer before, but the more he talked, the less that mattered.

"Teddy, you come up to New York one weekend, and we'll take a two-bedroom suite in a hotel. We'll get some women, some booze, and whatever else we want, and let's just party. And whoever stays up the longest, whoever's up first on Monday morning, wins. If you're still standing, I leave. If I'm still standing, I'm your manager."

"Deal."

We didn't totally seal it right then, but we agreed on enough major points that Shep left saying, "All right, let's get the wheelbarrows, because the money's going to be pouring in!"

From the very little that I recall of that weekend, it was everything I'd ever heard about the rock-&-roll lifestyle. Probably more. And best of all, I lost the bet. Who'd imagine I'd be outpartied by a white boy from Oceanside, Long Island? But I was, and it was one of the best things that ever happened to me. We shook hands, and that's been our contract ever since. No paper. His word was enough.

Shep is nothing if not honest, sometimes brutally so, and he told me quickly what he liked and didn't like about the show. To begin with, it was good-bye, Teddy Bear Dancers. I was sorry to see them go. I thought they brought something very special to the show, and they were all lovely young women. Because they were accustomed to a more traditional, sheltered work environment, I did all I could to protect them, as well as my three background singers, from problems on the road. As their employer, I had an obligation to make sure they felt safe and secure, and to see that they were always treated like ladies. Henry kept an eye on them for the most part, accompanying them back to their hotel and accompanying them to see a movie or do some shopping, if they wanted.

I was taken with Karen Still right away. She was then, and remains, a beautiful, intelligent, insightful woman. I first fell for her warm, happy smile, pretty brown eyes, and long beautiful hair (which I later made her promise not to cut). She has a lithe, graceful dancer's body and gorgeous legs. She's beautiful. As I got to know her, I admired her more and more and discovered that she is as beautiful inside as out. She is considerate and has a great sense of humor, but more than anything else, she is sweet. It's not a word you hear too much these days, but that's Karen. I felt a strong attraction to her, but I held myself to the rule I laid down for everyone who worked with me: no dating within the organization. I never wanted to be standing onstage and have anyone in my show go on angry with someone else in my show. It was a recipe for disaster. Well, at least that's what I kept telling myself. But one day in Detroit I left a message for her to come up and see me in my hotel room. As I waited, I worried that she'd think this was inappropriate or assume she was in trouble.

When she walked in the door, all I could say was, "I wanted to tell you I think you're a wonderful dancer. But more than that, I think there's something really special about you. And I want you to be my lady."

Karen was flattered.

"Teddy, I think you're a wonderful person, and talented, and all that good stuff. But I've seen the good, the bad, and the ugly, and I think you need somebody strong. I'm not that person, it's not going to work, and I think we should remain friends."

I might have said something else to try to persuade her, but my adopted daughter Joyce showed up with a bunch of people, and

Karen made a mad dash to get ready for the show. That night was one of only two times in my entire career that I went onstage with a few drinks under my belt. The audience never knew the difference, but Karen and the other dancers noticed it immediately.

"What was with you?" Karen asked me after the show.

"I got drunk because you turned me down," I told her. That didn't work either, but it was the beginning of a great friendship. So you can see why deciding to work without the dancers had its upside. The day they were let go, I said to Karen, *"Now* will you go out with me?"

The biggest, most significant change Shep made in my career concerned the venues in which I performed. From a business point of view, I was playing some great places, but I was also still doing dates that weren't so great. Without going into the lurid details, let's just say that there are concert promoters, club and theater owners, and other show-business "characters" who are not always as honest or as fair as they should be. Even when you have a written contract, a lot of cash changes hands, and you find yourself in lots of towns where the guy who owns the club is also the guy who owns the radio station. Or the popular disc jockey is the only concert promoter you can deal with, because if you don't, your records don't get played. It's not unusual to find that your sound system has just been trucked in from the lounge at the Holiday Inn down the road or to be told, "Sorry, you're not getting paid tonight." Suffice it to say, things could get ugly.

Having worked these places so much with Harold, I assumed these were the facts of life for a performer and didn't dwell on them too much. The first time Shep accompanied me to a show, the promoter never showed up afterward to pay me. When Shep confronted the guy's assistant, he took a ring off his finger and thrust it at Shep. "Here, white boy," he snarled. "Now *you* put it on."

This wasn't a side of the business Shep had much experience in. It was something I'd seen many times before. Later, Shep said to me, "I can't believe you stand for this crap!"

"This is the way it is," I told him.

"No, this is *not* 'what it is.' You can go out and get paid what you deserve and be treated like an artist, with respect."

"Shep, if you can do it, fine," I said. Frankly, I wasn't optimistic. What I didn't realize then was that I was becoming a big fish in a pretty small pond. There was a whole other world out there—of sold-out one-nighters in places like Madison Square Garden, of platinum hits—a world where I could be known as not just an R&B singer, but a singer, period.

From a career standpoint, my life could not possibly have changed more dramatically than it did in 1977. Back home in Philadelphia, things were changing, too, for many reasons. First, I suppose, was the fact that I finally had money. Real money. Mom always said that even as a kid, I spent my money like it was about to burn a hole in my pocket. Needless to say, suddenly having enough currency to set a small bonfire didn't exactly curb my impulses.

When I signed my solo contract with PIR, I celebrated by walking into a Rolls-Royce dealership, pointing to a light bronze-brown Corniche convertible, and saying to the salesman, "I want that one."

He looked at me and almost took me seriously for a moment, until he realized he'd never seen me playing ball or singing on television. After all, what other black men could afford a Rolls? I had some money for a down payment (which seemed to please him), but I had no bank account, no credit rating, and nothing you could call collateral (which did not). He was being obnoxious, so I opened up my recording contract and slapped it down on his desk. "How's that?"

He looked it over, and when he came to the dollar signs, his eyes bugged out. He looked up at me with a big ol' obsequious smile and in the most ass-kissing manner you can imagine, purred, "Why, Mr. Pendergrass, *of course* we have something for *you.*"

Unfortunately, the Corniche had been promised to a well-known New York disc jockey named Frankie Crocker. So instead I picked a two-toned blue-and-silver-blue four-door sedan off the floor. I think I drove it for two days straight without ever getting out of it. God, I loved my cars.

When you've got a car like that, you need a house that's on the magnificent side to go with it, right? Heaven forbid that Rolls should be parked outside anything less than an estate. So before long, I found my first real house: a ten-bedroom brick mansion at Latimer and Twenty-second that had once belonged to a former governor of Pennsylvania. Strangely, it had everything but a garage, so I parked my Rolls and my Mercedes out on the street, if you can imagine.

Even though my career had become very demanding, I never stopped looking for my daughters Tisha and LaDonna, and I tried to keep tabs on my son as much as I could. I was working in my Broad Street office one day when Rose's daughter Keya, whom I've always loved as though she were my own daughter, came by to see me with little Teddy in tow. He must have been two and a half or three then, and while I never found out exactly why Keya took it upon herself to bring him down, it was an act of kindness I never forgot. I'd had a good rapport with her ever since I'd started dating Rose when Keya was about six years old. It soon became clear that she hadn't told anyone she was bringing Teddy to see me.

My heart almost burst as I watched Teddy toddle around the office; he sat in my chair, behind my big desk. I'm not bragging when I say he was so damn *cute!* I held him and kissed him, and after a while Keya said she had to get back home. When she and Teddy left, I didn't know when—or if—I would see him again. I knew, though, that I had to have my children around me. All of them.

I was desperate to find my daughters, but wherever I turned I hit a dead end. Finally, a friend of Brenda's I knew in Baltimore gave me

Brenda's parents' phone number, down in Memphis. I phoned Mr. and Mrs. Hollerway, introduced myself, and explained all that had occurred between Brenda and me and why they hadn't heard from me before. I then asked if I could see my daughters and held my breath. Under the circumstances, they easily could have said no. I was so happy and relieved when they said yes and invited me to see the girls anytime. Brenda's parents kindly allowed me to be a part of my daughters' lives, and for that I will always be grateful. At first, things were a little complicated, because Tisha and LaDonna had been raised to believe that their grandparents were their parents; they called them Mama and Daddy. Now suddenly another daddy was coming on the scene, so their grandparents had to do a little explaining before I saw them for the first time.

We arranged a date, and I flew to Memphis and drove to their home. The whole time I wondered and worried: *What would they think of me? Would they accept me as their father?* By the time I pulled up to the pretty single-story house my nerves were jumping. Mr. and Mrs. Hollerway, or Louise and Elgie, as they asked me to address them, invited me in, and I was pleased for my daughters' sake to see that they had a beautiful, well-kept home. We talked for quite a while, and it was obvious that Tisha and LaDonna's grandparents were loving, protective, and concerned only with what was best for their granddaughters. Then it was time for them to meet me.

I was sitting in a chair, my heart racing with anticipation, when the girls—both then around three—came into the living room. Their grandmother said, "This is your dad. This is your father."

They were both so beautiful. Tisha I would have known anywhere, but this was the first time I'd ever seen LaDonna, and her close resemblance to her mother almost took my breath away. They were so small and beautiful, like little dolls. And I saw Brenda's Creole heritage in their café au lait complexions and wavy hair. *My angels!*

The two of them looked up at me with their soulful brown eyes, and responded in ways that I soon learned were typical of their different personalities. Without hesitation, LaDonna jumped into my lap and cried out "Hi, Daddy!" She snuggled up close against my chest and started playing with the gold chains around my neck. Tisha, however, held back, analyzing the situation and eyeing me closely, but before long she was sitting in my lap, too. Just to hold them . . . God! I'd finally found my babies, and I would never let them go again. My mom, too, shared in my happiness. It goes without saying that my mother was thrilled to be a grandmother. Despite her usually strict moral outlook, when it came to my children, she accepted them lovingly, without reservation. She never once made me feel that I'd done something wrong. In fact, she was extremely proud of me for taking responsibility for my children.

Even though being on the road and living in Philadelphia kept me from seeing them as much as I would have liked, I grabbed every opportunity to spend time with them. Whenever I was in Memphis, I'd surprise the girls by picking them up at school. I'd sneak down the hall and into their classroom, which was large enough that I could stand in the back without their noticing right away. The first time I visited, word that Teddy Pendergrass was in the school spread through the halls like wildfire, and I remember scooping up Tisha in one arm, LaDonna in the other, and running through the halls and out to their grandfather's waiting car as teachers chased us squealing, "Ooh! Teddy! Teddy Bear!" After that, the school permitted me to pick them up a few minutes earlier so that we wouldn't have to run for it.

When the girls were around four years old and after they'd flown with me a couple of times, I arranged for them to fly up to visit me at home in Philadelphia or accompany me on the road. I bought tickets for them to fly alone, even though they weren't actually old enough. Contrary to my swinging bachelor image, I was an attentive, protective father from the get-go. Wherever I went with them, they were constantly watched and cared for. As I became more successful, the possibility that someone might kidnap any of my children could not be ignored. I worried about them and always kept them very close.

One of the most frightening moments in my life occurred around this time. Despite everything that had happened between Harold and me, we still socialized now and then. Now that I wasn't working for him anymore, we could hang together. One day he and I were shooting pool on the second floor of my house when Harold looked out the window.

"Rug? There's a cop out there writing you a ticket."

I rushed over to the window, and sure enough, he was right. I ran downstairs and out onto the sidewalk with a pool cue in my hand. I didn't realize I was holding the stick; in fact, I'd run out of the house so quickly, I was still in my bedroom slippers. "Excuse me, Officer," I called politely. "That's my car."

Without looking up, he replied nastily, "Well, it's in the wrong place," and kept writing in his ticket book.

"But I live here," I said.

"I don't care where you live or who you are. I'm writing you up."

"Look, Officer, I can move the car in a minute. It's not a problem." This wasn't the first time I'd run afoul of the parking regulations, but the cops had let me move the car before. I'd never encountered such a hostile attitude over a parking ticket.

The policeman glanced up from his ticket book and noticed the pool cue in my hand. "What are you doing with that *weapon?* You gonna hit me with that stick?"

I was stunned. "No, no, Officer. I was just shooting pool, and I ran down here to try to talk to—" He slammed me up against a wall and slapped handcuffs on me in a matter of seconds.

"Let's go!" he snarled, gripping my arm roughly.

"What the hell are you doing?"

"Come on! You're going with me!"

"Wait a minute, Officer. My daughters—I have two little girls upstairs!"

"Shut up and get in the car!"

I glanced up to see Tisha and LaDonna at the front door, their frightened faces pressed against the glass, wailing, "Daddy! Daddy!"

I hadn't mentioned that there was another adult in my home, so as far as this policeman knew, he was leaving two preschoolers totally alone without regard for their safety or welfare. He didn't care. When I got home from the station a few hours later, I held my girls and comforted them. I seriously considered suing the Philadelphia Police Department over the incident—it wouldn't have been the first time I did—but, realistically, I knew what a hassle it could become, so I dropped it.

I hadn't lived in this house too long before the disadvantages of living there outweighed any advantages. With a couple of expensive cars parked out on the street, and word of my buying the house having been in the news, my address wasn't exactly a state secret. Everyone—tourists, women, jealous boyfriends—knew where Teddy lived. I had people sitting on my steps, leaning on my cars, ringing my doorbell, trying to peek in my windows. I felt like an animal in the zoo.

Through most of this time, I suppose you could say I was still a loner. I had a few close friends, my family, and Karen, whom I was now dating. It's funny when I think back on it now, but for all that Kenny Gamble, Leon Huff, and I meant to one another in terms of our careers, we never hung out together. I didn't go out much in public unless it was to a 76ers game or a private club. Then as now, those closest to me were friends I'd known for years and family. Through the years I briefly dated several famous women—among them Pam Grier, La Toya Jackson, Dionne Warwick—but nothing serious developed. They were all wonderful ladies, but there were times when I honestly wondered if being famous meant that you dated other famous people just because you could. Karen and I had begun dating, and she was always waiting for me.

With nothing really pulling me back home, I had no problem spending weeks on the road, doing two shows a night. Sometimes I headlined, sometimes I opened.

I opened for several other performers, including Marvin Gaye. I'd been a fan of Marvin's since I got my first transistor radio. In the years since, he had written and recorded music that was inspiring on many levels. As a singer and later a songwriter, Marvin never stood still. His first album was dominated by such classics as "My Funny Valentine" and "Witchcraft," yet the hits that followed were Motown classics: "Hitch Hike," "Pride and Joy," and "How Sweet It Is to Be Loved by You." His popular duets with Tammi Terrell (a Philadelphian, by the way), like the Ashford and Simpson masterpieces "Ain't No Mountain High Enough" and "You're All I Need to Get By," were followed by his somber number-one reading of "I Heard It Through the Grapevine." Three years later, Marvin wrote and recorded one of my favorite albums of all time, *What's Going On*. Then, a couple of years later, he changed direction again with the erotically charged *Let's Get It On*.

I don't think any popular singer before Marvin so freely and beautifully merged the sacred and the sexy, the political and the personal. As singers, our styles were too different for me to consider him an influence, but certainly in the mastery of his voice, his material, and his audience, he was an inspiration. In the years since Marvin's tragic death in 1984, much has been written of a supposed rivalry between us. I will not speculate about how Marvin regarded me, personally or professionally. I can only tell you what happened.

I first met Marvin in Lexington, Kentucky, at one of a few dates I opened for him in 1977, in the wake of his hits "I Want You" and "After the Dance." Marvin was a man I had admired and loved since my early teens, so it was a true honor to costar on a bill with him. Backstage at the coliseum one evening, I knocked on his dressing-room door, and he answered.

"Hello," I said. "I'm Teddy Pendergrass, and I just wanted to meet you."

Marvin, who was soft-spoken and a real gentleman, said, "Come on in and sit down. Let me introduce you to my wife, Jan."

"Hello, nice to meet you." Like many people who know Jan, I thought she was beautiful. But it was Marvin whom I'd really come to see.

We sat and talked for a while, and we just clicked, which is not all that common in show-business circles. With me, Marvin was open and kind, and that's how our friendship began. Watching Marvin up close from the wings every night was a revelation to me. He commanded his audience, but not in an aggressive way. I found it interesting that someone so deeply into his music was so laid back onstage. Even when he sang a song like "Let's Get It On," he projected a shyness that drew the audience to him.

Our styles may not have been similar, but we each ignited the same intense reaction from the audience. It's impossible to deny that Marvin and I were both viewed as "sex symbols," though I've always believed that the media went overboard on this point. Someone who knew us both then once told me that the promoter chose me to open in a conscious attempt to make the date more appealing to women. And it worked.

I respected Marvin immensely, and was honored to be on the same bill. But standing in the wings waiting for my cue, I never forgot why I was there: to get that audience in the palm of my hand. I'm not ashamed to say it: I wasn't interested in warming them up for somebody else; I wanted them burning for me. It wasn't me versus Marvin (or whomever else I opened for then), and I wasn't into blowing somebody off the stage just to prove I could do it. Marvin, who despite his laid-back demeanor was extremely competitive, understood and respected the fact that onstage I never held anything back. Each night, during his own show, he would acknowledge me and ask his audience to give me a big round of applause. Of course, it's a professional courtesy to acknowledge your opening act. But in his words, Marvin went beyond the call of duty, and I was flattered and touched.

Offstage, I got to know Marvin and his lovely wife, Jan, fairly well. Accompanied by whomever I was dating, I visited them several times in their California home over the next few years, and Marvin was always friendly. I never sought show-business friendships, so it's not my style to read more into the relationship than there was. Because Marvin's music made his life an open book, he was someone you could know a lot about without truly knowing him. I never got the impression then that he viewed me as a threat. That was about to change.

In the spring of 1978, PIR released my second solo album, *Life Is a Song Worth Singing*. The title track was cowritten by Thom Bell and the extraordinarily talented Linda Creed. I expect some people would be surprised to learn that a white Jewish girl wrote the lyrics to such R&B classics as the Stylistics' "Betcha by Golly Wow," "You Are Everything," "You Make Me Feel Brand New," and the Spinners' "Could It Be I'm Falling in Love." But Linda had a warmth and friendliness that transcended any differences, and whenever I'd see her we would laugh and joke around. Everybody there loved her. In fact, her office at PIR was specially furnished with a crib, refrigerator, and stove so that she could bring her baby daughter to work with her. "Life Is a Song Worth Singing" is such a powerful message. At the time I recorded it, though, I didn't know that my friend Linda had been diagnosed with breast cancer.

Within a month, *Life* was certified gold, and the first single, "Close the Door," was closing in on the top spot on the R&B chart and number twenty-five in the Hot 100. I'd recorded songs that were romantic, flirtatious, even mildly suggestive, before. I mean, I don't think anyone who heard me or saw me then mistook me for a choirboy. But for reasons my female fans would probably be better able to articulate than I can, "Close the Door" took the audience response and adulation to a whole new level. The screaming and swooning were great, don't get me wrong. And then the ladies started tossing flowers, notes with phone numbers, house keys, and teddy bears. Okay, that was still cool. But I will never, ever forget the night I watched a pair of silky panties sail over the crowd and land at my feet. If my face could have turned beet red, it would have. Believe it or not, I could stand on a stage entreating ten thousand women to "close the door and let me give you what you've been waiting for" or let them know, not so subtly, "you got, you got, you got what I want" and still be embarrassed. You don't believe me? What can I say?

That summer I was out on the road with R&B legends the Isley Brothers. Rudolph, Ronald, and Kelly Isley were like cats with nine lives. They burst on the scene in 1959 with "Shout," then through the 1960s scored hits with "Twist and Shout," "This Old Heart of Mine," and "It's Your Thing." They started the 1970s with a cooler kind of funk ("That Lady") and not only survived but thrived through the disco years.

We didn't hang out, but we got along well enough. I was backstage preparing to open the show when I got word that my first album had been certified platinum. *Platinum!* One million sold! I was absolutely euphoric. A few people congratulated me, but I soon sensed a different attitude from the Isleys. One of them came into my dressing room right before a show and said in a derisive tone of voice, "Oh, your album's platinum, huh?" Like it was no big deal.

Around the same time, the Isleys offered me the chance to play Madison Square Garden in New York with them. "It's ten thousand dollars for you," Kelly Isley said. "It's the most you'll ever make for a date in your life."

He didn't know it, but he'd just thrown down the gauntlet. With a platinum album and a number-one single, I was more than ready to meet the challenge. I'd show that Kelly Isley, even if I had to bide some time. The opportunity came sooner than expected.

After the Madison Square Garden date, the Isleys threw a lavish party in the penthouse of the New York Hilton. It had been a great date and a great party, and I was feeling good—until later that night, when word came down that the Isleys were canceling the next date, an arena show in Providence, Rhode Island. I forget what the reason was, but I remember thinking it was lame and being pissed at the prospect of losing money.

I told Henry, "Call the promoter. Tell him I'll headline the date. If I don't sell out, he doesn't have to pay me. If I do, he pays double." It was an offer no promoter could refuse, because whatever he sold beat an empty house. And since I was still brand-new to the platinum stratosphere, he might have been counting on my not selling out the place and being able to pocket everything he made without having to give me a penny. Either way, he couldn't lose. For me, however, this was a big risk, but one I had to take. Early in my solo career, I'd lost a lot of money when promoters canceled shows due to low ticket sales. Sometimes I didn't get the word I'd been canceled until we hit town. Then I had to pay everyone's salary and expenses out of my own pocket. So, yes, I had something to prove, but I was also trying to score big to offset those earlier losses. But more important, I loved a challenge.

And I won. Big. The show sold out, I muttered, "Screw you" to Kelly Isley, wherever he might be, and I never opened for—and never had to answer to—anyone else again.

SIX

❧

In July 1978 I returned to Los Angeles—scene of the Hollywood Bowl debacle—for eight sold-out shows at the Roxy, a rock club on Hollywood's Sunset Strip. The speed at which the place sold out set some kind of record.

However, this didn't sit too well with a local concert promoter who had some vague association with a disco on the Strip. At this time in the music business, many black promoters felt they were being shortchanged when it came to getting access to black performers. Their complaint was basically this: Once a black performer reached a level where he could sell out such large venues as New York's Radio City Music Hall or the Greek Theater in L.A., the chance to promote, and the profits, went to white promoters. According to the black promoters, they did not get to share in the "return" for what they had invested in these acts by promoting their shows when they were on their way up. They further argued that even though most of the concertgoers were black, their money was ending up in the hands of white promoters, who, they claimed, hired only white chauffeurs, caterers, and other related services, whereas by hiring black contractors for these jobs, black promoters recirculated those black dollars back into the black community.

I understood all that, but for reasons beyond any black artist's control at that time, white promoters were benefiting from their long-standing relationships with the bigger venues. Unfortunately, few black promoters were given the opportunity to promote bigger dates. This would soon change.

A group of black music-industry professionals banded together to form an organization they called the United Black Concert Promoters, and in 1979 held several press conferences to present their case publicly. Because of my high profile and the fact that I worked with white promoters, including my friend Dick Klotzman, they announced they were singling me out as the first black performer whose shows they would boycott. Fortunately, we were able to reach an understanding, and in 1979 I became the interim chairperson of the Black Music Association's Performing Artists Rights Committee, an organization founded by Kenny Gamble and committed to resolving these issues in all aspects of the industry. I had been using black promoters for my dates wherever it was feasible; for instance, my good friend Jesse Boseman had promoted many of my southern dates from the beginning of my solo career. And whenever possible I encouraged established white promoters to "copromote" with black promoters.

At the time of my Roxy engagement, however, some renegade promoters chose to deal with the problem street style. Because the Roxy usually presented white rock acts, my playing there was one more indication of my appeal to white audiences, and I became something of a poster boy for crossover success. I was never ashamed of it; I never saw anything wrong with being successful. But like any industry in America, the music business is plagued by racism and discrimination, both subtle and blatant. The problems faced by blacks in this business are too complex for me to do justice to them here. But suffice it to say that neither their causes nor their solutions rest on the shoulders of one man. Not everyone saw it that way, though.

Shortly before opening night at the Roxy I got wind that by not doing business with this other promoter, I was making a big, big mistake. The disgruntled promoter's threat was to the point: "Your life won't be worth a damn." Like any business where a lot of money changes hands, the music business has its dark side, a street element. I took the threats seriously—very seriously—and so did Shep and my new comanager, Daniel Markus. We called on the Los Angeles Police Department and the FBI, which provided agents to escort me to and from the show. They employed all kinds of tricks: Henry traveling disguised as me, decoy vehicles, and other evasive maneuvers. One time I arrived at the Roxy in the back of a laundry truck! And every night, plainclothes security guards roamed the club, looking for trouble. There was none in the club, thank God, but other people around me were threatened, and one of my managers' employees was pistol-whipped.

Amid all this tension and fear, the Roxy engagement was a triumph. Maybe it was having the chance to work a relatively small, intimate club, or maybe it was simply my belief that I had something to prove. Whatever it was, the shows were simply magical. It seems like such an obvious point, but standing onstage, it suddenly hit me that I'd achieved the dream I first glimpsed at the Uptown when I was fourteen. Earlier I compared singing live to making love to a woman. At the Roxy that metaphor took on a whole new meaning. After the opening-night show, Shep exclaimed, "Did you see all those women out there, Teddy? It's nothing but women!"

"So . . . why don't we do shows for women only?" I proposed. Shep nodded and said, "It's a great idea!" We both laughed. Artists often speak of their managers as their friends, their partners, their allies, but I've always thought of my relationship to Shep and Danny like a convict's to his lawyers. We always had to see how far we could push it, and they were with me all the way. Now, this was going to be cool, or hot, or both.

Like a dog with a bone, the press had long before leapt on the sex-symbol angle and chewed it just about to death. To be honest, standing onstage in a body-defining silk tank top and sweating off three pounds a night, I wasn't trying *not* to be attractive. The For Women Only shows, however, just put the period on it. These shows were fun, attention-grabbing, audacious, revolutionary, and ultimately a tremendous success. Print ads for the shows depicted an innocent, cuddly teddy bear holding a handwritten invitation to "Spend the night with Teddy." *(Ah . . .)* We also set up a Teddy Line, where you could call to hear a romantic recorded message from me. You have to feel sorry for the poor Philadelphia newspaper reporter whose phone number differed by only one digit and consequently was besieged by enough disappointed callers to make the news.

And the pièce de résistance: At each show, every woman in the audience was handed a teddy bear–embossed chocolate lollipop. Not exactly a subtle metaphor, I know, but the ladies loved it.

We put on the first For Women Only shows at Philadelphia's Shubert Theater, where ticket buyers stood in what the newspapers called the longest lines in the old venue's history. We recorded some of the concerts for *Teddy Live! From Coast to Coast,* which was released the following year. From there we took the show to New York, Los Angeles, Chicago, and San Francisco. While we were out on the road, *Life Is a Song Worth Singing* became my second album in a row to go platinum, and "Only You" was playing on radios everywhere. Life was good.

Well, most of the time. I was never more vulnerable or exposed than when I was onstage. Even though the theaters were nicer and the money was better, in some respects the crowds never changed. In November I was playing two shows a night at the Apollo in Harlem. Wherever you found pimps and players who resented entertainers, it was like Kentucky Avenue in Atlantic City all over again. The front few rows were overtaken by pimps and their prostitutes. They were screaming for me like all the other women in the audience, and their pimps didn't look too happy about it.

I was a few numbers into the first show when my eye caught a surly-looking guy pacing back and forth at the foot of the stage. He kept reaching to his side, and while I didn't actually see a gun, he made me think he had one. I wasn't about to stop the show and ask, "Is that a gun in your pocket or are you just happy to see me?" but you can bet I kept an eye on him. He'd glare at me, glare at his woman, glare back at me—this went on during the whole show. By the time I left the stage, I was truly afraid for my life.

I found Shep and Danny backstage and told them point blank, "I am not doing the midnight show! Cancel it!"

"You can't cancel the Apollo, Teddy!" Shep replied. "These people are going to demand their money back, and the promoter's going to want it from you. You're talking about a hundred thousand dollars!"

"Do what you gotta do. I'm not going on." I walked out the door and took the limo back to my hotel. Later Danny called my suite and implored me to come back, but I was firm.

"Then who's going to tell them you've canceled?"

"I don't know," I replied, "but I'm not coming back."

"Teddy, do you really want a white Jewish boy to tell the audience at the Apollo that Teddy Pendergrass isn't going on?" Danny asked a little nervously.

I appreciated Danny's concern, but I replied, "Danny, I'm not coming back up and get my ass shot over some dumb shit. No way. Nohow."

Now, this put my managers in a serious bind. Poor Shep. He had to hustle downtown and call in some favors to scrape together the $100,000 *in cash* on a moment's notice. Then the taxicab he took back to the Apollo broke down about ten blocks from the theater. So there he was, late on a bitter winter's night, walking through Harlem with one hundred grand in a brown paper bag. Did I mention how dedicated Shep and Danny are?

During this time I also performed on many television variety and talk shows. Over my career, I've been on everything from *American*

Bandstand (with Harold Melvin and the Blue Notes) to *Soul Train* (where we actually got Don Cornelius to do a whole show with me without his trademark suit and tie), *The Tonight Show,* and Merv and Dinah, to name a few. I even performed on a special with Oral Roberts and the Mandrell Sisters. I'll never forget that one. I took an early flight from Las Vegas, and between the dry Vegas air, singing two shows, and staying up late, my speaking voice was a little hoarse. During rehearsal, Oral Roberts insisted on praying for my throat— "Oh God, heal this man's voice"—as I stood politely, thinking, *Doesn't God have bigger things to worry about?*

I was a regular guest on Mike Douglas's show, which was taped in my hometown, and that's how I found the house of my dreams. During one appearance, Mike told me he was selling his hundred-year-old, thirty-four-room English Tudor mansion on fourteen acres. Located on Philadelphia's exclusive Main Line, the mansion was Mike's pride and joy, and the talk of the town.

I wasn't shopping for a place at the time. Then one night I came in extremely late (or very early in the morning, depending on how you look at the clock) and was exhausted. It didn't seem like more than a few minutes after I drifted off to sleep that a loud metallic banging jolted me awake. It was a damn garbage truck right outside my window, again. *That's it!* I thought. *I'm moving out!*

I loved my house in town. But between the parking problems and the people hanging out at all hours of the day, I needed something more secluded and quiet. I called a real estate agent and went house shopping, determined to find a new home that day, no matter what.

The money was rolling in, and, I admit, I was on my trip, so I told the agent exactly what I was looking for: "the biggest house you've got." We made an appointment to meet later that afternoon and look at some homes on the Main Line.

Wouldn't you know it, the first time Karen and I drove out there in my Rolls-Royce, I was pulled over by a policeman. Sad to say, I was getting used to being hassled for DWB—driving while black—

but I never accepted it. And this policeman was particularly insulting: What do you want out here? Where are you going? Who are you? Is this your car? It was humiliating. But the Main Line was where I wanted to live, and I was not going to let some racist cop convince me otherwise.

Karen and I were shown a few fabulous homes, including one that belonged to one of the heirs to the Campbell's Soup fortune. As it happened, though, the biggest house on the market turned out to be Mike Douglas's, and I fell in love with it. The first time I rode through those gates, I knew this was where I belonged. To a boy from the ghetto, it might as well have been a palace. Not only had I never set foot in anything so magnificent, I hadn't even known places like this existed. And just a half-hour drive from North Philly. It was situated at the end of Crosby Brown Road and had majestic wrought-iron gates. The gates opened to reveal a long driveway that took you toward the back of the house, then wound around the side and to the front, where you found a circular drive with an ornate fountain in the middle. The property included a large swimming pool, a tennis court, and a stream.

From the marble foyer and the spiral staircase to the *heated* four-car garage and the eleven fireplaces, this was a mansion with a capital M. Built in 1905 and originally owned by the millionaire banker named Crosby Brown, the estate was named Le Mesnil (the Little Farm) by its next owner, a Frenchman. I never knew what Mike Douglas called it, but shortly after I became lord of the manor, I christened it Le Chateau d'Amour: the House of Love. But of course.

Before I formally moved in, Karen and I would run through the house like a couple of kids. I didn't do much to change the house when I first lived there. Mrs. Douglas had done a beautiful job of decorating it, and I purchased a couple of rooms' worth of furniture from them. I brought only my master bedroom suite and then added a few more essentials: a stately rosewood grand piano, a large-screen television, and a comfortable chair.

The best part of owning my new home was seeing the expression on Mom's face the first time I walked her through it. Standing in the formal living room, which was bigger than any apartment we'd ever lived in, or the kitchen, which wasn't that much smaller than the one at Sciolla's, where I'd worked beside her, it dawned on me just how much the house meant to me. Owning it wasn't about showing off my success, though I had no problem doing that. It was about being independent and having the means to provide for and to protect those I loved.

When I was a kid, Mom would instruct me to "scrub the marble," the steps leading up to the front porch of the house on Eighth Street. It was many years before I realized that the steps weren't made of real marble. Now, seeing Mom run her hand over the smooth facade of a real marble fireplace, the distance we'd traveled never seemed greater and the connection between those two seemingly disparate places never seemed closer. My mother's sacrifices and struggles, her guidance and love, made me the man who could live out this dream.

One day after I'd bought the house but hadn't yet moved in, I took my friend Ronnie Butler up to see it. I don't know what she expected, but when she heard me tell the security guard I had posted at the front gate that I'd just closed on the house that morning, I think she thought I was playing a joke.

"Are you sure we're supposed to be up here?" she asked anxiously as we cruised down the drive. It was a clear, sunny day, and we saw a rainbow arcing over the mansion, like a big, luminous bow on a present.

Not long after I moved into the Chateau, I phoned Mom to say hello and found her uncharacteristically upset. The neighborhood around Eighth Street was at last succumbing to urban rot, and for the first time in her life, she was afraid to live in her own house. That was all I needed to hear.

"Mom, get ready, because I'm coming by to pick you up, and

we're going house shopping today," I said. A few weeks later she was living about a mile away from me in the home she picked, in the center of Gladwyne, next to a playground. My biggest pleasure was in knowing that Mom was secure, comfortable, and happy.

For me, the mansion and the property surrounding it were my own little slice of heaven. But as I learned shortly after I moved in, not all my neighbors felt that I belonged there. I admit that I was rarely home during these years, and you have to remember that in an area like this, "next door" may be hundreds of feet away. It's not as though we would all see one another every morning going out to pick up the newspaper. I lived my own life and kept to myself when I was home, which, with all my touring, wasn't that often.

In 1981, I applied to the local planning commission for permission to subdivide my property into three lots: a seven-acre parcel that would include the mansion, and two three-acre plots. I had no plans to build anything on these plots; the decision to subdivide was based on increasing the estate's value with an eye to the day I might sell it (which at the time I wasn't even considering). My neighbors' reaction to my proposal was enough to bring out a *Philadelphia Inquirer* reporter, who wrote a lengthy feature story, which ended with one of my neighbors being quoted as saying, "It is a tribute to this man that he can raise himself out of the ghetto. . . . We're just concerned about this magnificent place now becoming a ghetto." When I read the piece, I couldn't believe my eyes. It should go without saying that had I been white, no one, no matter how much they opposed my subdividing the property, would utter the word *ghetto*.

When the planning commission held hearings (which I did not attend), dozens of my neighbors—most of whom I'd never met—showed up and spoke freely with reporters. One called the proposal "a tragedy," while another complained, "It's not like before," because Mike Douglas's fans who drove by hoping to see him "were certainly different types of individuals" from my fans. It even got down to comparing the types of music he and I played when we entertained at home. One neighbor—still miffed because I didn't come to the front gate and personally thank him for returning one of my wheel covers that had fallen off on the road—even said of me, "He keeps more to himself than anyone else around. . . . He evidently is afraid of somebody killing him or something—all those guards and hidden cameras."

I'd never been rude to any of my neighbors, and when you stop to think about the distance between our homes, I can't imagine how anyone heard what kind of music I played. I couldn't even hear music playing on the other side of my house! I gave very serious consideration to filing at least one lawsuit against a neighbor on grounds of defamation of character, and my attorney was confident I could win. But after thinking it over, I realized that I didn't want to create a bad atmosphere for myself or my family. I didn't know why these comments were being made about me, or how far someone might go to show me I really didn't belong.

Let me just say, it was painful to realize that I couldn't feel comfortable living in a mansion I'd bought for myself with money I had earned. Sometimes, I felt more at ease on the streets of North Philadelphia. I still felt I was sitting in the corner in the booth in the dark. I could afford to buy the mansion, but the price of acceptance was not included. I taught my children to remember that no matter how successful you are, you are black first. And that no matter what they achieve or how much they have, there are some people who will judge them not by the content of their character but by the color of their skin.

I continued sending money to Tisha and LaDonna's grandparents in Memphis. Shortly after I moved into the Chateau d'Amour, when Teddy was about four years old, Rose called out of the blue and asked, "Do you want your son?"

"Yes!" I practically shouted without giving it a moment's thought.

"But why are you calling me now?" Rose explained that she felt Teddy needed to know his father. She is a devoted, loving mother, but—to her credit—she realized that a boy needs his dad. Growing up as I did, I understood Rose's concerns. Even though I was angry that my son had not been with me all along, I welcomed the opportunity to give him what had been denied me. Later, of course, I realized that my work commitments would make it impossible for me to be that home-every-night-for-dinner kind of dad, but I couldn't risk losing my son again. Fortunately, Mom lived close enough nearby to help, and I had a full-time live-in butler and housekeeper, a married couple named Johnson. Everyone agreed to pitch in and help with Teddy, and so he came to live with me.

In the beginning, it broke my heart to think of little Teddy coming from living in a city apartment to suddenly being thrust into this huge house. I realized this was a big adjustment for the little guy. I couldn't be home all the time, so the Johnsons, Mom, and Karen took care of him. But they did so lovingly, and I truly believed that in the long run it was the right thing to do.

On holidays, during summer vacations, and whenever else possible, Tisha and LaDonna came up from Memphis to stay with us. I believed it was important for my children to think of one another as family, not half-siblings. I don't believe in "halfs"; when you're blood, you're blood. Once I had my whole family back, I laid down the law. I'd seen enough people fuss and fight over whose kid was whose, and who was a "real" relative, or a "step" or a "half," and I wasn't having any of it. We were one family, all in it together, and the kids came first. I'm so happy to say that today, my daughters are welcome in Rose's home, Teddy has stayed with the Hollerways in Memphis (and Keya would be welcome there, too), and Karen has good relationships with everyone. In fact, Rose and Brenda will call the house to talk not to me but to Karen.

During these years, whenever they weren't in school, my children often traveled with me. I'd seen the damage from show-business parents hauling their kids around from one dressing room and hotel to another. That wasn't going to happen to my children. They needed a stable home environment and the best education they could get. Even though it meant I wouldn't get to spend as much time with my kids, the time we did share was quality time. Most important, they never had to doubt that I loved them, and I was always there for them.

In every way possible, I tried to make my children realize that even though I had an unusual job, I was still Dad and we were a family. While the press was busy writing about my private life as if the Chateau d'Amour had a revolving door leading straight to my bedroom, what really went on was even more fascinating: I had a happy, normal family. That's not to say I didn't have my fun, but if I partied, it was not around my kids.

Fortunately, I maintained a warm relationship with Tisha and LaDonna's grandmother and grandfather. One time while playing an extended engagement at the Sahara Hotel in Lake Tahoe, I flew the girls and Mrs. Hollerway out there to be with me. The only thing I objected to about Tisha and LaDonna's upbringing was their participating in children's beauty pageants. In Memphis, as throughout most of the South, these competitions are considered innocent fun, and I understood that. But seeing my girls overly dolled up, pretty as they were, it struck me that this conveyed the wrong message about what was important in life. I tried to raise all of my children to feel empowered, and I especially made sure my girls learned to value and respect themselves for their character and intelligence first. Besides, they didn't need a trophy to affirm their beauty, which was plainly evident.

Although the girls didn't live with me full-time, I was always aware of what they were doing. We spoke on the phone constantly, so when we were together, it was as if we'd never been apart. Still, I missed them terribly, often wondering what they and their brother were up to and wishing I could be with them.

My children learned at an early age that my fame had both its advantages and its drawbacks. I believe that their privacy is sacred, and they know I would never allow anyone to violate it, for any reason. Unlike some celebrity parents, I never lose sight of the fact that while I chose to be famous, my children did not. Interestingly, my kids could be as protective of me as I was of them. Once the girls and I were walking through a Memphis airport when Tisha remarked, "There's a lot of people here, Dad."

"Yeah, I know," I replied, holding their hands a little tighter and glancing around the terminal, where a few people were staring and pointing at us. Most politely kept their distance and gave us our space, but my girls spotted a woman who obviously had recognized me and looked as though she was trying to decide whether or not to approach.

The woman kept staring at us, so Tisha, who was always a little more direct, stood in front of me and in a loud voice warned, "Don't you bother my dad! You leave my dad alone!" Maybe she overreacted a little bit, but people around us giggled, and I had to smile. It was so cute: my little bodyguards.

Teddy would also join me on long trips and vacations, sometimes with his older sister, Keya. Even though Teddy didn't live with Tisha and LaDonna full-time, he too had a strong sense of family loyalty. One time we were all visiting Harold Melvin, and his kids and mine were upstairs playing in Harold's poolroom. Apparently, Harold's youngest son was tossing pool balls at the girls, and Teddy immediately rushed to their defense. I was so proud when he came downstairs and said, "Dad, you'd better tell him to stop messing with my sisters!" He was just four or five himself, but nobody was going to threaten his sisters and get away with it.

Before Teddy started school, I wanted to make sure he was prepared to meet the high standards of the local schools. I suppose because I had yet to complete high school myself, Teddy's getting the best education was especially important to me. Like all my kids, he's extremely smart, but I wanted to be sure he would get the most out of his education. He began attending an exclusive private school, and while I was pleased with the quality of the education he received, I wasn't happy with the rampant materialism and snotty attitudes he encountered. After fourth grade, I transferred him to a public school, where he would be exposed to children of all ethnic and economic backgrounds. Many a day, I snuck into my son's school and peeked into his classroom, just to see how he was doing.

I'd always felt that I could be an excellent single parent to my kids. After all, I learned from the master, my mother. But from the start, Karen earned my children's trust, respect, and love, and she has been a wonderful mother to them in every way. The Chateau d'Amour truly was a house of love.

The summer of 1979 saw the release of my third album, *Teddy,* which reached number five and included the hits "Turn Off the Lights" and "Come Go with Me," as well as another great McFadden-Whitehead song, "If You Know Like I Know." In addition to the garage full of cars, I now also had a Learjet with my Teddy Bear logo emblazoned on the fuselage. Whereas the year before I'd been playing midsize venues, we were now selling out arenas like Madison Square Garden, Atlanta's Omni, Comiskey Park in Chicago, and the Philadelphia Spectrum, in addition to doing weeklong runs at places with fewer seats, such as the Greek Theater, Westbury Music Fair, and the Circle Star Theater, near San Francisco.

By then, everyone working on the show, from the road crew to the musicians, had fallen into a real groove. I'm not bragging when I say that I had one of the tightest, funkiest, most dynamic damn bands ever. My musical director and bandleader, Sam Reed, was a fantastic saxophone player, who—as fate would have it—led the Up-town band when I was a kid sneakin' in. My Teddy Bear Orchestra was made up of local musicians from Philly and Baltimore: Robert

"Wah Wah" LeGrand on lead guitar, Norman Smith on bass, Cecil Duval and Alfie Pollite on keyboards, Joe Chohansky on trombone, Arthur Pugh and Sylvester Briant on trumpets, and my good friend James Carter on drums (who'd been with me since I left Harold Melvin in 1975). The Teddy Bear Singers—Melba Story, who was replaced by Connie Harvey, Harriet Tharpe, and Sherry Williams, who replaced Rudiero (whose last name escapes me)—were great singers, not to mention cute and sexy, too. Before each tour, we'd rehearse for a couple of months until we all knew the show inside out and could do it in our sleep. Once we had the discipline of it down cold, we had the freedom to be spontaneous onstage, to take the music wherever I wanted it to go. We had cues, of course, but my band and my singers learned to tell just by my body language where I was going with a song, and they were always right there with me. We were like a family.

From the outside, everything seemed to be going great. But there was a craziness swirling around me that sometimes came dangerously close. No performer could ask for more loyal, enthusiastic fans than I had, and I was grateful to them for everything I had. Still, there were moments that made me stop and ask myself, *What next?*

Like the night I was performing at a theater in the round. Singing onstage, all you can usually make out are the faces in the first few rows. The rest are mere silhouettes. I noticed one woman who seemed totally mesmerized, as if in a trance. Before and since, I've seen people in the audience who looked as though they had lost all sense of time and place, but this was different.

While I was singing, I saw her slip off her gorgeous full-length fur coat, toss it up on the stage, then turn and walk up the aisle. A stagehand scurried out and took the coat backstage for safekeeping. After the show, I held the coat as I climbed into my limo. "I hope we see her," I said to the driver.

It was a bitterly cold night. As I was getting ready to leave, I spotted the woman walking behind the theater wearing nothing but a dress. "That's her!" I shouted. "Pull over!"

Anyone else would have been shivering, but she didn't appear even to know where she was. I convinced her to get in the car, handed her the coat, and took her to my hotel room so that she could get herself together. We talked for a while, and after she calmed down, I had my limo driver take her home. Clearly, something wasn't right about her, and maybe she would have done the same thing at anyone's show. But I couldn't deny to myself that deliberately playing on people's emotions and whipping them into a frenzy had its risks. I'd toss a sweaty towel into the audience and watch the brawl that would erupt, as women pushed, clawed, and punched one another to get their hands on it. At one show, a woman even knifed another.

Once, a troubled young woman left her *two-month-old baby* in a seat at the Greek Theater for me. The story was front-page news, and the child's mother was eventually found, but when I stopped to think what could have happened to that poor baby girl, I wanted to cry with rage.

The most unnerving incident occurred when I wasn't even home. Now, you have to understand that the Chateau d'Amour was extremely secure, with gates, guards, guard dogs, and alarm systems. And I always kept a gun handy. I was always a stickler about putting on the alarm at night, but my housekeeper forgot one night, and the next morning she found a strange woman lying in my bed. My housekeeper called the police, and they took the woman away. When I heard about it, I was extremely upset. How did she get in? And what did she want from me?

In 1981 another woman managed to convince the media that I was about to marry her. And it never stops. You wouldn't believe it, but as I write this chapter, a strange woman has turned up in my driveway looking for me. Someone on my staff has intercepted her and discovered that she is a woman who has been trying to see me for years.

While in Los Angeles that summer I gave the ultimate For Women Only show at the California Institution for Women at Chino. Grinning, I asked the 450 female inmates, "What are nice girls like you doing in a place like this?" They whooped and cheered throughout the entire show. Looking into their faces as I sang "Close the Door," I felt like the biggest damn tease in the world, but they loved it and so did I. A few got so carried away, to put it delicately, that they lost every shred of inhibition. I couldn't believe some of the things going on in the audience.

It's no secret that people in prison often form homosexual relationships, and Chino had its share of butch–femme lesbian couples. At the start, the more feminine gay women who screamed for me got yanked back down in their seats by their partners the same way I'd seen pimps manhandle their women if they showed a little too much enthusiasm. Their glares and dirty looks were the same, too.

I was determined to win those ladies over. And just a few songs into the show, I did. They were standing alongside their lady lovers, screaming, too, which I took as the greatest compliment in the world. It was fantastic.

Even though Karen and I were dating seriously, we hadn't reached the point where it was an exclusive relationship. That summer my relationship with Jan Gaye evolved from a close friendship to a brief but intense affair. In the years since, both Jan and I have been hurt by some of the inaccurate information that has been written about our relationship. I want to set the record straight.

Contrary to a prevailing misconception, I did not "steal" Jan from Marvin. She is an intelligent, independent, and witty woman, and I became very fond of her. Jan told me that long before we began dating, she and Marvin had separated and that she had begun living in her own home. According to Jan, their marriage had been turbulent and not always happy. It was over. It was common knowledge in music-business circles that Marvin was going through some personal problems.

Although that phase of our relationship was brief, I cared a great deal for Jan, and still do. And so it hurts me to read that I pursued her out of some twisted rivalry with Marvin. I was with Jan because I wanted to be with Jan. And Jan was with me because, she told me years later, I was the first man who treated her as an individual, not just as Marvin's wife.

Marvin was a sensitive man who sometimes tried to give the impression that he was tougher than he really was. I never appreciated the degree to which Marvin perceived me as a rival, both personally and professionally. But, as I look back, this was a down time for Marvin on all fronts. After fifteen consecutive years of hit after hit, his career had shifted into slow gear. Knowing that his young wife was seeing a younger man—a younger man who happened to be considered a sex symbol and a star—upset him. Word quickly spread throughout L.A. that I'd better watch my back; Marvin was going to get me.

Whether or not Marvin truly intended to act on his threats, I can't say. Still, I wasn't about to leave anything to chance. Standing on a stage, you're completely vulnerable; an open target. So when I played L.A.'s large outdoor Greek Theater, for instance, security people mingled among the audience. But offstage, I felt that I could handle myself, and Jan and I dated openly. Marvin was extremely possessive of her, and I wouldn't have been surprised if he'd shown up and confronted me. But that never happened. Things eventually cooled between Jan and me, though not because of Marvin's jealousy. Today I'm happy to say that she remains a dear friend.

Stephanie Mills opened many shows for me during these years. While I've had some great male performers on my bills—Frankie

Beverly and Maze, for example—I always preferred strong women singers because I felt it balanced the show. Over the years I've been honored and pleased to share my stage with great singers such as Yvonne Elliman, Phyllis Hyman, Thelma Houston, the Pointer Sisters, Linda Clifford, Stephanie, and Patti LaBelle, to name a few.

Stephanie and I were rehearsing for a show when I heard her sing "Feel the Fire," a song she'd recently recorded for her album *Whatcha Gonna Do with My Lovin'*. Written by Peabo Bryson, it's a dramatic, passionate ballad, and Stephanie interpreted it brilliantly. A performer since childhood with extensive stage experience (she played Dorothy in the original Broadway production of *The Wiz* when she was still in her teens), Stephanie is an incredibly powerful and emotional singer. Singing the song to myself as I listened to her belt it out during her sound check, I couldn't help wondering how we would sound performing it as a duet. On a whim, I mentioned the idea to her, and she graciously agreed to share her song with me. We rehearsed the song just once and later that night, when we performed it onstage, we tore the place down. Stephanie and I then recorded the song for my next album, *TP,* along with an up-tempo, playfully sexy number, "Take Me in Your Arms Tonight."

I loved singing with Stephanie, because we had such a great rapport onstage. She may be petite, but don't let it fool you. Once she starts singing, she's a real powerhouse. I never had to worry about singing over Stephanie; if anything, I had to stay on my toes to keep up with her. We're both Aries, and neither of us gives an inch. When we toured together, I'd perform Lionel Richie's "Lady," then Stephanie and I sang "Feel the Fire," followed by "Take Me in Your Arms Tonight." We got so deep into it, it always felt fresh. I don't think we ever sang these numbers exactly the same way twice.

Our duets were so hot that, as with Marvin Gaye and Tammi Terrell, folks who didn't know us assumed our passion was more than an act, and there were some rumors. We were never more than good friends—still are, in fact—and as she left the stage each night, I always made it a point to stress, "She's going back to her *husband!*"

Around this time, I also met three other performers who would become lifelong friends: Nickolas Ashford and Valerie Simpson, and Luther Vandross. Besides being legendary partners in songwriting, producing, and performing, Nick and Val are also husband and wife. They opened a few shows for me in 1978, and from the beginning I was impressed by how down-to-earth they were. No attitude from these stars. Nick and Val were so gifted and talented, if anyone deserved to have big heads, they did. But they were also from the old school; they'd been around enough to know they didn't have to prove anything. They were easy to hang with—I've been a guest in their home many, many times—and wonderful to work with. They, too, contributed to *TP,* writing, producing, and providing background vocals for "Is It Still Good to Ya" and "Girl You Know."

I first met Luther when we were recording a commercial jingle for Miller Beer, which Nick and Val were involved in. In 1979, two years before Luther launched his solo career, he was a star among background singers. He toured and recorded with performers ranging from David Bowie and Chic to Barbra Streisand and Chaka Khan. It was a short session, so we didn't get to know each other that well then, but over the years we've become very good friends. As I look back, it's funny to think what roles these three would play in my life years later, and to think that I met them almost by chance.

Being famous made it possible for me to meet a few people that I truly admired. I was in Chicago in 1977, promoting my first album, when I asked a friend of mine if she knew where Muhammad Ali lived. She told me his address, and I was young and cocky enough to drive out to his place, ring his doorbell, and announce to the person who opened the door, "My name is Teddy Pendergrass, and I'd like to meet Muhammad Ali."

To my surprise, I was invited in and asked to wait in the foyer. A few minutes later, "the Greatest" came up from downstairs, shook my hand, said, "Hi, how are you?" and invited me to sit down and talk. We hit it off right away and spent some time laughing and getting to know each other.

That night the two of us went out to a club to see Wayne Cochran, a tall white singer with a towering platinum-blond pompadour that made him hard to miss. I'd seen him when the Blue Notes used to play Las Vegas, back in the day. Cochran, who dressed in Elvis-style jumpsuits, had a cocky attitude to match. He and his band, the C.C. Riders, put on an energetic show, complete with choreographed horn players. Cochran had all kinds of songs in his show, including black music that to the untrained ear might have passed for soul but really wasn't.

Muhammad Ali, my date, and I were enjoying ourselves when suddenly Cochran pointed to me from the stage and called out, "Teddy! Teddy Pendergrass! Come on up and sing with me!" I'm always reluctant to get up on someone else's stage, and I always decline graciously. But ol' Wayne wasn't taking no for an answer, so, with a shrug, up I went. There's an unspoken professional etiquette you follow when you share a stage: Never, ever deliberately show anyone up. But it quickly became clear that Cochran viewed this as some sort of competition. He instructed his band to play "Stormy Monday," a blues with plenty of room for improvising, and after we alternated on the first and second verses, I just went to town. I think once Cochran realized I wasn't a pushover onstage, the "competition" ended, and we had a great time. The whole audience loved it, and I must say it felt nice to hear Muhammad Ali encouraging me on.

During the following years, when Ali was still boxing and I was out on the road a lot, we crossed paths many times. I attended several of Ali's fights, and visited him in his homes in Chicago and Hancock Park, in L.A. If he happened to be in a town where I was playing, he'd surprise me by coming to the show and we'd hang out afterward.

Ali always had a wonderful sense of humor and a playfulness about him. Sometimes it was hard to reconcile that the champion who pounded his opponents to defeat was the same gentle friend. Ali liked to have fun, and one night in 1977 he surprised me and came down to see my show at the Swingers' Club in Miami. The dancers did only a few numbers, then usually retired to the dressing room. I looked out in the crowd and noticed he wasn't there. Later, the dancers told me he'd been backstage, trying to get into the dressing room to see them. He did like the girls.

Shortly after we met, he invited me to attend his May 1977 bout with Alfredo Evangelista, in Landover, Maryland, right outside D.C., and then spend some time with him afterward. Evangelista's gimmick was to appear with a boa constrictor, and I remember seeing one of his big snakes on display in the hotel lobby. Ali won after fifteen rounds, and afterward one of his assistants invited a select group of people up to his hotel suite. It was a tough fight, and Muhammad, then the two-time heavyweight champ (he'd win his third heavyweight title the following fall from Leon Spinks), was resting in his bedroom. He didn't want people to see him hurting.

After a little while, everyone was thanked for coming up but asked to leave the suite. The champ needed to rest. A member of his entourage whispered to me that I should stay, Ali wanted to see me.

To me and millions of others, Muhammad Ali was always such an inspiring champion. He was so majestic, in the ring and out, that it was impossible to conceive of his being hurt. But that night he asked me to help him up. Leaning on me for support, he rose slowly from his bed, and with one of his arms draped over my shoulder, we slowly made our way to the bathroom. Ali was obviously in great pain. I helped him back to his bed and we talked, which was always a pleasure. He told me how he was feeling and what he was thinking that night. I consoled him as much as I could, then left him to rest.

Our friendship was such that on a whim, I could drive up to his training camp at Deer Lake, Pennsylvania, arrive unannounced, and still be welcomed with open arms and a place at the table. In more recent years, the few times we've run into each other, we've always greeted each other with love and mutual respect. After my accident and before Parkinson's disease began to rob Muhammad of his ability to speak, he would say to me, "I think about you often. I love you. You're my friend. I pray for you." Even though we don't run into each other that often these days, when we do, I always see in his eyes the great spirit, the soul of a true hero.

No matter how many records I sold, the big money was still out on the road. And so was my passion. I know some performers grow to resent the rigors of touring, but I never felt that way. I was thankful to be given my gift and privileged to be able to share it on such a scale. Don't get me wrong; hit records are wonderful. I wouldn't trade them for the world. But if I'd ever been forced to choose between never making a record again or never taking a stage, so long, records. That's how much I love performing.

One reason the road never wore me down is that my organization ran with the efficiency and precision of a fine Swiss watch. I'm a tough, demanding boss, but I know everyone who worked for me and the artists who opened for me appreciated the professionalism. Ironically, the only person who ever had trouble getting to the airport on time was . . . me. In these years, Danny (whom Shep had hired to be my "everyday," hands-on manager to accompany me on the road) was with me constantly, and we became and still are very close. We didn't start out that close. I admit, I took one look at Danny, in his rock-&-roll clothes—with a dagger earring and jeans—and thought to myself, *Who the hell is this?* It took a week of driving up and down I-95 from North Carolina to South Carolina and back again during a series of concerts for us to finally get to know each other. Cooped up together in a limo, we had no choice. I remember once during this leg of the tour taking Danny and our white driver with me to a local club. We were not in a major city, so the place I found was very modest, with a dirt parking lot, and a clientele caught in a *Superfly* time warp. To me, they all seemed like good people out having a good time, but for Danny and our driver—the only white people in the place—the stares, the tough looks, and the gold teeth made for a heavy scene. I don't think anyone would have hurt them, but I think some people were having a little fun letting the white boys know they didn't belong. Our driver couldn't take it, so he went back outside, locked himself in the limo, and scrunched down in the seat so that no one could see him. Danny wasn't a lot more comfortable, but he felt he had to prove to me that he could hang, and he did. By the time that week was over, Danny had become one of my closest friends.

Danny's previous road experience had been with acts like Led Zeppelin and the Rolling Stones, who were notorious in those days for all manner of backstage and hotel room mayhem. A Teddy Pendergrass tour was a model of decorum by comparison—except for that time in Shreveport, Louisiana, when my bodyguard Soto got the idea to put dozens of chickens in Danny's hotel room. After a long day of work, he opened the door to find chickens squawking, feathers flying, and—thanks to the dose of Ex-Lax Soto gave the poor birds—chicken you-know-what everywhere.

It was Danny's job to make sure the boss stuck to the schedule. Since I couldn't go out on the town after a show, I got into the habit of entertaining people back in my dressing room. Stage crews are famous for not complaining about staying late, because it means overtime. But I would stay backstage so late, the union crews would be begging to go home. Obviously, I was in no shape to wake up all bright-eyed and bushy-tailed for that 8:00 A.M. flight. Danny now recalls the hotel-to-airport leg of the race as an "Olympic event." It never bothered me too much, though. If we missed our flight, I'd just lease a private jet. Whatever it took, as long as I didn't hit the stage late.

Even though my record sales showed no sign of falling off, at the ripe old age of twenty-nine I'd seen enough to know that no one can depend on selling records forever. As they say in the stock prospectuses: Past performance is no guarantee of future earnings. And nowhere is that more true than in the music business. Trends come and go, record companies change hands, time moves on, and sometimes it sneaks right by you. And it doesn't take much to turn last year's big thing into next year's "Who?"

I relished my recording success, but I was wise enough not to trust it. The artists I grew up admiring were performers first and foremost, and traveling around the country, I saw how a knockout show ensured longevity, even after the hits dried up. To me, records were stepping-stones to a long and stable career independent of hits and changing trends. Maybe I didn't need to work so hard anymore, but I wanted to, although it meant spending four days a week on the road. The doors were starting to open up, and Shep and Danny are unique as managers in their dedication to the long haul. For them, it's not about what we can get today but what foundation we can lay to build on tomorrow. To that end, in 1979, I was among the first singers to have a show broadcast on the then-new Showtime cable network.

Around the same time, Phil Walden, the head of Capricorn Records, happened to catch my show in Macon, Georgia. Before starting his own label, Walden had managed soul legend Otis Redding. He later told Shep that watching me perform was like seeing "Otis reborn." It had been twelve years since Redding died in a plane crash, shortly before the release of his biggest hit, "(Sittin' on) the Dock of the Bay." Walden wanted to produce a film biography of Redding's life, with me in the starring role. Naturally, I was flattered to be offered the part and gave it serious consideration. In the end, though, I felt that it wasn't the right project for me then.

When I finally got around to making my film debut—a cameo playing myself in 1982's *Soup for One,* shot the year before—the glamour of being up on the big screen faded real fast. You'd think since I was playing myself as opposed to "acting," it would be a piece of cake. While I appreciated the opportunity, the early hours, endless waiting, and drudgery of redoing take after take after take wore me down. It was one thing to record Nile Rodgers and Bernard Edwards's "Dream Girl" in the studio, but to put my heart into really performing for a bunch of guys in a film crew just didn't give me the same juice I got from those lovely ladies. You never say never, but I was happy to say "later" for this.

It was time to take my show outside the country, and in May 1979, I did a brief but exciting series of dates over Mother's Day weekend in Trinidad. Since my days with Harold and the Blue Notes, I looked forward to experiencing any island culture. I vacationed in Jamaica whenever I could. The climate was great, the people were friendly, but the music, the rhythms were infectious. Deep inside me still beat the heart of a drummer, and I loved hearing and learning new rhythms and styles.

As the 1970s drew to a close, the PIR machine no longer produced hit after hit. What happened? Who knew? Unlike the 1960s, when black music basically consisted of two styles—soul and Motown—now there were many permutations. Disco had faded quickly, but it still lingered. Rap had just arrived and soon began claiming younger listeners, while a new, more mature, ballad-oriented R&B drew the older fans. A producer, a songwriter, or a team might enjoy a streak here and there, but the dominance and consistency PIR built its reputation on was gradually becoming a thing of the past. In 1979 the label produced only a handful of major hits, including McFadden and Whitehead's "Ain't No Stopping Us Now" and the O'Jays' *Identify Yourself.* It was also a time of deep recession for virtually every record company. Across the board, record sales plummeted, concert revenues dried up, and the number of radio stations programming black music declined. That year ten albums went to number one: Only one was by a black artist, Donna Summer; another was two white comedians' lame excuse for a tribute to soul music, the Blues Brothers. Need I say more?

I accepted the possibility that someday people would tire of my style or be drawn away by the next phenomenon to come down the road. It was a time of transition. I'd never dream of disowning my hits with Harold and the Blue Notes (though, to be honest, it took me a long time to get comfortable singing a medley of them in my show), or not singing the more suggestive songs like "Turn Off the Lights" and "Close the Door." But it was time to move in a new direction. My fourth platinum album, *TP*, gave me the chance to redefine my persona, and in most of its songs, I'm more a devoted romantic than a seducer. Compared to my three previous albums, this one glowed rather than burned, especially the singles "Can't We Try" and "Love T.K.O.," a dark, emotional ballad by Cecil Womack and Gip Nobel.

TP came out a few months after that big thirtieth-birthday bash in New York City I was too high to enjoy. While my habits didn't change overnight, I felt older, wiser, and more responsible for my life, my career, and the image I wanted to project. I've been known to set a few fashion trends in my time, including accessorizing fine Italian suits with Western details and my trademark Stetson cowboy hat. (That look provoked some mighty interesting comments from women in the audience; "Ride 'em, cowboy!" is one of the few I can print.) I got the same thrill browsing the finest boutiques for full-length exotic fur coats that I'd gotten when I put on my first shark-skin suit. And I still do.

I had five huge closets to fill, so my lifelong love of fashion did not go to waste. Nor did it go unnoticed. There were times, I admit, when I went overboard. For a feature in the New York *Daily News'* Sunday magazine, a writer described my arrival at the cover shoot for *Teddy:* "Enter the Man. He is wearing a full-length sable coat, cuffed Sasson jeans, a white silk scarf, and at the cleft of his brown suede shirt enough gold chains to strangle Sammy Davis. He is not a clothes horse. He is a stampede."

In my defense, however, I did look pretty good. And, for the record, Sammy Davis Jr. wore more chains than I did. I know this for a fact, because when I appeared with the Blue Notes on Sammy's syndicated television show, he took one look at the chains around my neck, made a comment about how many there were, then returned a while later wearing more jewelry than I was!

I love trying new things. More important, though, I didn't want to perpetuate the stereotype. I put away the gold chains and buttoned up my shirt; I sported a stylish but more conservative look and even took to wearing my glasses during television interviews. For an appearance on Tom Snyder's show, I wore a gray suit, white shirt, and burgundy tie. I found that when you dress like a businessman, people know you're about business. I wanted to be taken seriously and regarded as a serious-minded person. And I was.

I was also ripe for change on a deeper level. I couldn't have been happier with my family, prouder of my children, or more in love with Karen. But life outside the Chateau d'Amour wasn't always so easy or so safe. Karen and I agreed early on that it was important to keep the public Teddy separate from the private Teddy. We tried hard to keep our relationship above the fray a star's life can become. Between the time she stopped dancing in my show in 1977 and 1985, when I sang at Live Aid, she did not attend any of my performances, nor did she go out on the road with me.

Looking back, I'm amazed at how wild and reckless everyone could be back then. Everyone drank without giving it a second thought, no one believed cocaine was addictive, and sex was everywhere. It was a hedonistic time, when the few consequences you might suffer seemed small and unlikely. I'll be honest: I worked hard and I played hard, but it was always about having fun and relaxing with friends, not destroying myself or escapism. After the show or when I had a few days off, I'd kick back with some fine wine or cognac and more than a few lines of coke. It was my reward, but it never went beyond that.

The road offered plenty of opportunities to indulge, and back in Philadelphia I frequented a private after-hours place a friend I'll call Big Mama ran in her home. Harold had turned me on to the place back in 1973, and Big Mama and I became so close, I felt she was my sister. In fact, I remember introducing her to Karen and telling her, "Karen's going to be my wife someday." If you were a friend of Big Mama's, she could get you whatever you wanted: girls, drink, food, drugs. And it was always discreet, always the best. Sometimes I needed to relax totally and be someplace where it didn't matter who I was. At Big Mama's, I never worried about anything.

I was lucky to come through these times without a substance-abuse problem or worse. For me, the real problem was being falsely accused of fathering children. It was, as most successful men can tell you, an occupational hazard. Part of it was my image, but I'm not going to lie: Part of it was me. Three women claimed I'd fathered their children, and I immediately assumed responsibility for two of them without insisting on any proof of paternity. You don't need a degree in psychology to figure out how having been abandoned myself, I was eager—maybe foolishly so—to step up and take responsibility for any child I believed could have been mine, even before there was definitive proof.

In one case, I took the woman's word for it, and when the child was born, I named him, and his mother gave him my last name as well. When he was old enough to travel, his mother brought him back to Philadelphia, where he was christened in my mother's church. The fact that this child was born while I was involved with Karen didn't diminish her willingness to accept him into our family as our fourth child. I later told Tisha, LaDonna, and Teddy about their new little brother.

I continued sending child support, even after my accident, and the boy's mother would send me pictures of him, but it became increasingly difficult for me to see him. Whenever I wanted his mother to bring him to Philadelphia, there was always an excuse. Finally, I decided to take legal action, and the boy's mother and I were assigned a family court–appointed mediator. The idea was that we could work out an arrangement without going to court. At that point I would have moved heaven and earth to have a relationship with my son. As a matter of fact, after my accident, he even spent time with me in Miami. So you can imagine my shock when his mother broke off negotiations, then said, "Teddy, you are not the father of this child anyway."

It felt as if someone had plunged a knife into my heart. I was devastated and furious, angry at myself for wanting to believe and to trust, and sad beyond words that I had "lost" a child.

But I was also angry because this had happened once before, back in the early 1970s. Then, of course, I was much younger. A woman I'd dated briefly claimed I fathered her son, and I accepted her word. I visited the boy a few times, but several things occurred to make me doubt that he was my son, and I stopped seeing him. That was fine with his mother, who never asked for my money or my involvement—until my solo career started paying off. Suddenly she had a lawyer and the child welfare bureau was on my back for unpaid child support. Although a blood test proved that I could not have been the father, this boy's mother let him grow up believing that I was and that I had abandoned him. I'll never know how he got my private phone number, but some time after my accident, when he was in his twenties, he called me. Perhaps because I understood his pain better than many men would, I invited him to meet with me so that I could explain the whole situation in person.

My heart broke when he asked me why I'd never acknowledged or honored him as my son. These were words I'd so longed to say to my own father, and it pained me to think that this boy really didn't have a father, and never would. Painful as it was, this boy deserved to learn the truth, and so I told him exactly what had happened through the years. Why any mother would so cruelly and deliberately mislead a child like that, I'll never understand. It would have been better for him to have grown up fatherless than to think he'd been abandoned.

I'm sorry to say, this young man is not alone. Another woman has publicly named me as her daughter's father, despite a blood test clearing me as a possible father. Even worse, she is raising her daughter to believe her daddy is Teddy Pendergrass. I dread the day she comes knocking on my door, though more for her sake than for mine.

As 1980 came to a close, Kenny Gamble and Leon Huff celebrated my fifth straight platinum album with an elegant party at the Franklin Plaza Hotel in Philadelphia. The guest list of over a thousand included Dionne Warwick, Nick Ashford and Valerie Simpson, ex–heavyweight champ Joe Frazier, Patti LaBelle, city managing director (later to be mayor) Wilson Goode, and the evening's emcee, Joey Bishop.

At one point, Kenny Gamble stood before the audience and, holding up a platinum album, said: "Teddy, the light you see shining from this album is the light of God. Don't ever forget that!" Kenny was, as I've said before, a very serious person, and while I certainly understood what he was saying, I'm not sure this was quite what the audience expected. A long silence fell over the room until I shouted, "Amen!" For the next few seconds, all you heard was "amen, amen, amen." Maybe not everyone fully understood what Kenny tried to put across, but I did. I was the first black male artist in history to earn five consecutive platinum albums. I was truly blessed.

Just a week before Christmas, December 17, 1980, was declared Teddy Pendergrass Day in Philadelphia. In January I hosted and performed at the American Music Awards, where I was nominated for Best Male Vocalist for *TP*. And Kenny Gamble and I had embarked on PIR's first foray into fashion with a line of Teddy Bear designer jeans, complete with my Teddy Bear logo on the back pocket. I have to hand it to him: Gamble was a man of vision, and he noticed that many sisters had trouble finding designer jeans that fit well because they were designed for ladies with—how shall I say this?—smaller derrieres. Teddy Bear jeans fit more shapely bottoms beautifully, and they were a great success. Wherever I appeared to promote them, a near riot broke out as ladies tore at my clothes as if they wanted to get me *out* of my jeans and everything else I had on. As for a marketing pitch, the possibilities were endless. I mean, what lady could refuse an invitation to get into the Teddy Bear's pants?

That spring Stephanie and I released our third duet together, "Two Hearts," which hit number three on the R&B chart and number forty pop. Through the spring and summer, we hit the usual spots across the country. In April I embarked on my first major tour of Britain, with dates at London's Victoria Apollo Theatre, where my friend Stevie Wonder made a surprise appearance during my last show and sang "Take Me in Your Arms Tonight" with Stephanie and me. The London date, originally a one-nighter, sold out so quickly that two more nights were added.

While the screaming never let up, people did notice my more subdued approach. From the beginning, there had been those who felt that the sexier aspects of my show and my public image were distracting from my singing. I'd been saying for years that there was more to me and my music than "Turn Off the Lights," and beginning with "Love T.K.O.," I think I proved my point. With my fifth studio album, *It's Time for Love,* and its first single, "I Can't Live Without Your Love," the Teddy Bear was doing more purrin' than roarin', and nobody complained. Anytime you make a major change in direction, you risk losing some fans. Fortunately, my fans never left me, and even critics who'd always been generous in their praise noted the improvement.

The next goal ahead was headlining in Las Vegas, and through the spring and summer, everything we did was working up to that. Since I'd first gone solo, the Greek Theater in Los Angeles always seemed to hold a special magic; the shows there were always exciting. Incredibly, the 1981 concerts there managed to top even that, and that's not just my opinion. The box office sold out in days, the audience was more diverse than ever, and the reviews were positively glowing. After a few dates at the Circle Star Theater outside San Francisco, it was on to Las Vegas.

Las Vegas . . . talk about a place with some memories. From the backseat of the limo, on my way to the Aladdin Hotel, I looked out at those hot streets I'd walked in my show shoes. I remembered the tacky little motels we stayed in when we worked the lounges, such as Nero's Nook at Caesar's Palace and a small showroom at the Flamingo. This time, I had my own house, complete with a cook, a driver, and servants at my beck and call—the royal treatment.

For me, Las Vegas was a talisman, a good-luck charm. If I could come out of my first headlining dates a winner, I'd be set. To be welcomed in Las Vegas signaled acceptance from everyone—men and women, blacks and whites. While I would always make records, I'd have the freedom to build a career independent of them and impervious to the fickle whims of radio programmers and the trend-driven tastes of the public. If there's anything close to career insurance in this business, it's Las Vegas, and in August 1981 I got it—signed, sealed, delivered.

Stephanie opened my shows in the Bagdad Room at the Aladdin Hotel, and as always, she set the stage on fire. As usual, I stood backstage, nervous as hell, but once I took off the glasses . . . well, you know the story.

The engagement was such a hit that in October, Stephanie and I returned to the Aladdin for another week of sold-out shows. The next month, PIR issued my last single of the year, "You're My Latest, My Greatest Inspiration." Early in 1982, Stephanie and I did another tour of England. At one point during my show there, a children's choir accompanied me on Nick Ashford and Valerie Simpson's "Reach Out and Touch (Somebody's Hand)." I loved the song

My mother made sure I was clean and sharp even back then.

(Photo courtesy of the author)

Safe in the arms of the woman who is the first and greatest blessing of my life, my mother, Ida Pendergrass. *(Photo courtesy of the author)*

Here I am, on the left, a three-year-old usher with my bridesmaid and the groom in a Tom Thumb wedding, at Glad Tidings Baptist Church. It was at this church that I made my singing debut, about the same time. *(Photo courtesy of the author)*

Even at this age, I liked girls. It was around this time that my Aunt Dee nicknamed me Teddy the Bear. (I wonder how she knew . . .)
(Photo courtesy of the author)

A photo from my elementary-school days.
(Photo courtesy of the author)

Sex symbol? Well, maybe not quite yet. With Delores,
the friend I accompanied to her junior prom. *(Photo courtesy of the author)*

My first big night out, 1964. For my cousin Pete Dent (left) and me, meeting the King of the Twist, Chubby Checker, in his dressing room at Sciolla's (where my mother worked in the kitchen) was a thrill. A year earlier I had seen Jackie Wilson and my life had changed forever. *(Photo courtesy of the author)*

The man who gave me my first big break in show business, Little Royal.
(Photo courtesy of the author)

On Don Cornelius's *Soul Train*, in our second lineup (left to right): Bernie Wilson, Larry Brown, me, Lloyd Parks, and Harold Melvin. *(Photo courtesy of Michael Ochs)*

Harold Melvin and the Blue Notes in the early 1970s (clockwise from far left): Harold Melvin, Bernie Wilson, Larry Brown, Lloyd Parks, and me. *(Photo courtesy of Michael Ochs)*

I don't recall the exact occasion, but obviously we were all very happy with the success of our first album, 1972's *Harold Melvin & the Blue Notes*. Clockwise from the left: Larry Brown, unidentified, Lloyd Parks, Bernie Wilson, me, unidentified, and Harold Melvin. *(Photo courtesy of the author)*

ABOVE: Celebrating the signing of my first solo contract with Philadelphia International Records in the fall of 1976. Left to right: PIR vice chairman of the board Leon Huff, girlfriend Taaz Lang, me, PIR vice president James A. Bishop, and PIR chairman of the board Kenny Gamble.
(Photo courtesy of the author)

LEFT: I was still playing small theaters like this one, in 1977, when my solo debut album, *Teddy Pendergrass*, had just gone gold. I was on my way.
(Photo courtesy of the author)

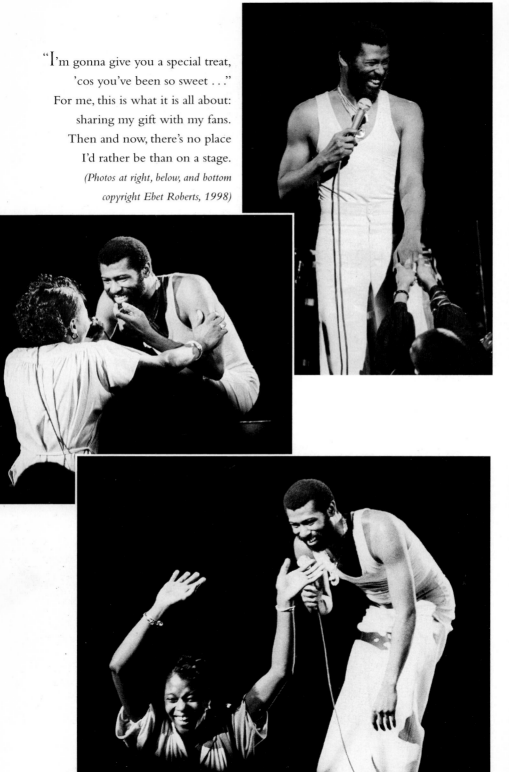

"I'm gonna give you a special treat,
'cos you've been so sweet . . ."
For me, this is what it is all about:
sharing my gift with my fans.
Then and now, there's no place
I'd rather be than on a stage.
(Photos at right, below, and bottom
copyright Ebet Roberts, 1998)

At the Greek Theater, Los Angeles, 1978: When you're hot, you're hot.

(Photo copyright Ebet Roberts, 1998; courtesy of Neal Preston)

On tour, 1979.
The Italian suit,
silk tank top,
those chains, and
the Stetson hat that
sparked a fashion trend
and incited some
interesting comments
from my lady fans.
"Ride 'em, cowboy"
is one of the few
I can print.
*(Photo courtesy of
Michael Ochs)*

Standing before a portrait I commissioned of my debut album's cover, around 1977.
The mansion, the Learjet, the luxury cars, and the other trappings of success could
make you feel sometimes larger than life. *(Photo courtesy of Neal Preston)*

"I go through life with a smile on my face, because there's nothing that I can't do."

(Photos top and above courtesy of Neal Preston)

I spent the first six months after my accident in a hospital and a rehabilitation facility, where I began rebuilding my life. *(Photos at right and below courtesy of Neal Preston)*

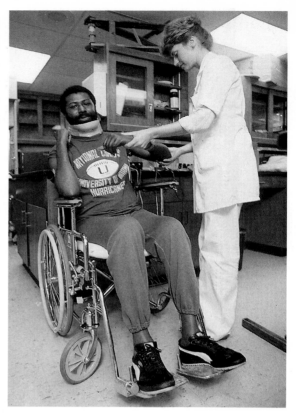

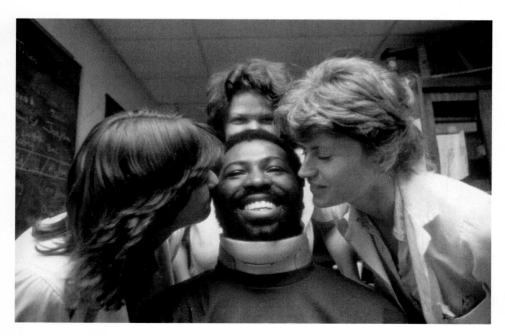

Teddy bears for the Teddy Bear: For years fans have showered me with my cuddly toy namesake, and they still keep coming in. *(Photo courtesy of Neal Preston)*

In the fall of 1982, I returned home to the Chateau, where thousands of cards, letters, and gifts awaited me. The love and support of my friends and fans around the world boosted my spirits.

(Photo courtesy of Neal Preston)

With my radiant bride,
Karen Still, on our wedding day.
(Photo courtesy of the author)

The wedding party, June 20, 1987: my beautiful children and their proud grandmother.
Left to right: La Donna, Teddy II, my mother, Ida, and Tisha. *(Photo courtesy of the author)*

The team that never let me down, sharing my joy in the gold album for *Joy*, in 1988. Left to right: my managers Shep Gordon and Daniel Markus, with Elektra Records chairman Bob Krasnow. *(Photo courtesy of the author)*

With my fellow Philadelphian and Uptown alumnus Miss Patti LaBelle performing "Can't Help Nobody," our 1993 duet on *The Tonight Show*. *(Photo courtesy of the author)*

Stephanie Mills and me at the American Music Awards in 1981. *(Photo courtesy of Archive Photos)*

Sharp as a tack in a suit I designed especially for the occasion:
my sixth Grammy nomination, for "Voodoo," March 1994.
This proved one of the best—and most trying—nights of my life.
(Photo courtesy of Chuck Pulin/Star File)

Accompanied by my very dear friends, the great singer/songwriters Valerie Simpson
and Nickolas Ashford, I made my first comeback appearance in my hometown,
at Live Aid, July 13, 1985. Singing "Reach Out and Touch (Somebody's Hand)"
and feeling the love of 90,000 people wash over me, I felt, for that moment, that
nothing had changed. I was home. *(Photo courtesy of Chuck Pulin/Star File)*

the first time I heard it, and I'd recorded the song earlier for a children's compilation album, *In Harmony 2*.

Flying home from England, I thought about what lay ahead. It was a new year and a new era. There were so many places I wanted to go, so many things I wanted to do, and the doors all were open. Shep and Danny had already begun work on the coming year's itinerary. On the table were more dates in Las Vegas, a concert with Stephanie that would be broadcast on HBO live from Resorts International in Atlantic City, product endorsements, a new album, another tour. Among people in the industry, Shep was a true visionary when it came to understanding and exploiting the potential for home video. My London shows had been filmed and were being released as *Teddy Pendergrass, Live in London*. It was one of the very first "long-format" concert videos for home viewing. Here was a new medium with unlimited potential, a new challenge. I could hardly wait.

I could tour less this year, spend more time at home with Karen, the children, and Mom. But I knew I would never stop; I can't begin to tell you how much I loved working a stage, pleasing a crowd, sharing the gift God gave me.

I was contemplating perhaps taking more control over my business; I'd recently begun suspecting that not everyone involved in my business had my best interests at heart. For a while now, I had been uncomfortable about some of the people around me but too busy and distracted to do much about it. I was getting tired of feeling suspicious all the time. That, I promised myself, was about to change.

I'd co-produced several of my recent tracks, and I loved flexing a different set of my creative muscles and being in charge. Although Gamble and Huff were still giving me great stuff to record, to be honest, I had a hard time singing songs like "Do Me." They struck me as shallow and repetitious. The overwhelmingly positive response I received to the less explicit, more mature songs and my reworkings of songs made famous by other artists (such as "All by Myself" and "Lady") convinced me that limiting my repertoire only to what came out of PIR—great as it was—wasn't the best way to go. I was anxious to stretch, even beyond the current pop format. Perhaps an album of classic ballads or gospel would work. I was talking to other producers and songwriters, and my leaving PIR sometime in the future, while not imminent, was a possibility.

But that was all for later. The plane touched down; I was back in Philly. There would be more time for Karen and the children, more time to relax, more time to just live. The big gates swung open at the end of Crosby Brown Road, and I was home.

SEVEN

Often I wonder as I sit all alone,
Is there anything in life guaranteed?

Happy birthday to you . . ."

Am I dreaming? Who's singing? It sounds like someone singing opera!

"Happy birthday to you . . ."

I struggled to open my eyes. *White! Everyone's wearing white. And looking at me. It's a doctor walking toward me, and I'm in a room somewhere. Where? I can't move.*

"Happy birthday, dear Teddy! Happy birthday to you!"

It was March 26, 1982, what I would later come to think of as the first day of my new life. This is my first clear memory since the night of the accident. It felt hazy and unreal, like a dream, but I suddenly realized that everything was real. My otolaryngologist, Dr. Robert Sataloff, was singing "Happy Birthday" to me.

The eight days between the accident and my birthday passed in a dark, painful blur. I wasn't in a state of unconsciousness or delusion. This was all too excruciatingly painful to be a dream. But I had no idea where I was, who was in the room with me, what time of day it was, or sometimes even who I was. People near me can recall speaking to me, and they recall my indicating that I understood what they were saying. But these moments elude me, and I don't think I'd wish to remember them even if I could. I believe there's a reason why my brain simply shut down and refused to process what was happening to me. There's a reason those days passed the way they did, but I don't feel that I need to know it. Mentally or emotionally, I really can't go back there.

I realize now that anyone who followed the news knew more about what had happened to me than I would know for many months. Later I learned that because the impact of the crash had jammed the car doors, it took the rescue squad over forty-five minutes to free me. They first rushed me to Germantown Hospital, but when the extent of injury to my spinal cord became known, I was transferred a few hours later to Thomas Jefferson University Hospital in downtown Philadelphia, which had a spinal cord injury center. The woman who had ridden in the car with me had been treated for minor injuries and released. It would be months before I learned that she was a transsexual and heard the ugly speculation regarding her possible role in the crash, months before I read the false reports that said I was drunk or high that night.

Beyond the hospital walls, life went on. News of the accident made headlines around the world, and the media duly reported daily updates on my condition. The press reported that I was awake, alert, and in no pain, but that was not the case.

The people closest to me remember these days more clearly than I do, but even their recollection is dimmed by the sheer, overriding shock of it all. Yes, I was injured, but my whole family was hurt, too. My mother recalls being awakened in the middle of the night and rushing to the hospital, where she saw me in the emergency room, lying motionless on a table with a brace on my neck. When I saw her, I pleaded, "Mom, make them take the brace off my neck," and she lightly touched the back of my head to make me think she was doing that for me. She remembers riding in the ambulance with me from Germantown to Jefferson. When we arrived, I looked up at her and said, "Mom, I'm back home again."

"Yes," she answered, smiling. "This is where you were born, at

Thomas Jefferson Hospital." Mom later recalled, "I tried to keep it together, but my heart went limp."

Karen remembers the shock of seeing me the first time and realizing how serious my injury was. She also remembers my saying to
her, "I may have to come home in a wheelchair." She replied tenderly,
"Thank God, you're coming home."

Danny and Shep remember flying to Philadelphia and being there
on the day the doctors told me I would never walk again. For me,
though, these weren't days of events and conversations. No calendar
or clock could mark what felt to me like an eternity of pure unrelenting terror.

My spine was injured and my spinal cord partially severed between the fifth and sixth cervical vertebrae, at the base of my neck,
right above my chest. In medical terms, this type of injury is referred
to as a "five-six incomplete." Because trauma to the spinal cord causes
bleeding and swelling that may affect sensation and movement, it
was a couple of days before the doctors were able to say with any cer-
tainty how extensive or permanent the damage was. In the very beginning, at least, there was some small hope that my condition might
improve, but it was not to be.

The most immediate problem was that the accident had broken
and twisted my neck in such a way that I was unable to move my
head or hold it up in a normal position. For a few days, I lay with my
head "resting" on my shoulder, as if I'd cocked my head to hear
something and it had frozen in that position. On March 24, the doctors performed an operation in which they took some bone from behind my right knee and fashioned a "splint" to stabilize the vertebrae
immediately above and below the injury site. This operation was not
intended to "undo" the paralysis. Nothing short of a miracle could
accomplish that. It did, however, make it possible for me to hold my
head upright, and it reduced the risk of further injury from the vertebrae "shifting" and creating pressure on my spinal cord. Later Mom,

Karen, and other loved ones recalled accompanying me as they wheeled my gurney to the operating room. When we got as far as they could go with me, Mom kissed me and said, "It will be all right."

Opening my eyes on my thirty-second birthday, I realized I was strapped to something. It was a Stryker frame, a large metal contraption made of metal tubing that looks like a wheel and encircles and supports a canvas "bed" in the middle. The frame can be rotated and adjusted to different angles, allowing caregivers to turn patients easily without risking further injury. Changing position regularly also improves circulation and prevents the development of pressure ulcers.

The Stryker frame reminded me of a high-tech torture device or sick amusement park ride out of a science-fiction movie. Danny once described it as looking like a spit you would cook a chicken on. You get the picture. I dreaded whenever a nurse would turn the frame (which was several times a day), because it felt like someone was jamming a sharp steel rod through my head.

Because of the operation to stabilize my neck, a metal "halo" had been surgically attached to my skull with two screws, one on either side. This exerted pressure that stabilized my head, neck, and spine. Of course, the rhyme and reason behind all this is far more technical than I can describe here. All I remember was unrelenting, almost unbearable pain. It was as I imagined some bizarre crucifixion.

In one single stroke, my body had been changed forever in ways that I could not even imagine, much less bear to think about. In my mind, though, I was still the same man I was when I started the drive back to Philadelphia that spring night. It's very difficult to describe facing a situation so intense you can't deny its truth while the whole time your mind is screaming that it simply can't be.

Once I began to understand the severity of my injury and the cir-

cumstances of the crash, I simply surrendered to the new medical re-
alities of my condition. That's not to say I accepted it; I didn't. But I
didn't ask too many questions, and I stopped fighting it in my mind.
I found it impossible to understand why I was still here. If this was
going to be my life from now on, why didn't God just let me die? It
would be a couple of years before I could thank the Lord for sparing
my life. At this time, I didn't feel that I had a life. Or if this was the
life I had now, I didn't think I wanted it. Yes, I had survived, but in
my soul, I was a man trapped between the life I once knew and the
death this new one felt like. The night my car crashed on Lincoln
Drive, the man I was died, and a new man was born. But who was he?

Looking back, of course, I can see that there were things to be
grateful for. For one thing, my injury was low enough on the spinal
cord that it did not affect my breathing. I didn't need a respirator, and
even when it seemed at one moment that I needed a tracheostomy—
an incision through the neck and into the windpipe to facilitate
breathing—I was able to forgo it (which saved my voice). My injury
left me with limited movement in my arms, though none in my
hands. And I survived the accident without head trauma or brain injury, so at least mentally and intellectually I was the same man. It
would be quite a while before I'd be able to appreciate fully these
"blessings" and the roles they would play in helping me adjust.

For the moment, though, I was consumed with a single thought:
What's going to happen to me? The question raced through my mind a
thousand times a day, relentlessly crowding out every other thought.
Obviously, I was going to live. But how? How? And why? My life
had been turned upside down. Confused, I found it impossible to
begin sorting out what it all meant. Whenever I tried, I felt myself
submerged in complete hopelessness and an overwhelming resentment toward everything and everyone. How was it that other people's lives were just going on, when as far as I could tell, mine was lost
somewhere out on Lincoln Drive? They say life goes on, but I
couldn't begin to imagine how mine would.

Lying in my hospital bed, I closed my eyes, tired of staring at the ceiling, exhausted with worry over what was going to happen from one minute to the next. I couldn't roll over, press the button to call a nurse, or pull up my own blankets. I glanced over at my mother, then sixty-four years old, sitting in the chair beside me. I'd had a dream, and I'd made it come true. I'd built the life I'd always wanted. Now it was over. Now I was thirty-two, and she was taking care of me again. One day I mentioned to her that the people at the hospital wanted her to take a course so that she could learn how to take care of me. I asked her if that was okay, and she replied it would be her pleasure. I was so thankful to have her there, but I couldn't bear the helplessness. I closed my eyes and tried to fall asleep.

In the years since, I've read the literature, so I'm up on the theories about how people respond to traumatic injury and disability. I can tell you all about disbelief and rage, denial, the bargaining with God, and the acceptance (if you can ever fully accept an injury like this). At the time all I felt was a profound sense of loss. Everything I had, everything I was, and everything I'd imagined for the future was utterly gone.

Some people believe that adversity comes to teach you a lesson. If that's so, this was one lesson I didn't think I needed to learn. Having grown up in the ghetto, I knew that much in life is beyond our control. Making it in show business, I knew, depended as much on getting the breaks as on having the talent. I didn't need anybody to tell me about chance and fate and the uncertainty of life, or to remind me that life isn't fair. I'd lived my life always working against the odds. I'd taken advantage of every possibility that ever came my way, because I *had* to be in control. I *had* to build that high wall between the life I wanted to live and the million obstacles that threatened to get in my way. Now the wall lay crushed in pieces. For the first time in my life, I felt my whole world had come to an end. I was totally helpless. Every day brought dozens of new reminders of how different life would be. If the phone rang, I couldn't answer it. My spoon slid off the tray? I couldn't pick it up. Karen hugged me? I couldn't hug her back. Nothing was the same.

Sometimes I'd look down at my body and feel as though it were no longer mine. It would be a long time before I felt reconnected to it. For now, I just lay back and closed my eyes, overwhelmed by the eerie realization that someone could put a knife in my leg and I wouldn't feel it. I felt powerless, vulnerable.

I could feel the warm air on my face, arms, and chest. If someone touched my shoulder or kissed my cheek, I felt it, perhaps even more intensely than I would have before. But the rest of my body had entered some dark and distant sleep from which it would probably never awaken, and I was its prisoner.

Probably the biggest barriers I faced were inside me. I'd spent my whole life striving to be independent. I prided myself on my perfectionism, my ability to move, to go, to do. Now the very qualities that had propelled me through life—my impatience, perfectionism, independence—were stones in my path. Now I lived on somebody else's time. I got dressed when someone got me dressed. If I needed to change my clothes, get a drink of water, wipe my nose, I waited for someone else. Television too loud? Room too cold? Pillows piled too high? Every little thing I wanted or needed required the effort and attention of somebody else, sometimes someone I barely knew.

When I was physically able, about two months after the accident, I was transferred to Magee Memorial Hospital, a spinal cord injury center, in downtown Philadelphia. Magee ranks among the nation's top institutions for rehabilitation. The people around me, including Danny and Shep, had wanted me to have the best care, and they looked into other facilities around the country. In the end, we agreed it was best for me to be near family and friends.

It was explained to me that in rehab I would be taught how to live with my injury. *How to live with my injury* . . . What the hell was that going to be like? I couldn't imagine and didn't even try. All I knew was that rehab was the bridge between now and the rest of my life. In my state of mind, though, it seemed more like an endless dark tunnel to nowhere.

I was rarely alone the whole time I was at Magee. Karen came by frequently. Mom spent the mornings with me, and Henry was there during the day, so that someone was always with me in my room. Because Tisha and LaDonna lived in Memphis, I didn't see them while I was in rehab. Yet whenever I thought of them and Teddy, it both brightened my day and reminded me of the responsibilities I still faced.

My cousin Pete's daughter, my niece Stephanie, attended a school right across the street from Magee. She would stop by with a hot Philly cheese-steak sandwich every day after school. For a native Philadelphian, it was really something to look forward to. I had so many visitors, it's impossible to remember them all. Even though my security guards Soto and Tylee let some inside, they kept many others at bay. Although I appreciated everyone's concern, the stress of having to be "on" for visitors was often more than I could handle, and I'm sure I missed seeing some people I really wanted to see.

As much as I understood that rehabilitation was essential, I didn't want to be there. The truth is, there were moments when I felt like I didn't want to be anywhere. I don't think anyone's invented the words yet that would convey the devastation. I felt as if part of me weren't even there. Merely concentrating on the simplest thing—how to feed myself with a device that strapped to my hand—demanded Herculean effort. I dealt with it by simply not doing it. I was confused, constantly being forced to accept things I felt I could not. I hated feeling helpless, but I found learning how not to be difficult and painful. I especially couldn't stand being dependent on other people, yet I looked forward to seeing those I cared about near me.

I wanted so badly to move ahead, to learn enough that I could get back to my own home and sleep in my own bed again. Then there were moments when I wanted to scream, *"I just can't fuckin' do it!"* My temper was short, my nerves were shot. I hated my life. And the irony of it all was, I couldn't have ended it if I wanted to. Without help.

Now, I imagine, this is the part where you expect to read about how I spent those months in rehab rising to every challenge, how I worked to perfect the life skills I needed to learn, how I never gave up. But the truth is, I did nothing. And I didn't give a damn, either. I couldn't. *From now on,* I thought, *I will always have people around to help me.* And if I didn't, I could hire someone! Sounds flippant, I know, but it's how I felt at the time. I was just not ready to accept the fact that I had to learn to do these things. What for? To feel worse about my life than I already did? It might sound crazy, but some days the only thing that got me through was watching *The Three Stooges* or anything else that would make me laugh. And, for a moment, forget.

While other patients went through their daily routines and had their bad moments under the shade of anonymity, I could not hide from being Teddy Pendergrass, the Entertainer. To be honest, I still wasn't clear where that guy ended and the real me began. Now it seemed that a chasm as wide as the sky separated him from me. I felt we were two different people—we certainly had two very different lives. But to the people who recognized me, we were one and the same. Walking down the hallway, people would peek into my room. Trying to be kind, some would say, "I love your music, Mr. Pendergrass." I knew they were trying to be nice, and I'd nod thanks, grateful for the compliment yet wishing they'd go away. Yes, I was that famous singer Teddy Pendergrass, but he wasn't everything that I was. Sometimes I wanted to say, "Even though you know my face and you've heard my records, you don't know me. You don't know the pain I'm going through. You don't know how badly I need to be left alone." Every look of recognition, every well-intentioned compliment, reminded me that there were people who loved me who didn't even know me, that I was famous for something I might never be able to do again.

I needed someone who could understand where I was coming from and reach out to me. Unfortunately, the physician in charge of my care at Magee wasn't that person. I realize that it's important for doctors and other medical professionals to be forthright and honest in dealing with patients who've suffered severe, life-altering trauma. I should mention that the other patients at Magee included people learning to cope with disabilities due to spinal cord injury, head trauma, and stroke. And I'm sure it's difficult and stressful to deal with patients who aren't always going to be "cured" or ever get much "better." Still, it seemed to me that, considering why we all were there, some who worked there could have been more compassionate. In hindsight, I realize they were doing a job, and I'm sure no one working there was without their own personal problems and difficulties. But God knows, I and every other patient I met there needed emotional support and encouragement as much as, if not more than, we needed to learn the mechanics of our new daily lives.

I left my first meeting with my doctor there feeling I was just another case to him, not a man. I felt he was more interested in exactly where my spinal cord had been severed, how much motion I had, and what I could expect to do with it, than in how I felt. I was in no state of mind then to commit our conversations to memory, but in every discussion we had about my body and my life, he made it sound like routine business. I got the impression that no matter what I did, no matter what anybody did for me, it wasn't going to make much of a difference anyway. It was at Magee that my full prognosis was determined, and I remember my doctor running it down for me as if it were a shopping list:

I would never be able to move or feel sensation below my chest. Period.

I would never be able to grasp objects normally. Period.

I would be in a wheelchair, dependent on other people, for the rest of my life. Period.

Chances were, I might not live beyond another ten years. Period.

For as long as I did live, I'd be prone to numerous serious, potentially fatal health complications. Period.

And maybe, because my injury was "incomplete," some ability might return over the next year and a half. Maybe.

Through the years, I've tried to get a new perspective on him. Maybe he simply couldn't mother each and every patient, or maybe he'd done that for a while and burned out. Whatever the reasons, his seeming lack of sensitivity colored my entire experience at Magee.

Most of my days in rehab followed the same basic routine: I'd wake up early and a nurse or nurse assistant would take me to the shower, help me use the bathroom, and do for me all the personal things I'd done myself from the time I was a little boy: comb my hair, brush my teeth, dress me. Then I'd be transferred into my wheelchair to go down for breakfast.

No one there could force you to do anything, but it was made clear that it would be better for you in the long run if you started doing as much for yourself as you could, even if that wasn't very much: feed yourself, dress yourself, transfer yourself from the bed to the chair and back, learn to use the assistive technology—in other words, the specially designed implements to help you do things—and so on. I chose to do none of it. I just couldn't.

Here's an example: We were all supposed to wheel ourselves down to breakfast every morning and try to feed ourselves. I knew I could do it if I set my mind to it. I just didn't have the will. Not yet.

Every day Mom took me to breakfast and fed me, much to the consternation of my therapists.

Every day included several hours of physical therapy, where I worked on further developing the muscles I still could use. Equally important, the therapist exercised the now-paralyzed muscles, to prevent my joints from stiffening and my muscles from atrophying due to lack of activity. As time went on, I learned how being paralyzed affects every system of the body, compromising its innate ability to regulate every bodily function, from the most personal and intimate to those we never think about, such as circulation, blood pressure, and body temperature. The physical reality is that bodies were made to be active. Once you are paralyzed, it is imperative that you make a conscious, continual effort to duplicate that "missing" movement by having a therapist or other knowledgeable person manipulate your joints and exercise your muscles properly.

A large part of rehab focused on adjusting emotionally to the situation. There were private sessions with a psychiatrist as well as group sessions where patients discussed their concerns and problems. I found talking to my psychiatrist incredibly frustrating. Though it really went against my nature then, I tried to open up and express my feelings. I struggled to overcome my usual reluctance to trust strangers. I'll admit it: I needed help sorting out what had happened to me and how I felt. I desperately needed answers and reassurance, maybe some hope, too. Each day, as Henry wheeled me down to the psychiatrist's office, I felt like just another patient on a conveyor belt. I know that everyone going through this has his or her unique problems. I also know that many of us experience the same emotions; that's why the group sessions could be so helpful at times. We'd all been there. But the fact is that I'd also been some other places because of my career, and my celebrity created problems for me that no one else there had to face. I didn't expect the psychiatrist—or anyone— to hold my hand and lead me, but I did expect them to at least show me a map and point the way.

I quickly discovered that there was no map, and the generic advice he offered was useless to me. I needed answers: How long was I going to feel this desperate and hopeless? Would I ever feel better? How could I start to rebuild my life? So you can imagine why it drove me crazy to sit in my wheelchair and be asked, "Why are you angry?" When I heard the doctor ask me that, I thought, *Have you lost your mind? What do you think?* But I said nothing then, and at every session thereafter I looked out the window in silence. When the session ended, Henry wheeled me back to my room.

The group discussions were more beneficial, I suppose. At least we patients understood one another in ways no one else could. Therapists presented informative talks about different aspects of coping with our injuries, and we were encouraged to ask any questions we had. Everyone had a million questions about all kinds of things, from how to protect our skin from pressure ulcers to how to hire aides to care for us at home. But by far the topic most pressing on everyone's minds was sex. Can we do it? What will it take? How can you accomplish it? We all wondered about it, but it seemed an especially frightening prospect for the young men, guys seventeen, eighteen, nineteen, some of them virgins. For them, the idea that they'd lost this ability was a possibility worse than death. I understood where they were coming from, but my perspective was a little different. Sure, I worried about it, but it wasn't the biggest or the only problem on my mind.

Sensitive, specially trained sex therapists and counselors talked to us in very specific terms about making adjustments, being creative, exploring different ways of thinking about and having sex. Some of this fell under the heading of alternative sexuality, and it was clear that many people in the group were uncomfortable with any kind of sex that wasn't straight intercourse. Because of my experiences, I had a better understanding of these other options and felt a little more comfortable with some of what they presented than some other patients did. The counselors answered our questions as best they could, but this was one issue—like virtually every issue in my new life—where the real answers came only with patience and time. The question is, What do I have to do now to have the feelings, the pleasure, and the experience I had before?

The most crucial element here was a patient, willing, aggressive, understanding, open-minded, adventurous, gentle, loving partner. And I know that's a lot to ask for, but that's what it takes. You both have to be willing to consider approaches you may never have even heard of before. With disability, sex goes from being one of the easiest, most natural, most pleasurable parts of your life to becoming a huge question mark for both of you. Everything changes except your innate human need to love and be loved romantically and sexually. To be loved and desired for the person you are, despite how much your body's been changed, is so important.

Speaking for myself, I know it was incredibly important to me to feel that I was still as desirable as I was before. The effect of spinal cord injury on physical sexual response can be very difficult to deal with. For so many men, the very definition of manhood is the ability to function sexually. For me, learning to redevelop and redefine my sexuality took some time, and I'm constantly learning new things about myself. I like to think that when people hear me sing about romance and sexuality, what they hear in my voice is true. I'm still singing from my experiences now, not just from memories.

Looking back, I know I had unrealistic expectations of what I'd learn from rehab. By that I don't mean that I'd figured to come out of rehab with solutions to all my problems; I knew that would be impossible. But I did expect to learn more about what my options might be. Nowhere was this more glaringly clear than in occupational therapy. As I sat in my wheelchair bored to death, forcing my now less able hands to draw countless figure eights on paper or build little wooden stools, I wanted to cry. On an intellectual level, I understood that these exercises were designed to help strengthen and develop the limited mobility I had in my hands and arms. But none of it would get me where I wanted to go, which was back in society as a productive, self-supporting man.

Personal computers weren't as common or as powerful as they are today, and assistive technology was in its infancy. I hope things are better in rehabilitation today. Still, I knew there were things that I wanted to do, things that I imagined there must be some way to do, like typing. Most troubling to me was the basic presumption that people who had suffered such a devastating injury wouldn't need or want to do much beyond the basics of survival. How could anyone even think that? Sit in a chair and imagine for a moment that you can do nothing beyond what you absolutely must to ensure your survival. Everything else is presumed to be beyond your reach. And remember, too, that this should be okay with you, because, after all, you're disabled. No one actually said that, but it's the message I got. And I could not accept that.

Everyone is different, of course, and I want to be clear about this: I'm not speaking for anyone but myself, nor am I passing judgment on those who take a different road. I understand why someone in my position would give up; I've almost done it myself a few times. But as I sat in my chair at Magee, overwhelmed by sadness and rage at the realization that my life as I knew it had been stolen, I desperately needed to be shown how I could get some of those pieces back.

At a time when it was assumed that returning to performing would be the last thing on my mind, I was dying for someone to show me how I could start on my way back. From the time I was a little boy, my ability to do for myself was an intrinsic part of who I was. My image of myself as a father, a son, a boyfriend—a man—revolved in large part on my ability to care for and to support the people I loved. This was the part of me that many of the people who worked with me at Magee did not understand. Maybe it was something no one would understand.

From the moment they pulled me from the car that night, the question of whether or not I would ever sing again haunted me. Granted, I had plenty to deal with besides that. I guess some people would argue that singing wasn't necessary to my physical survival. I could live without being able to sing, couldn't I? The real question for me, then, wasn't whether I could live without singing *but if I would want to.* Singing wasn't just something that I did, it was part of me, deep in my soul. My paralysis had so drastically reduced the ways I could express myself. I couldn't slam a door when I got angry, I couldn't surprise someone with a hug. Not sing? It was unthinkable to me. And on a practical level, if I couldn't sing, how would I provide for myself and my family?

I was lying in bed one day, with all this weighing on my mind, when Henry showed me the newspaper. There was my name in a front-page headline. I'll never forget the date: August 17, 1982. I scanned the lengthy article, curious to see what it was about. Within seconds, my heart dropped.

"VACANCY: IN SEARCH OF THE NEW PENDERGRASS." Under my photo ran the caption: "Teddy Pendergrass, the singer–sex symbol who has left a void." (When the article ran in a Los Angeles paper, the headline asked bluntly, "Who'll Be Their Next Teddy Bear?") My pulse quickened as I read: "The tall, bearded singer crooning flagrantly sexy songs in his gruff, powerful voice had"—*had?*—"a devastating effect on females, from teenagers to women in their forties. He was"—*was?*—"the cool, macho man with just a hint of sensitivity, exuding a kind of animal sexuality that seems to turn on many females. Since the late seventies, he has been the number-one black male singer–sex symbol . . . In March the thirty-two-year-old was paralyzed from the neck down in a Philadelphia auto accident. According to his doctors, he will probably be able to sing, but it's unlikely that he will ever walk again, which means that he probably won't perform. If he sang from a wheelchair, it wouldn't be the same. His accident left a void. Who's going to be the next Teddy Pendergrass?"

Tears welled in my eyes, and a lump rose in my throat. I looked up at Henry and shouted, "What the hell are they talkin' about? They think I'm dead? No one's gonna take my place. I'm still here!"

If I sang from a wheelchair, it "wouldn't be the same." What the hell did that mean? I was stunned, enraged, hurt, devastated. To say this added insult to injury—literally—doesn't even start to describe how diminished, worthless, and inhuman those words made me feel. Nowhere did the writer wish me well or express any hope for my recovery. Who the hell was he to tell the world that it was over for me? That Teddy Pendergrass no longer mattered? For him, my accident was merely an opportunity for ranking every other popular black male singer, as if we were not individuals but interchangeable cogs in the hit-record machine.

"Let's consider the characteristics we're looking for," the writer continued. "He has to be black, reasonably young, good-looking, virile, aggressive, and charismatic." Rereading this today, I wonder exactly which of these characteristics he assumed I no longer possessed.

I used to make it a point never to read reviews. I never cared what some writer thought of my show or my recordings. When it came to my work, the only opinions that counted were mine and the fans'. The writers who grilled and profiled me, the critics who believed themselves qualified to pick apart another person's life's work (and how, exactly, you get *that* job, I'd like to know)—I ignored them. In a way, it's ironic that it would be a music critic—one who had reviewed and interviewed me several times before—who would hurt me in a way no one else could. *The next Teddy Pendergrass . . .* My spirit collapsed under the weight of those words.

This wrenching moment served as a turning point. I've since come to realize how painful it is for many people to see someone who has suffered a tragedy and how hard it is for them to understand that even though that person is now wheelchair-bound, deep down inside, he is still the same man he was before his accident. The moment I finished reading that infuriating newspaper article, I vowed that nobody else would be "the next Teddy Pendergrass," and that I wouldn't rest until I was right back where I left off.

Not long afterward, I sang for the first time since the accident. I'd spent weeks and weeks terrified that I would no longer be physically able to, because the injury had paralyzed the muscles that support the voice. There's a lot more to singing than just opening your mouth. It's a very physical act, and the power and control you need to hold a note, to project your voice, to growl, to shout, even to sing very softly all depend on a finely balanced interplay between your vocal cords and the lungs, the diaphragm, and the muscles of the chest, abdomen, and back. You can sing your whole life and never be consciously aware of these things. Although I had lost the ability to control some of those important muscles, thank God neither my diaphragm nor the nerves controlling it were damaged. That meant that I could still draw a breath; that meant that I could still sing.

I didn't have much strength in my voice; even my speaking voice was noticeably softer than before. I desperately wanted to know if I could sing again, but at the same time, I didn't want to know. What if I opened my mouth and couldn't muster any of the old power? Or only a little of it?

My moment of truth came one afternoon when I heard a coffee commercial on television. I'd heard the jingle a thousand times before. *Okay,* I thought, *let's see . . .* I took a deep breath and hummed the tune aloud.

Now, I've sung literally thousands of songs, from the gospel at Glad Tidings to the Motown hits on the corner, to the sumptuous ballads and soulful hits that came later. But let me tell you, nothing ever sounded as sweet to my ears as my version of that silly damn jingle.

DAMN! I've still got it! I can still do it!

When I heard myself, I knew I'd taken the first step back. I closed my eyes and thanked the Lord.

I couldn't have seen then how long and steep the road was that lay before me. I couldn't know how many steps it would take to bring me back to where I belonged, back to where I was before my world shattered. And maybe it was better that way. At least for this one brief moment, I held hope.

Before my accident, I set goals and moved steadily but surely toward them. Sure, there were occasional setbacks, dreams that didn't come true. But I never stood still. Now things were different. You've heard the expression "one step forward and two steps back." Some days, learning to cope with my disability left me feeling as if I'd gone one step forward, twenty steps back, and a few dozen in circles. Every happy moment, every accomplishment—and there was no such thing as a "small" accomplishment—filled me with euphoria. But the feeling was usually short-lived, with disappointment and frustration following quickly and surely afterward.

Fortunately, I was able to take a few breaks away from Magee. One time Karen wanted to take me out for a ride. I'll never forget her struggling to get me moved from my chair to the car. I hit my head on the roof of the car, my glasses got knocked off. It wasn't easy, but from the start Karen showed a positive, can-do attitude. I trusted her and was willing to let her try, and she did it. *She did it.* When something would go wrong like this, we could even laugh about it sometimes.

Another time, Karen and I went the three-quarters of a mile from Magee to her apartment and back with Henry pushing me in my chair. Karen asked me what I wanted to eat that night, and she made me a special meal of oxtails and white lima beans. How much did it mean to me? The fact that I remember what Karen cooked but have long forgotten what I was served several years ago at the White House, when I attended a state dinner as a guest of President and Mrs. Bush, should give you some idea.

As Henry wheeled me through the streets of my hometown, I couldn't help but notice that almost everyone we passed had a surprised, quizzical look, like, "Is that Teddy?" A few called out to me—"Hey, Teddy, good to see you!" "Hey, Ted, how's it goin'?" Considering how desperately I didn't want to be seen, I was so glad to get out for a few hours, I didn't give a damn who saw me. And, I have to admit, it was nice to know I hadn't been totally forgotten. Still, I worried that the man they recognized no longer existed.

While I was in rehab, on more than one occasion total strangers would tiptoe into my room at night and flick on the light, just to see if the man sleeping in the bed really was "the" Teddy Pendergrass. Karen told me this much later, so as not to upset me. I was fortunate to always have someone with me in my room. God knows what might have happened if I didn't. To a certain extent, I can accept losing a little privacy because of my fame. But this seemed downright indecent. What did these people think they were going to see, anyway?

I was a loner who could now never be alone. I was a man in hiding—hiding from the world and, I now realize, hiding from myself. Those closest to me saw my anguish and knew my struggles. Everyone else I kept at a distance. While at Magee, I received many visitors, including Al Green and Jermaine Jackson. Al, who during this time had abandoned show business to preach and sing gospel, brought along a preacher and offered to pray for me. But prayer wasn't something I wanted to hear about.

No matter whom I saw, though, my wheelchair became my stage, and from it I gave some of the greatest performances of my life: Yeah, I'm doing fine. . . . Everything's going to be all right. . . . I'm gonna make it, man. . . .

It was all bullshit. The entire time I was sitting there, smiling and talking, I wanted to scream, "I am *not* fine! Everything is *wrong!* I can't go on like this!" But I hadn't yet fully admitted those feelings to my-self, much less to anyone else. I couldn't be honest with myself. I didn't know how.

More than anything, every waking moment reminded me of how every little thing, every step of the way, was an ordeal, a new problem I had to figure out for myself. When you're physically challenged, no one issues you an owner's manual for your injured body outlining every conceivable circumstance you might encounter. Everything I tried to do became an exercise in trial and error, and the problems were never simple. To do something I'd done a million times without a second thought—like getting in the car, getting a snack, opening the mail—suddenly took as much concentration, effort, and patience as climbing Mount Everest without a guide in the dark of night. Sometimes I felt even that might be easier.

Before, I moved through the world. Now the world moved around me, and usually got in my way. Where I wanted to go and what I wanted to do were no longer mine alone to decide. Before—like most people who never had to deal with it—I'd never noticed the height of curbs, the presence of stairs, the absence of elevators, the width of doorways. These are just some of the potential obsta-cles I face a hundred times every day.

One day that fall I got the news that I'd be going home soon. It was everything I'd been hoping for, and everything I dreaded, too. What would it be like "out there"? Karen had been with me at Magee almost every single day, helping me however she could. I wondered what would happen to us when I got home and started re-ally living my life as a quadriplegic. I tried not to think about it too much, but I—like most who go through this—feared I would no longer be lovable or attractive, that the relationship would end. You can imagine my joy when Karen announced, "I'm coming home with you." She's been here beside me ever since.

Not long before I left, my occupational therapist, Jerry, said, "Ted, before you leave here, I have to know that you can wheel yourself to breakfast and that you know how to feed yourself."

I knew Jerry was right, and he meant well. But I was in no mood to be told what I should be doing. Mom had been taking me down to breakfast and feeding me every day since I'd arrived. You might think I'd rage against that dependence, do everything I could to break it, even in the smallest ways. But I didn't. It doesn't sound like me, does it? But I didn't think I was me. And I saw it differently. How was feeding myself going to change a damn thing about my life? It wasn't. So why the hell should I bother? Obviously, this was not an attitude they liked to see in rehab. Nor, I should add, was it the one I should have taken. But no excuses: That's how I felt.

As I said, Jerry meant well. I just didn't want to hear it. "Damn it! I can do it if I want to!" I snapped.

"Okay, Ted," he replied coolly. "Tomorrow morning, I'm going to make you an egg, and you're going to feed yourself."

"Okay, I'll do it," I replied.

The next morning, Mom pushed me down to breakfast, and Jerry had the egg cooked and waiting on my plate. He strapped the assistive device onto my hand. I had never practiced this before, but I'd set my mind to do it. Then I did what I'd watched the other residents doing all these weeks. I stuck the fork in the egg and fed myself without dropping a single piece. There! After a couple of bites, I looked at Jerry and smirked, "Now what? You satisfied that I can do it?"

Jerry was astonished. "You *can* do it," he marveled. "You can really do it."

"Of course I can do it. I told you I could do it," I snapped, forcing back tears. "I also told you I just don't *want* to."

The day I left rehab, a cool, breezy autumn afternoon, I felt a mixture of relief and worry. I couldn't wait to get back home and be with my family, hear the dogs barking, smell the sweet country air, and—most important—be surrounded only by people I knew, loved, and *trusted*.

At the same time, I realized how much I'd come to depend on the doctors, nurses, therapists, and aides to guide me and my loved ones through this uncharted terrain. Karen, Mom, Henry, and others close to me had gotten a crash course in how to care for me, and I must say they couldn't have done a better, more loving job. No one's yet created the words that could express my gratitude for everything they did for me. But in the back of my mind, I worried. *What if I fall? What if I choke? What if the home-care nurses I hire aren't as proficient, as responsible, as caring? What if someone makes a mistake? What if, what if, what if.*

I'd done everything within my power to ease the transition home. While still at Magee, I personally interviewed several nursing assistants and hired a wonderful German woman named Jean, who would be with me for several years to come. Countless times her tireless devotion to me made the impossible possible. I got my motorized, or power, wheelchair, which I learned to control with a joystick (after running it straight into a wall the first time I tried it). Before I mastered driving the power chair, I was dangerous in that thing! It enabled me to move independently of anyone else, and I can't begin to describe what that chair symbolized for me. The feeling of being free to move without anyone else's help was simply exhilarating.

The insurance company made arrangements with the occupational therapist who would be treating me twice a week. And I got a luxurious, customized twenty-four-foot van, to which I added a comfortable reclining chair. My assistant, Sedonia Walker, had turned one of my downstairs dens into the Teddy Bear Productions offices, and the den across the foyer from it had been converted into my bedroom. It would be a while before the elevator was installed and I could move back into my old bedroom upstairs.

I faced going home with an overwhelming mixture of excitement, anticipation, relief, and fear. It was easy to get caught up in all the changes and the planning. There was so much to do, and I welcomed the distraction. At the same time, though, I couldn't avoid facing what these decisions and adjustments were all about: building a new life centered on my injury and my dependence.

The drive home took less than half an hour. As we approached the tall, black gates at the end of Crosby Brown Road, I breathed a sigh of relief. I was home, safe from the rest of the world. But as we neared my mansion, I was reminded, too, of what my life used to be like. Yes, it was home, but a home transformed, a looming stone reminder of a shattered dream. Outside the van's windows, autumn leaves glowed with the colors of sunset. It was beautiful.

I thought about how far I'd come to reach this day, then I tried to block it from my mind. I just wanted to savor this moment. It would be years before I could see clear to the future, before I understood that the changes I would make were not to the world around me but to the person inside me. There would be big changes in my daily routine, but it was still a routine, something I would have to do for the rest of my life. Over and over again, as far as I could imagine, my days would be dictated by my injury, colored by the same frustration, the same loss, the same helplessness, the same rage. *I can't live like this . . . I can't!* I thought.

Then I stopped and remembered, *At least I'm home.* The gates shut behind me, and I felt safe for the moment. I closed my eyes and wondered if I'd ever want to see those gates swing open again.

EIGHT

Yes, there are times when my road gets so long,
And I stumble alone in the dark . . .

Other people could move and live independently. Why couldn't I? I knew the medical reason, but now I was asking God. I'd grown up my whole life believing—knowing—He was there with me. But where was He now?

To be honest, I'd fallen out of touch with the Lord by then. As a teenager, I had drifted away from the organized aspects of my faith, though I never totally lost my spiritual connection to the Lord. I'd heard my calling, and I knew I had a purpose. Still, there were times when I wrestled with what it all meant and questioned my beliefs. Part of losing touch with my faith, I'm sure, was also just a teenager's natural rebelliousness. I thought I knew it all, and I had "better" things to do than sit in church six days a week.

As a kid, I never doubted the moral authority of the church, the Bible, or the people who claimed to speak for them. In my mother's house, preachers and ministers were men and women of God who could do no wrong. Once I got out on the road, however, I saw a different side: so-called preachers and ministers hanging around private after-hours joints and people's homes, drinking, snorting cocaine, and spending their Friday and Saturday nights carrying on in ways that, come Sunday morning, they'd all be denouncing from the pulpit. In my youthful idealism and shortsightedness, I could not separate the hypocrisy of these individuals from the church and the religion they claimed to represent. I drew away from what I saw as a sham.

As I grew older, I came to see it in a different light. I credited God for the gift I'd been given, but I never forgot that while He gave me these many blessings, it was my responsibility to use them wisely. Though I grew up among people who believed Jesus would pay the light bill if you prayed hard enough, I knew better: God helps those who help themselves. And from the streets I learned other lessons, too. From my experience growing up, I knew that the passivity and acceptance the church taught didn't always work in real life. I knew you had to fight for what you wanted. In North Philadelphia the meek inherited nothing but trouble. No amount of praying and singing could do for me what I had done for myself.

I saw nothing sinful or wrong in the music I sang, the money I spent, the way I lived my life. Sure, I had a big, fancy house, but I took good care of my mother, too, giving her a home and a car and making her feel secure. Yes, I was a single father, but I was deeply involved in the lives of my children. Yes, I lived the life and I loved every minute of it, but I also gave of my time and my money to charities. Yes, I was proud; I had something to be proud of.

So by the time of the accident, I had begun to see my relationship with God as something different from what I'd learned in church. Inside, I knew He was with me. The things I did that may have gotten between me and what I'd been taught were my choices, and I did not feel compelled to justify them to anyone.

My accident forced me to redefine my relationship with God. I can't preach; I can barely explain. The Lord was with me, but it was up to me to find Him again and to rediscover the connection I'd felt so intimately as a child. In a sense, I was a child again: My life was so new to me, and every moment seemed to bring something new for me to learn or to understand. And I cried out to Him, and He was there.

Now, this didn't happen overnight, and it wasn't an experience as vivid and definitive as my calling when I was ten. But when I surrendered in my heart as I had surrendered kneeling at my mother's bed, I knew that He would walk alongside me. And He has. The Spirit was always there for me, and I wanted to get closer.

Over some time I came to see the accident as something that happened, not something that God "did" or "let happen." God doesn't stop bad things from happening to you. But He does help you deal with them when they do. Even as the car hurtled out of control that night, I had a feeling I knew why, and years later my suspicions would be confirmed. In the meantime, in the back of my mind, I wondered if part of it was my fault. I was painfully aware that there were those who viewed my tragedy as "punishment" for the rock-&-roll lifestyle and my playboy image. The fact that my passenger that night was publicly revealed to be a transsexual certainly didn't help. It hurt me to realize that for some my accident would remain a topic of sordid speculation, not the very human tragedy it was.

Most people, though, were concerned and supportive. I was grateful for the well wishes and the encouragement expressed to me in calls, letters, cards, flowers, and—of course—teddy bears. Friends who took time to see how I was doing and offer to help were like angels sent from God. For the most part, though, I lived the life of a recluse, still hiding from the world and my worst fears of how people might look at me now.

Some showed such incredible thoughtfulness. Dick Gregory, the comedian, activist, and entrepreneur, came to my home and offered his support as well as a lot of advice about nutrition. There were no cameras, no media. Dick was truly there to help, and I appreciated that so much. While in town for their Victory Tour in 1984, Michael, Tito, and Marlon Jackson called and asked if they could come by and see me. Sure, I said. Now, I understand their having to travel with some security, but before they even drove through the front gates, their security staff had combed the entire property. Why, I don't know. They finally arrived—safely, I should add—and we had a pleasant visit. They invited me to come see the show, but I was too self-conscious to appear in public. It was too painful.

The little things really did mean so much, more than you can ever imagine. Another friend, Charles Huggins, called before coming over to the house and asked if it would bother me to see him driving his Rolls-Royce. If it did, he had no problem driving a different car; he just didn't want to remind me of the accident. What a thoughtful, sensitive gesture.

But as so often happens when someone suffers a devastating loss, it became painfully clear that many people I'd thought of as friends weren't calling or coming over, now or ever. Naturally, I didn't expect everyone I knew or worked with to show the same devotion as my family, Karen, Henry, or Danny and Shep, but when I thought about the people I never heard a word from, my heart broke. Always a loner, I surprised myself by how much I needed to know that people still cared, that I still mattered.

I've since learned that when people stay away, it's because of their inability to deal with another person's pain. To be honest, before the accident, I might have reacted the same way; I can't say. But no matter how well I understood the psychology behind their staying away, I could not accept it. I couldn't help but feel that I was being rejected because I wasn't the same person, and that I wasn't the same person because I couldn't do all the same things I had done before. It's funny how when you're "healthy" and "able-bodied" the person you are inside and the body you live in are two separate entities. To some, though, once your body is dramatically changed, it's as if your personality, your character, the "you" inside you vanishes. I sometimes felt my name was no longer Teddy but Teddy-in-the-wheelchair.

Even with my family and friends rallying around me, I felt more alone than I'd ever felt in my life. My estate became my whole world. Every day I wheeled myself around the property, trying to lose myself, or at least not be seen by anyone. I didn't feel like talking. Some-times I didn't even feel like being.

The only person I allowed in from the world outside was a Lower Merion Township police officer named Joe. Because of the size of the properties in the neighborhood, the local police regularly drove up to each house and looked around just to check that everything was okay. Joe was a tall, stocky, middle-aged white man with a warm, friendly manner. Most days, he would come by, and we'd spend half an hour or so just talking and having a few laughs. It's hard to de-scribe how much these visits meant to me.

During those six months of hospitalization and rehab, I lived in a world where everything revolved around my physical condition; I essentially blacked out the rest of the world. I mean, I worried about the kids, Karen, Mom, money, and the other issues that once consumed my day-to-day life. But the truth is, there was little I could do for anyone else besides tell them that I loved them. The other problems paled in comparison to adjusting to my new life. Barely able to cope with my personal challenges, I had to leave everything else alone. Was I selfish? Yes. But it was the only way I knew how to fight. And if I didn't fight, I was going to die.

Once I got settled in the downstairs den that had been renovated to accommodate my hospital bed, the routine of my new days quickly fell into place. I had full-time nursing care, which could be either a blessing or an incredible source of stress. Maintaining a "nor-mal" home life in the constant presence of nurses and other em-ployees was one of the most difficult things for me to get used to. I say "get used to" rather than "accept," because there will always be some aspects of it that I can never accept. Nurses are essential; I couldn't live as well as I do without them. But that care comes with a price. Having a nonfamily member always in our midst, my family and I have lost a lot of the privacy most people take for granted. Not always being able to say or do exactly what we feel simply because someone else is here can create a strain on relationships, too.

Of the hundreds of nurses I've had, I have been fortunate to find several extremely good ones—both male and female—who were competent, caring, and pleasant to be around. When this relationship works best, it's like a partnership. But like anyone who finds himself suddenly completely dependent on strangers for many things, I've had my share of bad experiences, too. Things have been taken from my home, including Karen's diamond-and-sapphire necklace I gave her for our first anniversary and my wedding ring. My family's plans can be thrown into turmoil by the nurse who can't make it in for a shift. Now, I'm not saying that my nurse has to be my best friend or an endless source of good cheer. People are people, and we all have our problems that we can't help but bring to work sometimes. But I've often wished that a nurse could lie in my bed one morning, when I've just awakened and begun thinking about all I want to do that day and wondering, even if only for a second, if anything un-expected will interfere. To me, there's a big difference between a cheerful "Good morning, Ted," and a grudging, apathetic "Hi." When a nurse signals that she's unhappy to be here or that she's got other things on her mind, it creates a tense atmosphere. There have been some who develop an attitude when I ask for something I need or ask that something be done for me in a specific way—for example, how my clothes are cared for or how my papers are arranged on my desk. They might think I'm being unreasonable. It would be one thing if I could do these things for myself, but there are times when I wonder if they need to be reminded that I'm not asking just for the hell of it. I'm asking because being dependent on others doesn't mean you have to give up running your life the way you want to.

No matter how many years' experience a nurse may bring to the job, the fact is there is no greater expert on the care of Teddy Pen-dergrass than Teddy Pendergrass. I'm willing to listen and to learn, but ultimately I know what works for me. I know what feels right and what doesn't, and it never ceases to amaze me how many arguments I've had with people telling me they know what's best for me when they don't even know me. Because I have struggled so mightily with issues related to trust, opening my home and the most intimate aspects of my life to strangers has been very, very difficult. It's not always easy to set boundaries diplomatically. A request to open my mail is not an invitation to read it over my shoulder. We have to strike a fine balance between my privacy and my dependence when, for example, a nurse accompanies me when I'm visiting friends. It's a unique and complicated relationship, and with every new person, you start from scratch and hope for the best.

My physical therapist worked with me at home a couple of times a week. On the other days, Karen would be my therapist. I had a large padded mat table, which measures about four feet by six feet, where I'd lie for therapy. Karen did everything she could to make it more pleasant, including buying me five different-colored terry-cloth sweat suits. Being a dancer, she understood how to stretch my muscles correctly. Sometimes, like when she'd try to stretch my heel to my ear, I'd shout, "Karen, I'm not a dancer!" One exercise she did with me, which greatly improved my singing, was to sit on my stomach and force me to push her up using my stomach muscles. Karen is slim and petite, but a person sitting on your stomach is still a person sitting on your stomach. It was tough, but with her encouragement, I kept at it. Between Karen's vast knowledge of exercise and physiology and our determination, we went above and beyond my regular exercise program, and it paid off. She worked tirelessly to keep me in shape and healthy. We even tried a strict health-food regimen, and Karen learned to prepare tofu in every way you can imagine. Still, it was tofu. One day I looked up from a big plate of steaming tofu and said, "Karen, get me a steak!" Not only was I happy, Mom was ecstatic. She was tired of eating tofu, too.

I knew what I had to do; I just hadn't fully come to terms with why. The desire to move and do and just live the way I used to still burns inside me, and will until the day I die. It would be a long time before my mind stopped telling my body to answer the door or pick up a book.

Karen's selflessness, dedication, and love formed a beaming ray of light, urging me forward when I felt I couldn't go on. Her positive attitude was a blessing to everyone. Here's what I mean: To welcome me home from one of my many hospitalizations, she and the kids put on a show for me. They created a stage in the living room, then she, Tisha, and LaDonna sashayed out all dressed up like my background singers, followed by "Teddy Pendergrass"—little Teddy in a cowboy hat and my cowboy boots, doing a dead-on imitation of his old man.

Being just eight years old the year of the crash, there wasn't much my children could do for me, but, boy, they tried. In my coldest moments, the glow of their love has kept me warm and alive. They have tried to be strong and put my feelings first. They may have cried on someone's shoulder, confided their fears to someone else, but they never wanted to burden me.

Still, my children needed a father, Mom needed her son, and Karen needed me. Traumatic injury doesn't change the nature of your relationships or the roles you play in other people's lives. In my mind I knew I couldn't hold a door open for Karen or help Mom, but, damn it, I wanted to. I think the most terrifying part of being paralyzed struck me one day when I saw Teddy trip and fall while he was playing. He wasn't seriously hurt, but he cried, and I couldn't do a damn thing for him. Before, I would have run to him and scooped him up in my arms, taken care of his scrape, hugged him—did whatever it took. Now it was different. To be lying in my bed or sitting in my chair and hear one of my children cry or call for help—it's one of the worst things I can imagine.

I'd never been much of a talker, always keeping my deepest feelings to myself. My injury forced me to express my emotions; to say

"I love you" instead of giving a hug, or "I'm angry" instead of storming out of the room. And I had to learn to trust people in a way I never would have—never could have—before. It wasn't all about me anymore. By myself, I could do nothing. Everything now was a team effort.

There was still so much to learn about what I could and could not do, and how even the simplest things—like being around someone who has a bad cold—could have unimaginable consequences. For instance, as with other paralyzed people, my immune system isn't as strong as it was before. I run a higher risk of contracting potentially deadly pneumonia. Before my accident, I hardly ever got sick. I never cared if someone around me sneezed or coughed. Now, like so many things, it was a problem, one more thing to worry about. Sometimes just thinking about what I had to do could be as exhausting as actually doing it.

My personal issues were daunting but not big enough to eclipse what was going on outside my immediate circle. The issues and problems that had been too heavy for me to bear before were suddenly thrust onto my back, and I admit I faltered under the weight. I came home to face endlessly mounting bills, employees I had to worry about, and business commitments I had to buy my way out of at great expense. Before, I'd never had reason to worry about what my health insurance would cover and what it wouldn't. Now I counted my money not in the finer things it would buy but how I'd be spending it to stay alive and live to my fullest capacity. *Thank God I'm a millionaire,* I'd think as I lay wide awake for hours every night. *At least I don't have to worry about that.*

All those years, I'd never wanted to be bothered knowing how much I had or where it was going. I knew what I made—and it was sweet, believe me—but I didn't follow it once it wended its way through the Teddy Bear Productions accounts, streaming out into salaries, employee benefits, taxes, and expenses. I looked around, and I knew broke sure as hell didn't look anything like this.

For some time before the accident, Shep and Danny had been encouraging me to be more directly involved in my business. They were right, but I already had a job: being "Teddy Pendergrass." I also had a great assistant in Sedonia Walker. Even if I'd had the time, I lacked the intricate knowledge and experience to take control in any meaningful way. And unless I earned degrees in law and accounting in my spare time, I'd still be dependent on the advice of other experts.

In this regard, my story is the old, familiar lament of singers, actors, athletes, and anyone else who gets rich quick doing something besides playing with somebody else's money. Once the dollars started piling up, I was the shiny golden lure in a sea full of hungry sharks, and when they bit, they got me good. In addition to the fancy cars and the magnificent house, I unwittingly collected some of the other accoutrements of success you don't always hear about: a messy and convoluted financial situation and the very expensive attention of the Internal Revenue Service. Before long, I was up against the wall. My only recourse was to file for bankruptcy, abandon my responsibilities, and start fresh. It sure would have been a hell of a lot easier, but I just couldn't bring myself to do it. I'd worked too damn hard, I was too proud. I was Teddy Pendergrass. As vague and slight as my other options were then, I still believed I could turn it around, so I held out.

I didn't need to look at a bank statement or a ledger sheet to know that my situation probably wasn't good. My lifestyle was built on the assumption that there would always be another tour, another long, lucrative engagement, another hit pumping up the bank balance. It was widely reported that PIR awarded me an unusually generous royalty rate on my records, when in fact the deal was way below what other multiplatinum artists commanded from other labels. Out of loyalty to Gamble, Huff, and PIR, I'd let that slide for

many years, but before the accident, I had been planning to renego-
tiate a more equitable deal and make other major changes in how I
ran my business and my career. There were so many things I had been
primed to set in motion. Now it was too late.

In the days immediately following the accident, Shep and Danny
took it upon themselves to exploit every possible source of income
for me and my family. This wasn't their responsibility; they weren't
hired to manage my personal finances. Still, they tried to help in any
way they could. With my mother's permission, Shep went through
my house collecting all the tapes of unreleased recordings. He then
appealed to Kenny Gamble to release the songs as an album, for
which I'd be paid my customary advance. *This One's for You* came out
later that summer, and spun off a couple of minor hits in "This Gift
of Life" and "I Can't Win for Losing." The money it earned didn't
even begin to cover my expenses, but it was something.

Given my long and lucrative association with Gamble and Huff,
you might assume I could have turned to PIR for some help. But less
than two months after my accident, the label began what would become a near-fatal slide into insolvency. No company or artist
emerged from the industry-wide recession unscathed, and—to Gamble and Huff's credit—PIR held out as long as it could. In November 1982, CBS Records dealt the knockout blow when it announced
it was terminating its eleven-year distribution deal with PIR. Gamble, a black man trying to hold his own in a white man's world,
didn't stand a chance. He was a brilliant artist who did the best he
could to be a businessman. In the end, though, he was no match for
the suits in New York. Less than a year after my accident, PIR would
exist in name only, the music that carried the message silenced.

But there were other factors that would profoundly affect my
recording career. As Kenny Gamble told me many years later, the relationship between PIR and CBS had been deteriorating for some
time. Once the independent label's sales began sagging, CBS
amended the deal so that it was obligated to distribute PIR product

by me and only four or five other PIR acts. I never recorded for PIR again.

Despite what occurred between CBS and PIR, I strongly feel that given my phenomenal record sales and the millions of dollars I'd made for CBS, I should have at least had the option of signing to CBS directly. It hurt me deeply to realize that they simply assumed that I would no longer be a creative force in the music business.

I was home only a couple of months when I developed a stubborn infection and had to be rushed back to the hospital, just two days after Christmas. Out of frustration, I raged at my body, which I was now obligated to care for and protect. I felt it now did so little for me but seemed to run my life. As I quickly discovered, unplanned trips to the emergency room and the doctor's office are part and parcel of life with paralysis. For me, the hardest part is not knowing what the doctors will discover is wrong and what they will have to do to correct it. A doctor I'd never met before examined me and explained that I'd have to be admitted to the hospital. *It can't always be like this,* I prayed, but deep inside I feared it would be. Since then, I've been hospitalized over a dozen times, for everything from the treatment of mild infections to extensive, life-altering surgery.

When I got home again, I simply continued to retreat inside my-self, not appearing in public again until February 1983, when I introduced Bill Cosby, who was being honored by the Afro-American Historical and Cultural Museum at the Academy of Music, in Philadelphia. I was so apprehensive about being seen in public, and very self-conscious about having to be pushed onstage in a manual wheelchair, but I was told that Bill had especially requested my presence and that I would receive an award from the museum. My appearance would be brief, and I'd have to travel only about half an hour from my home. Maybe this would be a good way to get out and test the waters. I said yes.

Over the years I'd crossed paths with Bill several times, but we were not close friends. I didn't see him before I went onstage. All he knew of my condition and my ability then was probably what he'd read in the newspaper, like everyone else. That is why what happened onstage that night so took me by surprise.

Henry pushed me out onto the stage, and I received a heart-warming standing ovation before I even spoke, which felt wonderful. Wonderful! People were shouting, "God bless you, Teddy!" and smiling and cheering. I read in the paper the next day that some people were even crying. I said a few words, and when I paused at one point, someone shouted, "Sing a song, Teddy!"

"Just because I stopped walking, I haven't stopped singing!" I replied, which set off more cheers and applause. God, it was good to be back. Then I spoke from my heart: "I live with all of your prayers, and I know things will be just fine."

Then it was time to introduce Bill. He came onstage, then surprised me and everyone else there by walking up to me, dropping a microphone in my lap, and saying, "I'm not leaving here until you pick up that mike." This was totally unplanned, and I was so taken aback, I couldn't do anything but shake my head no. I can't even venture to guess why Bill was doing this. Did he think he was "helping" me? That putting me on the spot like this and making me struggle was somehow "good" for me? If Bill really knew me, he'd know how much I'd overcome just to *be* there. I thought Bill would get the message when I refused, so you can imagine my shock and horror when he shouted, "I'm not leaving here until you pick up that mike!"

A nervous silence fell over the crowd. I was embarrassed, humiliated, and—most important—furious. Didn't he realize how devastated I'd be if I failed? I was fuming inside, but I was trapped. I maneuvered my hands to my lap, grabbed the microphone between them, held it up to my mouth, and announced, "I have it! I have it!" The audience cheered and shouted, but I don't think anyone there that night thought what had happened was okay. It wasn't. My son

Teddy came onstage, and I received my award, then said good-bye and left the stage. I retreated back into the Chateau, more depressed and withdrawn than ever.

I had good days as well as bad. I'd once envisioned my recovery and adjustment as an ascending staircase. Some steps rose steeper than others; others were plateaus where I might be stranded for a time. In reality, the road to recovery was more like the haunted house ride in a boardwalk carnival. Breathtaking acceleration, then a sudden stop. A sudden twist here, a turn there, around and around, out into the daylight, then—*Slam!*—back down into the dark. Nothing you can anticipate or brace yourself for. Where will it end? I'll let you know when I get there.

Shortly after coming home, I'd locked myself in a room and cried the whole day. Sometimes Karen or one of the kids would make me laugh, or Mom would gently stroke my head with her hand and comfort me as she'd done when I was a child, or Henry would remind me of some crazy thing that had happened on the road. That would make it a good day. Other times, the slightest thing would send me into a rage of curses and tears. I was feeling more depressed more of the time. Emotionally, I just shut down. I didn't want to feel anymore, it was too painful, and there was no end in sight. The ride got darker and darker.

Then Karen surprised me by announcing that she'd rented a van. "Teddy," she said, "we're going to Ohio to see Johnnie Wilder."

"We're what?"

"We're going to Ohio. Right now."

"Right now?"

"Now!"

I didn't know it then, but Karen had phoned my friend Johnnie Wilder and explained to him how depressed I'd been. I'd known Johnnie for years, but we'd never spent a lot of time together or been close friends. He's a talented singer, songwriter, and musician. You'd probably know him best from his group Heatwave, who in the late 1970s topped the charts with "Boogie Nights," "The Groove Line," and the classic romantic ballad "Always and Forever." Johnnie understood my problem in a way no one else could: A 1979 car accident had rendered him quadriplegic. While I was in rehab, he paid me a surprise visit, and I remember seeing him and thinking, *If he can do this, then maybe I can, too.* My spirits rallied for the moment, and I never forgot the tremendous effort he made to come and see me.

I'd known Karen long enough to know that once she made up her mind, there was no stopping her. We'd been together over five years by then, and I thought I knew her so well. But every day she showed more courage, a renewed commitment to me and my rehabilitation. Naturally, at first I'd worried that she would leave me. Instead, time and again she confronted every problem that came our way, even after I'd long since given up. Her positive spirit set a great example for me, although it was one I couldn't always follow.

That day she and my nurse struggled to lift me up out of my chair and gently laid me down in the back of the van. I fell into a deep sleep. Ten hours later, we arrived at Johnnie's house in Dayton, Ohio.

Johnnie is a warm, talkative guy who's quick with a smile and always upbeat. I've never known anyone like him. Despite what had happened to him, he seemed at peace with himself and his situation. Johnnie had continued to write and record his music, and when he showed me around his house, he was especially proud of his home studio. It was designed so that he could use it without help from anyone else. I remember watching him and thinking, *How can he be so happy? And how can I be so damned depressed?*

Over the next few days, we went out a few times; we attended church together, but mostly we talked and laughed and cried.

At one point, Johnnie and I started working on some music in his living room. Johnnie had a drum machine, which I played with a pencil, and we probably could have really come up with something if I hadn't kept falling asleep. Of course, every time I nodded off a little, the drum machine would lock into an infinitely repeating pattern until the sound of everyone laughing woke me up and I'd start again.

Johnnie was the first person who really understood what I was going through. He was a living example of how life after paralysis could be if you decided to make it so. Up until then, it was easy for me to dismiss the well-meaning encouragement of able-bodied doctors, therapists, even Karen and those close to me. What the hell did they know about how I felt and how hard everything was for me? They didn't need someone to help them all the time.

Johnnie, more than anyone I'd met up until then, helped me see around the bend. When Karen and I were leaving, Johnnie and I looked at each other from our chairs and said good-bye. I never wanted to hug a guy as badly as I wanted to hug him. I hope Johnnie knows how much those few days meant to me, and how they changed my life.

In early 1983, I traveled to Miami for surgery. While there, I rented a beautiful house on Biscayne Bay, and Karen threw a fabulous party for my thirty-third birthday. My family and close friends were there, as well as Shep and Danny and my new hero, Elektra Records president Bob Krasnow.

In order to survive, I had to make records. I had to move on with my life, but how? While I knew I could sing, I was keenly aware that my voice was less powerful than it was before. Also, I hadn't yet learned how to fully control it. Bob offered to take a chance on me without ever meeting me. He was a friend of Shep's, a true gentleman, and my champion. Before he committed, though, he asked for a demo tape of my singing. In came Luther Vandross, who had written a song for me—"You're My Choice Tonight (Choose Me)"—and offered to produce the demo. Luther had come a long way in the few years since we'd met; he now had a couple of platinum solo albums under his belt.

There were several state-of-the-art recording studios within a short distance of my home, but the prospect of being seen out in public terrified me. Luther prerecorded the instrumental tracks, then Shep and Danny arranged to bring a state-of-the-art mobile studio to the Chateau. With the ten-wheel black semi containing the studio parked in the circular drive near the front door, the house was wired up, and I was able to record my vocals while sitting in my wheelchair in the foyer! Being a singer himself, Luther understood how my voice had changed and how difficult recording could be for me now. His involvement helped to put me as much at ease as I could ever hope to be.

I didn't have to say what everybody understood: My life depended on having a viable career, and at that moment it was all riding on this five-minute track. Who knows what my life might be like today if the song hadn't come out so beautifully? It's simply unthinkable to me. Hearing the playback reminded me of my first sessions with Gamble and Huff. That was me singing, all right, but I wasn't hearing what I was used to hearing, and that took some getting used to.

"You're My Choice Tonight (Choose Me)" is a catchy, sexy ballad, and what Bob Krasnow heard in it was enough to clinch the deal. Not only did I have a new record label and some hope of a future career, but as executive producer of my records, I now had more control over and more responsibility for my work than ever before. It was everything that I needed then: a challenge, a distraction, a chance. (For contractual reasons too complicated to get into here, my recording a "soundtrack" made it easier for me to switch labels. In order for "You're My Choice Tonight (Choose Me)" to be considered a soundtrack, there had to be a movie to go with it. Once again, Shep to the rescue. After we recorded the single, Shep got into the motion-picture business, producing *Choose Me,* the first of several dozen movies he's made.)

As executive producer, my deal was basically this: Elektra gave me a large sum of money, and I handed them a completed album. Sound simple? I thought so, too. How little I knew. If I'd never fully appreciated the magic of Gamble, Huff, and the whole PIR operation, I certainly would by the time this album was in the can. Until then my concept of recording was that you showed up and sang and sang and sang. I'd never thought about where songs came from, what music publishing was, or what went into finding and hiring musicians and background singers. It had always been enough for me to show up and sing. Cold, hard reality check comin' up! Here's what recording *Love Language*—and every album since—entailed:

Find an experienced producer who understands what I want to achieve, contact music publishers and songwriters for material, plow through a mountain of demo tapes for the eight to twelve perfect songs, hire and schedule musicians, background singers, and studio time. Find the studio with the best sound for each song, then negotiate the cost of studio time. (Obviously, I couldn't record a whole orchestra in my foyer.) And that's just the business side. There's also the art of it all. Analyze each song: How should it be arranged? What instrumental and vocal backing would work best? How long would it take each musician and singer to lay down his or her tracks? Fortunately for me, my producer, Michael Masser, brought a wealth of experience and seven perfect songs, including a couple that were cowritten by my friend Linda Creed. He oversaw hiring musicians, singers, and studios, and arrived on my doorstep with completed instrumental tracks to which I then added my vocals, so it was not as daunting a task as it might have been otherwise.

While I was grateful to Michael and at that point in no position to assume all these responsibilities myself, in the end, the first album cost me far more than I expected it would. That was a serious problem, since my sole income didn't come from making my albums but from what was left of the advance after all the expenses of producing the record. Seeing the final production figures for the first album was a blaring, screaming wake-up call. Beginning with my second

Elektra album, *Workin' It Back,* I handled every aspect of production personally, as difficult, time-consuming, and exhausting as that could be.

Before we began recording, I consulted with Dr. Robert Sataloff. In addition to being a brilliant otolaryngologist, Bob is an accomplished amateur opera singer, so he truly understands the mechanics of singing. For me, the biggest difference in my voice was the lack of power that resulted from not being able to use all the muscles I'd used before to exert pressure on my diaphragm. Bob and I experimented with a homemade contraption: sort of a wide elastic belt that could be tightened to press against the diaphragm whenever I needed a surge of power. It sounded like a good idea, but it was impractical and unpredictable, and we soon gave up on it.

Clearly, I wasn't going to sound like the old Teddy, at least not right away. So I had to critically evaluate my singing the way an artist studies a painting. The accident had muted and washed some colors on the palette, so to speak, and now I had to figure out how to create the same emotional and musical effects without them. I'll give you an example of what I mean: Early on I simply didn't have the power to sing a long, high note with volume. So I had to approach it differently, maybe through how I phrased a line or held a lower note. There were infinite possibilities. As I reacquainted myself with my voice, the years I'd spent singing classics and ballads proved more valuable than a vocal coach. Everything I'd learned from listening to the phrasing and style of pop singers, such as Nat "King" Cole, Tony Bennett, Frank Sinatra, and Marvin Gaye, gave me a head start in finding my new voice.

Fortunately, Michael Masser brought me songs that not only fit my new vocal capabilities but reflected what was going on in my life. The leadoff track, Michael and Cynthia Weil's "In My Time," set the tone, acknowledging the setbacks and triumphs and proclaiming that love endures over all. Originally, this track was intended to be the first single, and we shot a video for it. For years, the buzz in the business was how video would revolutionize the way music was marketed and promoted. I'd been so focused on performing live, I didn't give it too much thought. Besides, a lot of the early videos were unimaginatively staged clips of singers lip-synching to their records.

With my new album nearing completion, I started paying serious attention to the business again. Not long before we shot the video, I happened to catch Bruce Springsteen's video for "Dancing in the Dark" and fell in love with it. Although it was not really a live performance, it was shot like one, and it was one of the few videos I'd seen that depicted a singer's pure joy in performing before an audience, something I now missed so much. I wanted to put across in a video the emotions I used to communicate live onstage. For the foreseeable future at least, this was going to be the only way my fans would see me perform.

The video for "In My Time" was filmed in the gym of my old high school, Thomas Edison. Everything about it was simple and understated, from the bank of colored lights behind me to the "Teddy Who?" I had sewn on my jogging suit. (You can read into that all you want; I still can't say exactly why I did that.) I'd spent so much of the past two years hiding from the world, there was some relief in the opening shots of me, alone in my wheelchair in the dark, empty gym. It seemed to say, "Here I am. This is how I look now. This is who I am." I trusted my fans to accept me, and they did.

We were in the midst of recording the album and still hadn't decided on a title. None of the individual song titles seemed appropriate. And as for variations on my name, PIR had exhausted all those long before.

I happened to be talking to my friend Stevie Wonder about the record, describing the songs, what they sounded like, and why I recorded each one this way or that. It was a conversation between musicians, and Stevie is peerless for his musical insight and creative vision. But I also found talking to Stevie inspiring in a way I didn't appreciate as much before my accident. In addition to everything else we had in common, there was now disability. Only he, Johnnie Wilder, and a few other people could understand the challenge of appearing and sounding confident when in fact you feel vulnerable, even helpless.

"What I want this album to do," I told Stevie, "is to make people see that despite everything that's happened, I've still got a heart, and I want the songs to reflect that."

"You know what, Ted," he mused. "This all sounds like love language."

"Love language! Yeah, that's what it is!" Thank you, Stevie.

Love Language was set for spring 1984 release. We were all ready to go with "In My Time" as the first single, when someone at Elektra decided that since duets were hot, the first single should be "Hold Me." It's a sumptuous Linda Creed–Michael Masser composition that I had recorded with a singer named Tenita Jordan, whom I was producing for Teddy Bear Productions. (I thought then that developing talent through my own label, Top Priority, was a viable option. For many reasons, it didn't work out as planned.) Tenita had toured with me on those dates when Stephanie couldn't join me. I thought she had a lot of potential and that our recording of "Hold Me" was fantastic.

We were just weeks from releasing the album when Clive Davis brought to my attention a new young unknown singer named Whitney Houston. I knew Whitney was Sweet Inspiration Cissy Houston's daughter and Dionne Warwick's cousin; just twenty years old, she'd already made a name for herself as a background vocalist for Chaka Khan and Lou Rawls. Would I be willing to give Whitney a shot at "Hold Me"?

The final decision was mine, and I figured, why not? Whitney recorded her vocals, and when I heard the finished track, I was amazed, astounded, totally knocked out. Tenita's version was wonderful, too, but it was clear that Whitney had a rare quality that transformed "Hold Me" into something truly special. Millions of record buyers agreed. "Hold Me" went to number five on the R&B chart and Top Fifty on the Hot 100, and *Love Language* went gold, after spinning off a second hit single in "You're My Choice Tonight (Choose Me)." The video for that song, which used scenes from the movie, met with some controversy, largely because it contains one very wet, sensual kiss, which was fine with me. I never shunned controversy.

We launched the album with a documentary special on the Cinemax cable network and lavish parties at Lincoln Center Library for the Performing Arts in New York City and at the Franklin Plaza Hotel in Philadelphia. Friends, family, and other stars showered me with congratulations and good wishes. It was wonderful to be out, to be back, to be alive.

There was a time early on when I would have done anything to be able to walk again. My pride, my will, my determination, I was going to harness them all, and one day, by God, I was going to walk again.

Long before I got home from the rehab center, I was besieged with calls and letters from strangers and people close to me claiming they could cure me or they knew someone who could cure me, through all kinds of folk remedies, herbs, high-tech contraptions, and laying on of hands. A lot of it sounded just plain crazy. Those who offered to heal me through prayer or the laying on of hands presented an awkward situation for me, because I have witnessed healers perform miracles. Still, it's my basic nature not to take anything at face value. Especially in light of who I am, I always have to question other people's motives. I refuse to submit to the laying on of hands. I even told Al Green no when he came to visit me in rehab and asked if he and another minister could put their hands on me and pray.

Over the years, this has caused some uncomfortable moments. Once, a woman preacher from out of town approached my mother in church and told her that the Lord had led her to Mom to heal me.

She told Mom that she had no idea who she was, that she was being guided to her. Even though Mom had her suspicions, this preacher made quite a convincing pitch, and I agreed to meet with her. It soon became clear that the only thing this lady preacher wanted to do was relieve me of enough money to build herself a new church. I saw right through her and told her so to her face. As you can perhaps understand, Mom was upset, and I was furious that she'd been deceived by this holy-talkin' charlatan. But this woman was not the first, and she wouldn't be the last.

In the year after I left rehab, there was a remote chance that I might regain some movement and sensation. No one could say for sure. Like most folks in my situation, I grabbed on to this faint hope. The medical establishment had given me all it had to offer. There *had* to be something else, and I was determined to find it. I was desperate and, I see now, gullible. And I paid the price.

A woman friend of mine swore by a herbologist I'll call Dr. N. He spoke of how the medical establishment lacks the knowledge to cure paralysis and the secret power of specific herbs to "regenerate electricity" in my nerve cells. Looking back, it all sounds like bullshit, but I was vulnerable then, and what he said made a lot of sense to me. I must say, Dr. N was extremely persuasive. He had an answer for every question and a cache of arcane knowledge beyond the realm of traditional doctors, and he seemed *so sincere.* He gave me a supply of pills and potions concocted from familiar and exotic herbs along with specific instructions on how and when to take them. I must be patient, he cautioned, but I would see results.

I dutifully followed Dr. N's directions. The herbs didn't seem to exert any effect on my paralysis, but I did begin to feel better. Be patient, he counseled, so I waited. Shortly after I started the therapy, Dr. N suddenly became very difficult to reach by phone. When I did get through to his office, he would return my calls, but before long, he stopped speaking to me personally. Instead an assistant would relay his message to me. Ten thousand dollars later, I realized I'd been had.

Compared to what I've heard other people have spent on quackery, I got off pretty easily. If there's a hell, there ought to be a special table reserved for people who shamelessly exploit the hope of the physically challenged and ill. By the time I finished with Dr. N's "regimen," the window of time during which any improvement might emerge had closed.

The holy grail of research in paralysis is finding a method of regenerating nerve cells so that an injured spinal cord can be "regrown." While there have been hints of progress in that area, it's my understanding that a cure for paralysis is years, if not decades, in the future. During my trips to Miami for treatment, in 1983 and 1984, I also had the opportunity to meet with doctors who were conducting research that involved applying electrical stimulation directly to muscles to do the work of useless, "disconnected" nerves.

In theory, it makes a lot of sense. The first time I traveled to Miami for surgery, in 1983, I underwent a regimen of functional electrical stimulation (FES). I had electrodes placed all over my body, and then the doctors studied how each of my muscles responded to electrical stimulation (which can cause muscles to contract as they would if they were functional). I got myself "wired up" every day for six weeks. The electrical stimulation would contract my muscles in a way that, theoretically, mimicked the way they would have contracted naturally were I not paralyzed. Of course, for someone to walk using FES, they would have to be tethered by countless wires to a computer, so its practical use is extremely limited.

When they asked me to come back down and let them work with me for six months, I said no. Not only would doing that essentially put my life on hold—I wouldn't be earning money and they were not offering to pay my expenses there—but it didn't seem like something that was going to help me move in the direction I wanted to go. I was not willing to become a guinea pig for a doctor or an organization that wanted to use my name. Not everyone sees it the same way, but for me, getting on with my life as a quadriplegic seemed a better use of my time and energy than submitting to experiments.

Of course, I dream of the day when there will be a cure, and if not a full cure through spinal cord regeneration, for example, then perhaps better technology that might make it possible for me to use my hands more effectively than I can now, perhaps even to walk someday. The question isn't whether or not you're "for" a cure or "for" research, but how you can contribute to the cause in a way that is meaningful and comfortable for you. I've met, spoken with, and received mail from thousands of people with disabilities, and I know that simply by being a public figure and continuing to achieve and succeed in the public arena, I have helped others. But this has taken time, and before I could realistically choose how best to help others in my situation, I knew that I had to heal myself first.

There was one incident in Miami that literally changed my life, or at least how I would think about my life from then on. From the moment I woke up in the hospital after the crash, it seemed that all I heard from doctors and other medical people was how difficult my life would be, how striving to lead a long and relatively healthy life would be an uphill battle from then on. Because I had been told that being paralyzed would probably shorten my life considerably, I had no concept what the future held for me, or if I even had one. In my darker moments, the paralysis seemed like a delayed death sentence. I really didn't think I would live very long.

One day in the doctor's waiting room I saw another of his patients, a gorgeous woman in a wheelchair, being pushed by a man who I learned was her boyfriend. Later, my doctor mentioned that she'd been in the chair for ten years.

I looked up. "Ten years?" I exclaimed with surprise. "You mean you can live that long?" It was like a light went on in my head. *There is hope. I can live.* It was such a small thing, and yet it changed my life, or at least how I saw it.

And with my new record deal, I had something else to focus on.

Love Language was on the verge of being released, and I was in a very positive state of mind when I gave *Life* magazine my first in-depth interview since the accident, which was published in spring 1984, to coincide with *Love Language*'s release. It mentioned that I planned to become a "spokesman" for spinal cord injury and paralysis research, and I'm quoted as saying, "The knowledge is there to get people out of chairs. We need the funding."

I truly believed that then, and I was more than willing to help get out the word. Now, more than fifteen years down the road, I can see that I so desperately wanted to believe simply because there was no other choice. Until you've had time—and I mean many years—of living with paralysis, you simply cannot imagine what your life will be like. To blindly embrace optimism is sometimes all that keeps you going. It's easier to picture yourself walking again—as unlikely as that might be—than to imagine yourself in your chair or bed forever. Sometimes false hope is the only kind you can muster.

Since then, I've decided *for myself* that it's best to focus on living to the best of my ability with paralysis. Obviously I would welcome a cure or a new technology. But I can't put the rest of my life on hold waiting for it. And, remember, I saw developments over fifteen years ago that still have yet to fulfill their promise. Doctors and researchers have made some very impressive strides, and I support their work wholeheartedly. But the hard truth of the matter is that for all they've accomplished, the ability to apply any of that knowledge or technology in ways that can improve physically challenged people's lives today remains very limited. I find this especially troubling in view of how much people with disabilities could be helped to live more productive, fulfilling lives if they only had access to the technology and medical interventions that already exist. A seemingly small thing, like having a motorized wheelchair or a personal computer, can literally change a person's life.

Whether I'm in this chair or—God willing—out of it, life will still go on. I know that some people in the disability community may

disagree with me, but I don't believe that because I happen to be famous, I'm obligated to allow organizations to trade on my name. I
constantly field "offers" from researchers and organizations to get involved promoting their work, offers I would never receive if I weren't
already well known.

Overall I was pleased with the *Life* magazine piece. But in it a
doctor who had treated me was quoted as saying that I had agreed
to perform at a benefit concert. I didn't recall making any such
promise, and I felt I was being exploited in the name of the "cause."
It would not be the last time. These experiences, as distressing as
they were, weren't without value, though. They taught me that I'd
have to approach my activism the same way I'd done everything else:
on my own terms.

One of the questions the writer from *Life* had asked me was,
"What did the accident tell you about God?"

"I've gotten a chance to catch up on a lot of praying time," I told
him. "For years I was running. I might have wanted to take some
time to talk with my Creator, but it was always thirty seconds to show
time. Now I'm not busy when He wants to talk with me."

I felt a deep, renewed spiritual connection. I'd proved I could return to my craft and support my family. I'd made a major comeback.
But even that would not be enough to carry me through.

My nurse, Jean, and I flew home from Miami after my stay. Both trips
to Miami had been unmitigated disasters. Between the two trips I'd
endured every conceivable mishap, from being heavily sedated into
a state of oblivion by a doctor who thought I needed to "relax" to
having my specially prepared food stolen from the hospital
refrigerator. The airline mishandled and damaged my wheelchair,
the hospital staff resented my private nurse, and everything, it seemed,
went wrong. On several occasions airline employees would stare idly
as my nurse struggled to help me into or out of a seat by herself. And

the times they did try to lend assistance, I got hurt and was almost dropped. By the time our plane landed in Philadelphia, Jean and I were exhausted. I had never felt so angry.

Karen met me at the airport, she and Jean helped me into the car, then Karen went around to the trunk, where she folded and stowed my chair. *Was this what the rest of my life would be like?* By the time she got back behind the wheel, I was sobbing so hard my body shook.

"Is it always going to be this way? Is it always going to be like this? I can't fuckin' take this!"

Back at home I gave in to everything, it seemed. Because my paralysis makes it impossible to feel hunger or to know when I've eaten enough, I had been eating enormous amounts of food the past two years, and being immobile, I soon had the extra weight to show for it. I'd always loved good food, and eating was one of the few sensory pleasures I could enjoy. Eggs, bacon, grits for breakfast, a full lunch, a full dinner, then a big late-night sandwich. Second helpings, third helpings—hey, keep it coming. When I wasn't eating, I was *thinking* about eating. It was the happiest part of my day, but I was depressed and it was getting out of control.

For years after the accident I was plagued by insomnia. The fact that I could no longer roll over and settle myself into a comfortable position had a lot to do with it. Then there were the dreams. Every night for the next couple of years after I got home from rehab, I could never drift off to sleep without finding myself behind the wheel of the Rolls, heading south on Lincoln Drive, across the intersection at Wissahickon, then—I'd wake up gasping, looking around the room for reassurance that, yes, it was a dream, just a dream. *The* dream.

I was prescribed sleeping pills, which helped, but they never completely banished the dream, which seemed to stalk me, returning night after night until I thought I'd lose my mind. Even when I couldn't sleep, my mind would drift back to that night, that place. If each of us has his own personal hell, this would be mine: reliving the accident over and over again.

I started out taking just one pill a night, but after a while I developed a tolerance to it, so my doctor upped the dosage to the max: two pills. Before long, those didn't work, so I started taking three, the whole time wondering, *Where's this going to end? What's the point?* One day I was so depressed, I said to Karen, "I can't go on like this. Let me just go to sleep and be done with it."

More than anyone, Karen knew how I felt and how futile everyone's efforts to bring me out of my depression had been. "Would you give me all the sleeping pills I needed so I'd never wake up again? Would you do that for me, Karen?" I pleaded.

Karen looked at me with tears streaming down her cheeks. "Teddy, I can't do that for you. You have so much to live for, and I love you."

We cried together. The thought of suicide had crossed my mind before and would several times again. But whenever killing myself seemed like my only choice, I would remember how easily Karen could have done my bidding and the love and the faith that never wavered.

I sought out the help of Dr. Dan Gottlieb, a remarkable psychotherapist who is also quadriplegic.

The first time we met, Dr. Gottlieb asked me point blank: "Why did you come to see me?"

"I feel that you will be able to help me," I replied.

In Dan I discovered not only a wonderful therapist but a good friend. As you can imagine, I didn't hold therapy or therapists in very high regard then. Being disabled, Dan broke through my defenses. He knew enough about disability and depression to recognize after only a few sessions that I was suffering from a deep clinical depression that called for a drastic solution.

"I don't know of anything else that will help you," he said. "I think that maybe we should hold a mock funeral for you."

A mock funeral? It's exactly what it sounds like: Family and friends gather around and act as if they were attending your funeral.

While I sat in my living room with a sheet draped over my face and body, Karen, Danny, Henry, Mom, and other close friends and family dear to me stood and "eulogized" the dead, departed Teddy Pendergrass. I listened as everyone sang "Reach Out and Touch (Somebody's Hand)."

Now, in the made-for-TV version of my life, this moment would have instantaneously turned me around. With tears running down my face, I'd promise to go through the rest of my life with a great big smile. But life ain't that simple. The truth is, I was so mired in depression and so resigned to dying that the mock funeral had little immediate impact on me. The one thing I realized within a few minutes under that sheet was that I didn't want to be dead. I wanted to live. My problem was finding the next step, the step back, away from suicide. I recall very little of what happened that day in terms of who attended and what was said. The most anguished emotional pleas for me not to take my own life meant nothing to me. I was not paralyzed just physically, but emotionally, too. In my heart, I was already dead. Still, I knew this wasn't the way I wanted to go. I wheeled out of the mock funeral believing it had failed.

I didn't realize it at the time, but this symbolic event had planted seeds of hope, seeds I'd recognize only months later, after they began to take root and grow.

So many people helped me through this time, it's impossible to name them all. Two, however, made a dramatic difference in my future. My friend Ronnie Butler took it upon herself to see that I got my high school diploma. Once or twice a week she traveled up from Washington, D.C., to visit and to help me study. She would climb up on my bed and sit beside me, patiently helping me memorize everything I needed to know. She was incredible. I knew one day I'd want to attend college—which I've now begun—and Ronnie's determination, time, and effort made that possible. It was the first thing I accomplished that wasn't something I'd done before. Ronnie's dedication was a blessing to me.

Linda Creed played a very special role in my life as well, and I love her, not only for what she gave to me but for what she had to sacrifice to do so. By the time I came home from rehab, Linda had been battling breast cancer for over five years. She was a courageous woman with incredible spirit, and at a time when she faced so many problems of her own, she gave so much to me. She often came to the Chateau, sometimes with her two little girls, and we'd sit up in my room and talk about all kinds of things, but mostly songwriting. If she felt fatigued, as she often did, she'd crawl up on my bed and lie next to me.

As pleased as I was with *Love Language,* I realized that I was losing a lot of money by not writing my own songs. But where to start? I'd written some lyrics here and there and cowritten a B-side Evelyn Champagne King recorded in the 1970s, but I wasn't certain I had what it took to write songs good enough that I'd want to record them.

Linda gets the total credit for pushing me to try. We would lie in bed and talk about songs: how they were constructed, what worked, what didn't. Linda was a genius, and I couldn't have asked for a better teacher. A few times, she brought along a songwriter named Dennis Matkosky, and Bill Neale, who played guitar, and we started writing three or four songs. One of them, "Let Me Be Closer," appeared on my next album, *Workin' It Back.* (More recently Dennis and I collaborated on "Slow Ride to Heaven" on *You and I.*)

More important, though, Linda could always make me smile and laugh. Even when it was clear that she was losing her battle, she found a way to cheer me on through mine. For this, she will always be special to me, and when I stop to think about how my ability to write songs changed my life, I thank Linda, wherever she is. When she passed in 1986, at just thirty-seven years of age, the world lost a brilliant writer, and I lost a dear friend.

I could sing, I could record, and now I could write songs, too. It felt good to know that there were new challenges I could meet and new ways to express myself and grow artistically. But composing and recording could never replace the experience of performing onstage. For me, that had always been what it was all about. God, how I missed it: the audience's love, the sense of transcendence, the joy—even the panties. It was always about so much more than getting my ego pumped (though that did happen now and again). I missed the immediacy, the intimacy. I felt as if part of me would always be on a stage somewhere, and if I couldn't make it there, I never would be whole. In the three years between the accident and the summer of 1985, I'd suffered more losses than I could count, much less grieve. But this proved one of the hardest to accept.

I knew in my heart that one day I'd perform again. I had no idea when or where, but it had to be right. In the early summer of 1985, Philadelphia was gearing up for the biggest pop-music event of the year, if not the century: Live Aid. The largest, highest-grossing benefit concert ever mounted, Live Aid made history on several fronts. It was initiated by Irish rock star Bob Geldof to raise money for famine relief in Africa. Geldof's first effort for charity had come the year before, when he assembled a group of English music all-stars to record "Do They Know It's Christmas," which in turn inspired an all-star American effort on Michael Jackson and Lionel Richie's "We Are the World." The concert was mounted on two stages an ocean apart—London's 72,000-seat Wembley Stadium and Philly's 90,000-seat John F. Kennedy Stadium—then linked and broadcast live via satellite. Over 1.5 billion people in 160 countries saw the all-day, star-studded show, which included Tina Turner, David Bowie, the Pretenders, Queen, Eddie Kendricks and David Ruffin with Hall and Oates, Bob Dylan, Patti LaBelle, and reunions of Led Zeppelin, Crosby, Stills, Nash, and Young, and the Who, plus many other acts.

Early in the planning of the Philadelphia show, I had been invited to perform. I was flattered and excited to be asked, of course, but I had to face the fact that I hadn't sung live since the accident, and I worried about how people would respond to seeing me perform in my wheelchair. I still wasn't comfortable going out in public because I felt my soul wither under people's stares and well-meaning, pitying glances. Would an audience hear and see *me,* Teddy Pendergrass the singer, or would they see that poor disabled guy who used to be Teddy Pendergrass?

I played out every imaginable scenario, from my being unable to control my chair to missing notes. There was only one way to find out what I could do, how the world saw me, and what my future might hold. I said yes to Live Aid.

Shep worked hard to ensure that my return to performing live would be as comfortable as possible. When he told me I would share the stage with Nick Ashford and Valerie Simpson during their set, I was pleased and relieved. And when I heard we would be singing their "Reach Out and Touch (Somebody's Hand)," I thought, *Perfect!* It was the right message for the event, and the right message for me. I was ready.

Well, almost. Up until the night before the show, I considered backing out. I remember discussing it with the kids, weighing the pros and cons and telling them how I felt. But their decision was unanimous: "Go for it, Dad!" That's all I needed to hear.

Saturday, July 13, 1985, was a scorcher. Although I wasn't scheduled to appear until later in the afternoon, I arrived at JFK Stadium that morning to discover that no one had made provisions for my wheelchair. I was nervous enough as it was, and every time my chair hit a bump, I felt like crying. I couldn't wait to get to my air-conditioned trailer dressing room.

Guess what? The promoters had spent untold millions heading off every possible technical glitch to transmit the show around the globe, but hadn't thought to provide a ramp so that I could get into my trailer.

Sitting there sweltering, I felt tears coming on. "Damn it!" I muttered in despair. One result of my injury is that I can't regulate my body temperature. I simply don't sweat, which can result in my becoming dangerously overheated. For the first of several times that day, I was tempted to go home. Henry, Karen, and other people with me appealed to the organizers, who hurriedly transported me to a makeshift dressing room: a tent with several groaning electric fans to "cool" it down to about eighty-five unbearable degrees. All they did was blow hot air. I wheeled over to Nick and Val's trailer. They came outside and we ran through the song once or twice, and it all fell into place. Then I returned to my tent, where I waited and searched my soul for the old killer instinct. Everyone I saw had encouraging words and told me they believed in me. The question was, Did I?

Santana was just finishing their set, and Nick and Val's band was setting up while the show switched to London for Elton John's set with George Michael's duo Wham! As Henry pushed my chair up the ramp to the stage, I closed my eyes and heard my heart pounding. We stopped in an area that was upstage, out of sight of the audience, where I was fitted with a headset mike. I looked out at the huge crowd and savored the cool, calming breeze, the first I'd felt all day.

After Nick and Val performed a couple of their hits, their band started vamping the introduction, and Nick announced, "We have someone very special to us, and someone we love very much. Mr. Teddy Pendergrass!"

When I heard my name, I almost started singing right there. Rolling out onto the stage in my chair, I might as well have been barreling down the steepest incline of a roller coaster: There was no turning back now. As I approached my mark, the audience rose up like a wave, and cheers of encouragement and love engulfed the stage. Just when it seemed the adulation would die down, it started all over again, and I could hear people screaming, "Yeah! Teddy!" "Come on with it!" "Let's do it!" "We love you!" I stopped my chair and let their love and support wash over me like water. With Nick and Val on either side of me, I began to weep.

"I am truly grateful to be here today," I said. "And I surely feel your love." After a few words about the reason why we were there, I led off the song, "Reach out and touch . . . somebody's hand . . ." as the whole crowd swayed in unison. I could feel where I didn't have the same power, and it did feel strange to be working the stage from a chair. I felt worn out from the heat and self-conscious about the weight I'd gained. But the audience embraced me and let me know none of that mattered to them. I was too occupied with my performance to think or feel much of anything, and before I knew it, the song was ending.

Rolling offstage to a deafening ovation, I felt like a new man. I could do it. Within minutes, I was in the back of a limousine, with the air conditioner blasting and bags of ice packed under my arms and all over my chest to cool me down. I was exhausted. But it was all worth it. For the first time in three years, I allowed myself to dream.

NINE

Now that I know just what I must face,
And see exactly what life can put you through . . .

Those incredible five minutes onstage at Live Aid seemed to say it all, didn't they? I felt reborn and resurrected. *Back.* I'd scaled that mountain I set my sights on back in rehab. The world saw a man at the pinnacle, but where I expected to find a wide, open horizon, other mountains—higher and steeper—surrounded me. For a while, there was no place to go but down.

My future was so uncertain, I thought it best to sell the Chateau. I loved that house (still do, in fact), and I'd sold some other property that allowed me to pay off the balance of my mortgage. I didn't have to leave the mansion, but I wanted to. I needed to make a new start, and despite all that the Chateau once meant to me, my heart just wasn't there anymore. Before the accident, I'd begun to feel that it was more a warehouse than a home. When I first moved in, I would fill the mansion with people, because it was such a showplace. When they left, though, it always felt empty.

Even though it was I who had changed, the house suddenly felt like a different place. Now, being paralyzed, all those things about the house I'd reveled in before—the space, the quiet—terrified me. The whole family seemed always to be gathered in the kitchen, at the opposite end of the house from my bedroom, a distance of about 150 feet—about the length of half a football field. My kids' rooms down the hall might as well have been miles away. Lying in bed, I felt cut off from everyone else. Isolated. Alone. Behind the heavy wooden door and thick plaster walls of my room, I could scream, or fall, or choke and never be heard. So, yeah, it was time to move.

For two years, Karen and I looked everywhere around suburban Philadelphia, Pennsylvania, and New Jersey for a more suitable house, but nothing felt right to us. I knew the kind of house I wanted to live in, but my future was uncertain, and I worried what I could handle over the long run. I'll never forget telling Karen this and her saying, "If we have to live back in North Philadelphia again, we'll be okay."

No matter how attractive the home or the price, once we figured in the costs of constructing ramps, adding an elevator, widening doorways and hallways, modifying kitchen and bathroom fixtures and appliances, and the dozens of other changes we'd have to make, it always seemed like more aggravation than we were willing to take on. The two of us finally decided that the easiest and most logical thing to do was design and build our own home. We found a beautiful piece of property about a mile or so from the mansion and began building a new home for our new life.

The mansion sold almost immediately, and in June construction on the new house began. We spent the six months between selling the mansion and moving into our new home with my mother in her three-bedroom Gladwyne home. All the bedrooms were on the second floor, so I slept in the dining room, which also served as my therapy room, makeshift bathroom, and so on. My bed fit in only one way, so we slept with the air conditioner blowing right on our heads. There was no room for my mat table, so I did my exercises on the bed. It was rough.

Between Karen, me, Teddy, Tisha, and LaDonna (when they were in town), my nurses, the visiting physical therapist, my special bed, the wheelchair—the list goes on and on—quarters got a little tight. It was wonderful being with Mom, but not without a few tense moments, as you can imagine.

There was no room at Mom's for Teddy Bear Productions, so we took some office space nearby. Most days found me either there or in the studio working on my second album for Elektra. Mom, the kids, everyone pitched in to help, but Karen especially rose to the challenge, as usual. Her typical day consisted of driving Teddy to and from school, and stashing my wheelchair in a mini U-Haul trailer and taking me to and from work. In between, she'd check up on the construction of our home-to-be and deal with the seemingly never-ending problems the builders encountered. Then Karen went to work. She was exhausted and remembers this as one of the roughest times. Yet she never lost her spirit or strength. She was simply incredible, and she never let me forget how to laugh.

Because Mom's house wasn't designed to be wheelchair accessible, my friend Ernie built a couple of plywood ramps, including one at the side door, which, because of space considerations, was pitched at a slightly steep incline. It isn't anything an able-bodied person would notice, but in bad weather, it could be a killer. One day I'll never forget, it was pouring rain and Karen tried to push my chair up. Each time, we'd get to the top, and the chair would start rolling backward. Tisha then came out to help. They started pushing me up the ramp again, and—again—a few feet from the porch, the chair started rolling back. Once the chair tilted as if it were going to topple over. I was scared to death, and we were all soaking wet. They carefully guided me back to the bottom, and we started again, only to start slipping back at the top again. It was like a scene out of a cartoon, and after a couple more tries, the three of us were laughing so hard Tisha and Karen didn't have the strength to try again. Finally, we called Teddy out, and the three of them together finally got me into the house. At the time, I was absolutely terrified, but I smile today just thinking about it. In that period, moments like this were too rare.

This was just one of countless times Karen and my family came to my rescue. I can't say enough about Karen. There was nothing she couldn't do to help me. She learned everything, from how to care for me to how to fix the lift on my van. We became self-sufficient. There's never been an emergency or a situation Karen couldn't handle. Here's an example: To get from the ground into my van, I use a lift, an automated rising platform I wheel onto, ride on up to the van door, then wheel off to go into the van. It's like a forklift with a platform. Because my chair weighs nearly 330 pounds and could seriously injure or kill me if I ever fell in it, everyone around me follows strict safety procedures. Whenever I'm on the lift, one person spots me from the front and another spots me from behind, just in case something goes wrong and the chair begins to roll. The lift also has a lip in the outside edge that lowers when the lift is at ground level (so that a chair can wheel off smoothly onto the ground) and rises, to keep the chair from rolling forward, when the lift is being raised. I was on the lift one day when it malfunctioned. Karen, who was bracing the chair from behind, felt the chair move slightly forward. She immediately called to the nurse standing in front of the lift, who pushed against the front of the chair so that it could be maneuvered into a safer position. If that chair had fallen, I might have lost my life, but Karen's vigilance and care saved me.

It was a time of unimaginable stress on so many levels. So much was riding on my next album, tellingly titled *Workin' It Back*. (I always title my albums according to how I feel at that time in my life.) How I'd have loved to park that mobile recording studio in the driveway and hand off some of the production responsibilities, but it was out of the question. If I was going to make it work, I'd have to do everything I possibly could, with the help of my staff.

Recording *Workin' It Back*—and every album since—I began with a vision of the theme, or message, I wanted the album to express and then set to putting it all together like a puzzle, where each "piece" illuminates and completes the bigger picture. My assistant, Sedonia Walker, helped me find the pieces, the songs, by contacting many different music publishers and asking them to send demo tapes of the type of songs I wanted. We then listened to hours of tapes in search of the perfect one. Next we found the producer or coproducer who I felt had the insight and the talent to translate my ideas into a finished track (the "right" ones being those I shared a good rapport with and who were available). Then we hired and scheduled musicians, background singers, and, for each song, studio time in the place that not only had the best sound but was wheelchair accessible to me.

Then it was down to business: For every person involved, my staff and I negotiated contracts covering everything from the cost of studio time to fees and expenses for producers, arrangers, drum programmers, background singers, and musicians. We faced the same problems I face with every album. If you want to use someone who's already signed to another label, you must negotiate with the label. Then you have to keep track of all these credits for the liner notes, as well as those for assistant producers, engineers, second engineers, mixers—even the person who goes out for sandwiches. To give you some idea of what that involves, *Workin' It Back* used four different studios, nine producers, and over a dozen background singers. And that's just the business side.

There's also the art of it all. Analyze each song: How should it be arranged? What instrumental and vocal backing would work best? How long would it take each musician and singer to lay down his or her part? And then the scheduling, making sure everything dovetailed, all within the budget set for each track. Sometimes I felt it would have been easier to plan a mission to the moon.

And then—I almost forgot—I had to sing. Back in the PIR days, I could go into the studio and sing one song for three weeks, if that's what it took. Now, with the meter running, every second in the studio had to be about business, and that created a new kind of pressure. After working this way for nearly fifteen years, I can say it's made me more focused and disciplined in the studio. But at first it was a tough adjustment to make.

The mere thought of going into a recording studio made me extremely anxious. So much of my singing was still trial and error, and

I imagined the pitying looks and forced encouragement I might get as I struggled through take after take. I never wanted people to compare my life before and after and think of me as "poor Teddy." But there was no denying it: My singing was different now; things didn't come as easily as they did before. I'd spent my entire career making records at Sigma, so I naturally gravitated back there. To be singing in the same studio I'd used before the accident brought back memories, of course, but I felt comfortable there. And at that time in my life, that's what mattered most.

In October we released "Never Felt Like Dancin'," a moderate hit, followed by *Workin' It Back* in November. Though it was a little more aggressive than *Love Language*, *Workin'* showed me still, well, workin' it back. Vocally, I'd recovered a lot of my sound, but my confidence wasn't quite there yet. Singing a song, every vocalist has a place he instinctively goes to where everything feels easy and natural. I knew I had that place inside of me, but I couldn't always find it. Most of the songs are lovely and romantic but lack that spark I wanted so badly to rekindle. For the moment, though, it was the best I could do. Learning to accept and work around limitations in so many aspects of my life has been one of my greatest challenges since the accident.

Critics were generous, and the public was still cheering me on. In January 1986, I appeared on the American Music Awards show, where I sang my Top Ten single "Love 4/2" (cowritten by Jimmy Carter with background vocals by Tenita Jordan) and received a standing ovation. Wonderful moments like this were precious reminders of where I'd come from and where I was going. My problem was living with where I was.

It should have been a joyous time. A couple of weeks before Christmas 1985, we'd moved into the new house, which was structurally complete but without the finishing touches that would make it feel more like a home. Although it was significantly smaller than the mansion, it was still a roomy seven thousand square feet, designed to be open and spacious, so that I could get around easily and hear and be heard throughout the house. I couldn't afford to go to town decorating or landscaping. What we moved into wasn't finished in all the details, but the heart was there. We'd built it specifically to provide everything I needed, especially rooms for Mom, Teddy, Tisha, and LaDonna, and space for a home recording studio (which I decided not to build soon after I moved in).

Over the years, we have continued to build and extensively improve our home. When we first moved in, it was a house on a rocky lot that even grass wouldn't grow on. I excavated the entire property, had it landscaped gorgeously, added outdoor walls, gates, a courtyard, a swimming pool, and changing rooms, and I'm still at it. This too was named Chateau d'Amour. Let me explain. If I'd named this house for what it *really* symbolized to me, it would be forever known as the House of Struggle, and that didn't have the right ring.

Though we'd scaled down somewhat, this house cost as much to build as the mansion cost to buy. We moved in certain I would receive a large lump of money, which we were depending on. It didn't come through, and within a month of moving, we were facing the possibility that we'd have to sell this house and move again. How bad was it? I was so strapped for cash that I had to borrow $5,000 from Karen's sister Donna to make the first mortgage payment. And I had to charge $10,000 on my credit card to buy drapes and carpet; when the bill came, I couldn't pay it. I can't begin to express how frightened and desperate I felt then. Yet, somewhere inside, I knew this was a house of love, too.

Obviously, the circumstances surrounding the accident never completely left my mind. I knew that *something* had happened that night when I crossed that intersection before the fateful curve. I felt it in the way the car was handling right before the crash, and every night in my dreams I relived that same sensation of trying to control the car and the panic of realizing it would not respond. I believed that some mechanical malfunction or failure contributed to my accident, and in 1982, after consulting with my attorneys, I filed a lawsuit against Rolls-Royce. The irony of it all was that I'd bought the Rolls in 1980 because I knew that my children would be riding in it, and I wanted the safest car money could buy. I even recall a discussion I had with Teddy, when he was about five years old, telling him why I chose that car and how important his and his sisters' safety was to me.

A few weeks before the accident, I'd been driving on City Line Avenue when the engine suddenly cut out. Although I was able to restart the car about ten minutes later, obviously something was wrong, so I took the car in to be serviced immediately. At the time, I remember thinking it was odd to have this kind of problem in a new Rolls-Royce, but I assumed that whatever it was, the mechanics had corrected it. The night of my accident, the car felt that way again—I knew it. I'm well aware that lots of people have lots of ideas about what went on in my car that night, and I admit that there have been times in my life when I've been irresponsible, even downright stupid. That night on Lincoln Drive wasn't one of them. I sometimes wonder how I would have lived with myself if it had been my fault.

I met with several top attorneys, and I swore to see the lawsuit through, no matter how long it took or what it cost.

Ironically, at a time when I couldn't have felt more dispirited, I learned that I had been chosen to receive the Victory of the Spirit Award from the National Rehabilitation Hospital. I was deeply touched, but it was the proverbial best of times and worst of times. In the weeks before, I'd developed a severe pressure ulcer on my behind. The constant pressure of extended sitting cuts off circulation, which then can lead to the total breakdown of the skin. Untreated, these pressure sores can result in life-threatening infection. For the severest cases, the only treatment is surgically grafting new skin to the spot.

I needed that surgery, and right away. But I also wanted—actually, needed—to be able to travel to Washington, D.C., and attend the ceremonies at the Kennedy Center for the Performing Arts. Understanding how much it meant to me, my personal family doctor, Dr. Brower, agreed that I could go, but only if I sat as little as possible. I called the event's organizers in Washington, and it being Washington, they arranged for a helicopter to fly me there and back.

The helicopter landed on a large piece of cleared empty land near our house. Accompanied by Karen, Teddy, and my male nurse, Skip, I rode in my manual chair from my house to the helicopter, was lifted into the helicopter, lay down on a cot for the flight to Washington, landed at the Kennedy Center, transferred back into my chair to get backstage, lay down there in a bed they had waiting for me, got up to prepare, went out onstage, sang a song, and received my award. Along with actress Ann Jillian, Edward Kennedy Jr., and Senator Bob Dole, I basked in the applause—for a few moments.

Then I rolled backstage, got ready to leave, rolled back out to the helicopter, transferred from my wheelchair again, lay down for the trip back, then transferred back into my chair, went down the street, and was home again. I am told that had I been able to feel pain, it would have been excruciating. Within a few days I entered the hospital, where I underwent surgery to repair my skin (an operation I've had to repeat since then). It was a lot of work and worry, but I made it to that ceremony. I made it.

For the first four years after the accident, I'd been pretty fortunate in terms of avoiding serious complications. Come 1986, my luck ran out big time. I'm not going to lay out my entire medical history for you; it's too painful. Let me just give you an idea. From the time I had corrective surgery after returning home from Washington, D.C., in April 1986 to April of the following year, I practically lived in the hospital.

My independence is so important to me, and I wanted so desperately to go out on my own, I took driving lessons as soon as I could. I purchased a used van that I had modified with special hand controls that I could operate. I cherished the sense of freedom I got from just being able to go anywhere I wanted, whenever I wanted. No waiting, no planning, nothing but get set and go. God, I loved it.

In early July 1986, after a period of bedrest, I was dying to get out. Even though I hadn't fully recovered my strength, against my better judgment I decided to go out, with a nurse along. The controls felt hard and stiff to me, and I could feel that I wasn't as strong. Still, I was driving along well enough until I made a right and couldn't straighten out of the turn. I hit an electric pole and suddenly felt myself growing faint. In the split second before my eyes closed, I saw an ambulance pass us. Thank God, the ambulance attendants saw the van. They turned around and came to my rescue, which very well may have saved my life. The pressure of the seat belt had lacerated my liver, and I was hemorrhaging internally. Had the ambulance crew not spotted my van, I easily could have bled to death. My nurse suffered a few minor injuries, but I underwent emergency surgery to stop the bleeding (I'd lost about five pints), then spent a few days in intensive care. Once I got home, I decided not to drive anymore and asked Henry, who'd stopped working as my driver after I got the van, if he would come back and drive for me again. He agreed.

Initially, I hesitated to tell this story, because I worried people might blame my disability for the accident or conclude that perhaps physically challenged people have no business driving. I'd driven safely for quite a while before this accident, and I admit that the real cause was my impatience to get back behind the wheel before I had the strength.

After two weeks in the hospital, I came home, only to be readmitted in August, for pneumonia. Later that year I began running a high fever of 102 to 103 degrees. My doctor insisted I go to the hospital, but I refused until Tisha and LaDonna came up from Memphis for Christmas. By the time I was hospitalized and the cause of the fever was discovered—osteomyelitis, a serious infection, in my hip joint—it was too late, and my hip joint had to be surgically removed. From that point on, I wouldn't see the outside of the hospital for nearly eight months. In that time, I experienced two bouts of pneumonia and a bleeding ulcer (whose symptoms I didn't feel, of course, so had no idea until it had ruptured and Karen noticed blood running onto the floor), and underwent a second skin graft on my rear end to replace the skin that had been grafted there the year before.

During this time, Karen quit working to spend days with me at the hospital. One day she came into my room to find me shaking and saying only, "Hi, hi, hi!" She found a doctor and said, "You've got to do something! That's not Ted. Something's wrong." They tested my blood-oxygen level and discovered that it was so low, I was on the verge of slipping into a coma. I was immediately put on a respirator. For a while it seemed that I might need a tracheostomy, but thank God I got by without having my throat and windpipe cut open to accommodate the respirator tube (which instead was lodged very uncomfortably down my throat). A tracheostomy would have meant the certain end of my singing career.

Another time, I experienced ICU psychosis, a severe psychological reaction to the ICU environment. I heard people talking to me, saw them on the ceiling, and warned Karen, "They're trying to get in!" For most people, ICU psychosis is temporary, but there are some people who never snap out of it. When I finally came out of it, I was moved to a regular private room, where I suffered a few seizures. In desperation, Karen called some friends, and they prayed over me. The next morning I woke up feeling like a new man.

Mom has been with me during every hospitalization, and between her and Karen watching out for me, I'm in good hands. After a more recent surgery, Karen noticed what, for me, was an alarming change in my behavior. Not only was I talking about how I'd just had breakfast with Bugs Bunny, but I was agreeing with everything everyone said to me. Imagine that. Karen told my doctor, "Something must be wrong. Ted's agreeing with everything. That is not Ted." Suspecting that the cause was the medication I was taking, Karen told the doctor to stop my medication. When he argued that it was saving my life, she replied, "You're saving his life, but he's losing his mind." Two days after the medication was stopped, I was back to normal again.

I could go on and on with these war stories. There were so many times during these years when I thought, *Dying would be so much easier.* Sometimes I'd close my eyes and just wish it could all be over. Forever.

Outside my hospital window, the world kept turning. My attempts to establish my own record label, Top Priority Records, did not pay off as I'd hoped, and while I was hospitalized my longtime assistant Sedonia Walker held down the fort. Unfortunately, after I got home, I realized she also had made some business decisions that I disagreed with, and so we parted company. Soon after that, I closed my office. The lawsuit against Rolls-Royce was dragging on with no end in sight, adding more to the stress of meeting my ever-escalating bills.

I was too much of a realist and knew myself too well to believe that I'd ever truly accept how my life had turned out. Sitting in my wheelchair, I felt cheated, not only by the accident but by the loss of hope as well. They say the Lord giveth, the Lord taketh away, but to me it all looked like a shell game on the street. It was as if some hustler had flashed all the good moments before me for a tantalizing second, then whisked them away. I bet my heart and my soul and my trust in God, and for a while at first I won enough to make me believe in the game. But then everything started coming up empty. Now those first couple of years looked like a con, like somebody had let me win just enough to keep me in the game.

Around this time, I decided to stop playing for hope. There wasn't any, and I wasn't going anywhere, and what I'd once seen as the inspirational force that pushed me forward now looked like one cruel, elaborate joke. Live Aid wasn't about what I could do; now it was about what I couldn't. Johnnie Wilder and Dan Gottlieb weren't examples of who I could be; they were reminders of who I was not. And that productive, fulfilling life with disability I'd heard so much about, *well, where the fuck was that?*

I escaped the only way I could: through my mind. For me, substance abuse was always a package deal. I couldn't smoke cigarettes without drinking, and I couldn't drink with doing some cocaine. Although I'd led a relatively healthy life right after the accident, little by little, the old bad habits started creeping back in. I took up smoking again right after I got home from rehab, even though it compromised my already diminished lung function. (Plus, think of the effort involved—I had to have somebody hold the cigarette to my lips!) Thinkin' I was slick, I'd lie in bed with the ashtray on my chest, praying to God a burning ash didn't fall onto my clothing or my bed.

After we moved into the new house, the pressure became unbearable. Initially I had my "reasons" for doing what I did. But by the time I came out of the hospital in April 1987, all I could think was, *I'm getting out of here,* "here" being reality, my emotions, the truth. I had come to grips with being in the wheelchair, but the rest of my life seemed to be spinning out of control. I couldn't make sense of it all. I started doing cocaine a little bit on the weekend because it helped me escape, and alcohol because it brought me down from the cocaine. Gradually, though, I was doing it more often. Nobody was going to help me purchase that one-way ticket to oblivion, so instead I took the big vacation package, with a vengeance.

How I got the stuff, why people who loved me "let" me have it, I won't say. My life was unbearable, and *I* was unbearable. I wasn't out to get high or have a good time. I was out to *get out*—out of my body, out of my mind, out of my life. Everyone around me, everyone who loved me, kept urging me forward: *You can do it! You can do it!* It was all well-meaning and encouraging, true. But it also put such incredible pressure on me, there were times when I felt like screaming, "I can't do it!" Yet I never let myself do that. I don't think I could have lived with myself if I had said what I truly felt then. Instead, I looked at my life and worried. Worried that I wouldn't be able to support my mother anymore and would have to send her to live with someone else. Worried I wouldn't be able to support my family. Worried that I'd lose the new house.

The alcohol and drugs took me to a place where I could be oblivious *and* powerful, where I didn't know what the nurses were doing to me or how much my kids, Karen, or Mom depended on me. I'd figured out a way to give myself the coke, so nobody had to compromise themselves to help me. I would go into a room and get high. I had to, but I could never let the words that explained why pass my lips. I was sitting in my chair one day, stoned out of my head, cocaine all over the front of my shirt, when Teddy, then about fifteen, came in to see me. He looked me in the eye and without saying a word, he gently brushed the white powder from my shirt. Then he walked out. Somewhere, I'm afraid, he understood.

Of course, eventually I'd come back down to reality. There were periods of clarity and relative stability where the need to be emotionally present in my own life was stronger than the compulsion to escape. My family never gave up on me, and they never stopped loving me, although there were moments when I probably didn't make it too easy.

Little by little, though, things began looking up. In 1987, while I was in the hospital, the suit with Rolls-Royce was settled out of court. Part of me wanted to see it go to court. You can be sure the opposing lawyers looked everywhere they could for evidence that it was me, not the car, that was responsible for the accident. For the most part, I ignored the rumors about the transsexual and the allegations that I'd been high at the time, but I was also amazed at how they seemed to have taken on a life of their own. When we'd initiated the suit, I'd been so hungry for vengeance and vindication, I could taste it. But five years down the road, I knew the publicity and the stress of a protracted trial would drive me deeper into despair, not to mention bankruptcy. I had to make a clean break, get some distance from the accident and get on with my life.

It was also time for Karen and me to move ahead. We'd discussed marriage many times and agreed that when we did marry, it would be for the right reasons. I did need her, and she did feel committed to me, but I'd rather have seen her walk away than marry me more out of obligation than love. We were old enough and wise enough to know we should wait for the right time.

This was it. I proposed by sending Karen roses every day for several days, and finally one with an engagement ring around the stem. She said yes. My lengthy hospitalization postponed the wedding, but once it looked as though I would finally be discharged, Karen started making arrangements. Even though we'd agreed it would be a small ceremony at home in front of family and friends, Karen wanted everything to be perfect. We planned it for Valentine's Day, but that didn't work out. So we chose a date in March, and had napkins with our names and the date printed up. When *that* date had to be canceled, Karen accepted it philosophically, the way she accepted everything else. We used those same napkins on our wedding day, June 20, 1987, as a reminder of the uncertainties our love would face in the coming years.

Having just come out of the hospital, I wasn't up to a big honeymoon trip, so we decided to drive down to Atlantic City for a few days. All my children had been in the wedding, and they decorated our van in the traditional style, with streamers and a "Just Married" sign on the back. A typical boy, JR threw the rice at my face. With Henry driving and my male nurse Skip along, we waved good-bye and took off. Karen and I rode in the back and Henry and Skip up front. All the way to Atlantic City, people drove up alongside us, honked, waved, hollered, and seemed so happy for Karen and me. Sitting in the back, we smiled. It wasn't until we got into town later that day that we realized that people weren't cheering us—they couldn't have been, because they couldn't see us. All they saw were the "happy newlyweds"—those two burly guys sitting up front.

As I look back on this time, my most frightening realization is how easy it can be for a person to give up, say to hell with everything, and lie down to die. It's one of the few things you can actually *do.* It's the end of struggle, of disappointment, of being angry. It's the only option that you always have, and it can be as tempting as a dream. Getting high let me escape not only my pain but also the pull of total surrender. It was a third option. While it threatened to destroy my life, in a strange way it also saved me. I had to be able to get up again, someday. Just not today.

Oddly enough, it was during these dark years that I found myself again artistically. I didn't write any of its songs, yet my album *Joy* expressed those aspects of my life, my faith, and my belief in love that I knew survived. Dedicated to Karen, *Joy* was, for me, the real comeback.

I discovered another recording facility, Kajem Studios, a little closer to home. When we arrived on that first winter day, I took one look at the two steep flights of steps leading to the front door and just about turned around and headed home. Henry had scouted out the place beforehand, so I knew I'd have to be carried in my manual chair up the steps. The thought of it scared me beyond words, but I went ahead with it; that's how badly I wanted to record again. With my wheelchair facing backward, Henry pulled me up the steps while another guy lifted the chair from the front. With the chair swaying, and me tilted back a little, I looked up at the sky and just prayed to God nobody slipped. Once we were inside, it was up another short flight of stairs to the studio. Then, when we were done working, it was back down, which was equally frightening. It would be bad enough to be dropped, but knowing I couldn't even lift my arms to break my fall terrified me. Until my accident, I would have bounded up those stairs and never once thought about the obstacle they posed for someone in a wheelchair. Fortunately, the studio owners thought enough of me that they soon installed an elevator and a ramp.

Joy took more than a year to record and involved several different production teams, including Reggie and Vincent Calloway, but it proved well worth the wait. The title track from the Grammy-nominated album was my first number-one R&B single since "Close the Door" exactly a decade before, followed later that summer by the number-three hit "2 A.M." (written by James Carter) and "Love Is the Power." I believe the videos for "Joy" and "2 A.M." broke new ground by showing a physically challenged person—yours truly—as the object of romantic, erotic interest.

By the end of summer, *Joy* had been certified gold, sparking the most media coverage since the accident. Although I'd never paid much attention to what critics had to say, the unanimous praise for *Joy* truly touched me. It's one thing to feel that you've hit on the right thing, but to have the world confirm it for you makes it especially sweet. The first time I heard the title track, I knew it would be a hit.

While the music press concentrated on my music, the general media was more interested in—"obsessed with" might be a better description—my injury. I welcomed any opportunity to increase public awareness about the plight of the physically challenged and to let the world know that I was still here. I agreed to talk to the press because I felt I had a positive message to share. But, as I discovered, some interviewers took this opportunity to expose and exploit my vulnerability. Some parts of my interviews with Bryant Gumbel and Barbara Walters made me feel as if I were on trial. Because *Today* airs live and Gumbel has a reputation as a tough, overbearing interviewer, when I arrived at the studio that morning, I requested and received a list of the questions I would be asked. I wanted to be prepared. In the first minute of the interview, I was caught off guard when Gumbel began asking completely different questions. I don't recall every word that was said, but his point seemed to be, "What makes you think you can still do this?" Considering all that I'd been through and the fact that I was there to promote and celebrate the success of *Joy*, Gumbel's provocative approach struck me as inappropriate and insensitive. I rolled out of the studio that day with the feeling I'd been kicked to the curb on national television.

Anyone who saw Barbara Walters's Thanksgiving 1988 *20/20* profile would think she thought the world of me. But off camera, while walking with me outside my beautiful new home, she asked abruptly, "So, are you broke?" I didn't understand why she asked that or what she was getting at. Later, when she asked about my sex life, I struggled to be good-natured and honest but general in my answers. But I couldn't help wondering, *Why would anyone think I would answer a question like that?* Even though I have a sex-symbol image, my private sex life had been private before the accident. Did the wheelchair really change that? And why? Just because people wanted to know?

In May I testified before the Senate Labor and Human Resources Subcommittee on the Handicapped about how available technology can transform lives. I spoke at length about how my use of MIDI (musical instrument digital interface) and an array of other new technologies freed me to "play" any instrument and compose and record music using my personal computer. With MIDI I can write and record a demo, and with the push of a key change the tempo, alter the instrumentation, rearrange notes—you name it. To give you an idea of what a big deal this is, just a few years before, I'd have had to hire a studio, arrangers, producers, and musicians, at a cost of tens of thousands of dollars, to accomplish the same thing. In the years since I testified, technology has evolved at an astounding pace. I've found that for me, working with a partner who can jot down my thoughts or work it out on a piano as ideas come is most comfortable. Technology is wonderful, believe me, but nothing is more conducive to reaching that magical state of creative flow than two people sitting in a room bouncing ideas off each other. If I didn't have the luxury of being able to work with my partners in person, I'd be using MIDI more than I do. For the physically challenged, it all comes down to having options.

I arrived on Capitol Hill with a message to deliver. Even though I had memorized a speech (written with the help of John Hartman, who worked for Shep), I was damn nervous beforehand. This wasn't my usual audience. When I finished, committee chairman Senator Tom Harkin led the gallery in applauding me. I later discovered that this was a break with congressional tradition, which made me appreciate the gesture even more.

The success of *Joy* didn't solve all of my problems, but it certainly gave me a lift that carried through on 1990's *Truly Blessed,* an album that is special to me for other reasons. In contrast to that wild thirtieth-birthday party in New York City, the big four-oh was relaxed and easy, a time of introspection. Even with all that was wrong about my life, I couldn't deny that so much was right.

When it was time to start work on the follow-up to *Joy,* I kept hearing the phrase "truly blessed" in my head. For me, work on an album doesn't really begin until I have that first song, one that sets the tone for everything else. There was a song inside me, but I couldn't hear it clearly yet. I wanted to express how I felt then, where I'd been and where I was going. And without shoving any particular religious philosophy down anyone's throat, I also wanted to praise and celebrate my relationship with the Lord and thank Him for all the blessings that He'd bestowed upon me from birth. The challenge for me was to write honestly of my life in a way that would inspire hope rather than pity. As the song began taking shape, I knew I wasn't writing a smash hit for radio, and that was okay. It had to be right, no matter what it took. I called in my good friend and collaborator Gabriel Hardeman, a songwriter who's written in almost every genre but has a particular affinity for gospel. Four or five months after I started hearing the words "truly blessed," I completed "Truly Blessed." With the help of gospel singer-songwriter-producer-arranger John Kee and backing from his New Life Community Choir, the finished track captured the spirit I first discovered in church as a child, swept up in a gale of glad tidings and joyful voices.

The rest of the album flowed after that. I cowrote four of the eleven songs with Terry Price (whom I'd known from our days at PIR), including my third number-one single, "It Should've Been You." My cover of the Bee Gees' "How Can You Mend a Broken Heart" (which I arranged) was nominated for a Grammy Award that year, and the album also included the singles "I Find Everything in You" (another Jimmy Carter tune) and "Glad to Be Alive," a duet with Lisa Fisher, a gifted background singer.

Truly Blessed proved to be a prescient title. Shortly after its release, I received one of the greatest honors of my life at the Soul Train Music Awards in Los Angeles. Knowing the audience was filled with other singers and musicians, I was more than a little nervous. I rolled out onstage, ready to begin singing "Make It with You," when everyone rose up in applause. I'd expected to be welcomed, but nothing like this, and it was heartening to look out and see it wasn't just the older, established artists I came up with back in the day. A whole new generation was up and cheering me, too. I remember seeing LL Cool J smiling at me, and the next night I joked to Arsenio Hall on his TV show about how much that meant, since the new guys like LL never seemed to smile at *anybody!*

I'd promised myself that for my fortieth birthday I would give up alcohol, cocaine, and cigarettes. I guess it was a combination of having a clearer sense of myself and my direction, plus being disappointed in myself for letting things get out of hand. I finally began to fully believe what I'd known intellectually for a long time:

Living a long, healthy, productive life would be an uphill struggle for me. I had to begin making it easier for myself instead of harder. While I still believe those temporary excursions from reality served a purpose, I always returned to the same place I started. Now that I felt stronger, the need to be here now in every way prevailed over the desire to escape. I was on the verge of becoming a grandfather, and no grandchild of mine was going to grow up seeing Granddad with a nose full of white powder. My life had to be about something else: I had to find a way to reclaim my ambition so that I could resume being productive and successful—in other words, *me.*

There were lots of reasons, but mainly I was fed up. As you'll often hear former substance abusers say, I got sick and tired of being sick and tired. But it was more than that. I looked in the mirror and asked myself, "What's it gonna be? The drugs or me?" I knew what I needed to do, and one day in the summer of 1991 I stopped everything cold turkey. No twelve-step program, no drug house, nothing—cold turkey, and it was done. I kept telling myself, "Teddy, you're bigger than all this, you're better than this," and I believed it. Karen helped me by quitting smoking a little before I did. I know it's rarely that easy for most folks, but except for the occasional glass of wine with dinner and a few beers in the summertime, I'm clean.

In 1993 I released *A Little More Magic,* which garnered another Grammy nomination—my third since the accident—for "Voodoo" and spun off hit singles in the title track and "Believe in Love." I was especially proud of the socially oriented "Can't Help Nobody," a duet with Patti LaBelle, which we later performed on *The Tonight Show.* I used to think it was hard following Patti when she opened for me; singing beside her, man, you've got to be ready! Another track, "My Father's Child," is a spiritual song that is a companion piece to "Truly Blessed."

Having "Voodoo" nominated for a Grammy was especially sweet, since the song was written for me by Gerald Levert, son of the O'Jays' Eddie Levert and an accomplished singer-songwriter-producer in his own right. Eddie and I went way, way, way (that's far enough!) back, and I'd been Uncle Teddy to Gerald and his brother Sean since they were little guys.

In March 1994 I attended the Grammy Awards ceremony at Radio City Music Hall in New York City. The Grammys being the Grammys, the nomination alone is something to be proud of. But I wanted to win, too. "Voodoo" was my sixth nomination, and, having had a song nominated from each of my last three albums, I had some momentum going. Maybe this would be my year. Baby, I was ready. I designed, and my haberdasher, Charlie Marotta, instructed his tailor to whip up, an elegant burgundy velvet jacket with black quilted lapels and a brocade vest that were the epitome of sharp. And that's not just my opinion. As we were taking our places in the audience before the show, my good friend Aretha Franklin came over to me, looked me up and down, and proclaimed, "God damn, boy! You're clean!"

No matter how long I'm in this wheelchair, it's impossible to venture out into the world and be completely at ease, because being paralyzed affects so many personal bodily functions. Over time, you learn to deal with the adjustments you have to make, and even though I insist that whoever's helping me check and recheck everything, in the back of my mind, I'm always conscious that something could go wrong. Just the fear of embarrassment is enough to keep some people in their beds or locked up in their homes forever. Any physically challenged person who has ever suffered an embarrassing accident can easily understand why.

Obviously I couldn't walk up the stairs from the floor to the Radio City stage. So the plan was that about ten minutes before the nominees in my category were to be announced, I would be accompanied to the backstage area to wait in the wings. This way, if I did win, I could easily roll out onto the great stage to receive my award.

Only a few minutes before I was to go backstage, I felt myself urinating and instinctively glanced down, as I always do. You can imagine my horror when I saw that the front of my pants was wet. *Oh, my God,* I thought, *what am I gonna do now?* Wherever I go, I'm always prepared for any emergency, and I had a duplicate pair of pants with me. It was a problem I could have solved if I'd had time to get to where I could change, but I couldn't. I was on the verge of tears, trying to figure out how I could make it to the bathroom quickly and get back in time, when I heard someone say, "Ted, it's time to get in position for the announcement."

Luckily, my pants and my seat cushion were black, and because I was seated, my problem wasn't immediately noticeable. But dammit! I knew I was sitting on a wet cushion, in wet pants. During what should have been a thrilling moment, I was mad as hell. *The only thing that's gonna make this fuckin' situation worthwhile,* I thought to myself, *is winning.* But the award went to Ray Charles and I breathed a sigh of relief, though I was extremely let down. Learning not to sweat the small stuff is crucial, but it's not always as simple as that.

It isn't easy for me to tell you a story like this. But I think it's important for people to realize that physical disability goes far beyond what you can no longer do. There are difficult moments, but you reach a point one day where the details of your disability can be taken in stride. You can lose yourself in the moment—whether it's having a fabulous meal out, or a romantic evening, or taking a spin on an amusement park ride—because you do learn how to prevent and solve problems. It does get easier.

One reason I throw my support behind projects and organizations that focus on empowering physically challenged people is that I've seen how crucial to my survival that's been. In the beginning, when you first realize that you are physically challenged, your worldview shifts from what you can do to what you cannot. Every change in your life happens because of what you cannot do, and before you know it, you're defining your environment, your life, even yourself in those terms. Do it too long, and you end up disabling your spirit and your will. I know.

After I got over mourning the many things I could no longer do, I took control of whatever I could still do. For me, the "big" accomplishments were in regaining control of my life: being able to sing, write songs and produce my own records, run my various entertainment and non-entertainment business ventures. But, as I learned after a few years of living in this wheelchair, sometimes the bigger accomplishments inadvertently underscore the loss of those "little" things. To sing and receive a standing ovation from thousands of people, then come home and have to ask someone else to get you a glass of water, tarnishes even the sweetest triumph. After all, there are moments when you'd give everything—including the standing ovation—to be able to walk to the sink and fill your own glass.

Everyone in this situation finds his or her own path. At least I hope so. For me, it's wonderful beyond description to be able to wheel myself into my combination music room and office, close the door, and run my business without help from anyone. Thanks to my personal computer and the Internet, I can compose music, write all of my own correspondence, and stay on top of my finances, not to mention research my college term papers. I have a wireless phone system with a headset receiver and a dialing pad that fits on my lap desk, so I can make and receive calls without any help. Because I have some limited use of my hands and arms, I can turn pages and read a book; operate my radio, audio system, and television; use the computer; feed myself; and do dozens of other things that remind me that I haven't lost everything.

When I began recording, artists routinely released an album a year. Now it's not uncommon for two, three, or more years to pass between releases. Realistically, there wasn't going to be a return to the concert trail anytime soon. Music was so vital to my life, but it wasn't my whole life. Before the accident, I was the type of person who immersed himself in work, to the point that I couldn't wait for vacations to end. It took about ten years after the accident for me to start feeling that way again, except now I expanded my efforts beyond my own music.

Of all the projects I involved myself in, the two closest to my heart had roots back in my North Philadelphia childhood. In 1994 I founded the Pendergrass Institute for Musical and Performing Arts, a nonprofit organization to give young people an alternative to the streets. An outgrowth of the Institute was the Teddy Pendergrass All-Star Community Choir of Philadelphia, made up of sixty-five exceptionally gifted teenage boys and girls between the ages of thirteen and eighteen. It was an ethnically diverse group—which I felt perfectly represented the City of Brotherly Love—and the choir's repertoire was equally wide-ranging, including pop, jazz, classical, R&B, you name it. My dream was to have the choir perform across the nation, even around the world, a shining example of what people from all walks of life, all backgrounds, could achieve by working together.

I wanted to create something that would endure for many years to come, and we got off to a fabulous start with a sold-out benefit concert at the 2,500-seat Valley Forge Music Fair in 1995. The Music Fair's owners generously donated the venue for the night, and all the stars—Chubby Checker, Ben Vereen, and Sean and Gerald Levert—donated their time. Being onstage with a choir brought me back to my childhood, as did the sight of Chubby singing (and doing) "The Twist." I joined the choir for "Truly Blessed" and Chubby, Sean, Gerald, and Ben joined us all for Kirk Franklin's "The Reason Why We Sing." Believe me, I got teary-eyed more than once that night. When the choir presented me with a plaque in appreciation of all I'd done, I felt humble and grateful.

The second project I undertook was even more ambitious: the revival of the Uptown Theater. The venue had closed in 1978, and since then several groups had tried to raise money to restore it. A host of causes, ranging from economic deterioration to political ambivalence, had sent my old neighborhood spiraling into decline, but other arts-based renovation projects promised to make North Broad Street a destination for tourists and a source of economic revival. Returning the Uptown to its former glory wasn't going to be enough, though. Our plan was to transform it into a complete, multipurpose, state-of-the-art entertainment complex that included a theater for live shows, and recording and broadcasting facilities, among other things. The renovation plans encompassed the entire 2200 block on the west side of North Broad and called for creating new spaces for restaurants and retail stores.

It was an ambitious plan, and I accepted that it would be years before I moved into my top-floor executive office in the new complex. But it was also a race against the clock, because by the time I formed my partnership and announced my intentions, the Uptown had been closed for a year, the roof was falling in, and over 50,000 gallons of water had flooded the basement under the stage. Structurally speaking, for the Uptown, it was now or never.

Going into it, I knew I'd have to wear several new hats: fundraiser, politician, diplomat, urban planner, architect, cheerleader. I also understood that it would take time and hard work and would be an uphill battle all the way. What I didn't figure on was the slippery slope of political interests, shaky funding, and bureaucratic bullshit that sent the project sliding back down ten feet for every foot closer we got to the top. After we failed to match through private donations a crucial $10 million grant from the state (which Pennsylvania State Representative Dwight Evans was instrumental in our obtaining), I had to let this dream go. And though it didn't become what I'd hoped it would, the whole experience was a great education for me. No matter what I do, no matter what the outcome, I never regret trying.

I was looking forward to starting my next album. I'd reached the point where the details of executive producing that had been so overwhelming to me before had become almost routine. In *Joy, Truly*

Blessed, and *A Little More Magic,* I felt that I'd built a strong foundation from which to grow creatively and commercially. My first Elektra album, *Love Language,* was on the verge of going platinum. I don't want to appear immodest, but the fact is, my career had grown stronger. The entire *Joy* album and a track on each of the two next albums were nominated for Grammys; among my dozen-plus charting singles were two R&B number ones—"Joy" and "It Should've Been You"—and three Top Twenties—"2 A.M.," "Believe in Love," and "A Little More Magic." Times had changed (as reflected in *Billboard*'s ever-multiplying chart categories), and I'd changed, too, as reflected in my getting plenty of airplay on both R&B and adult contemporary stations. I'd found my position; now was the time to consolidate it and keep moving up. It had been nearly a dozen years and several million records sold since Bob Krasnow had signed me to Elektra. My relationship with my label was solid and secure.

When I heard that Krasnow was leaving the label, in 1994, I was sorry to see him go. Upon hearing that he would be replaced by Sylvia Rhone, I sensed that I would be in very good hands. Not only is Rhone the first woman in history to head a major record label, I was proud to know she's a black woman. Sylvia brought the benefit of her extensive experience in the trenches of record promotion and a strong reputation for the R&B and rap acts she'd championed at previous labels. Considering where I was and where I wanted to go careerwise, Sylvia's taking over Elektra seemed like a gift.

I had already begun working with my songwriting partners, mainly Jim Salamone, on songs for my next album and had a few demoed on cassette tape. Sylvia called, introduced herself, and agreed to come to my home so that we could get to know each other and she could hear what I was doing.

The day she came to my home, Sylvia and I spent a lot of time together, and after I played her the demos I'd done, she said, "Those are great! I want you to do those songs for the album." With Sylvia sitting with me, I phoned Jim, put him on the speaker phone, and she

repeated to him what she told me. I took this conversation to con-
stitute the record company's approval that I needed to proceed with
recording these tracks. I went ahead and spent hundreds of thousands
of dollars and many months' hard work recording what would be my
next album.

Another reason I proceeded with such confidence is that Sylvia
and I also discussed a concept for a second album, one involving
several producers. I was very excited about this, because it indicated
that she was developing a long-term strategy.

Then things got confusing. Despite all her enthusiasm for this
album, we never got a release date, and Sylvia became less available
to me. I began to lose heart, then months later Sylvia surprised me
by inviting me and my comanager, Ed Gerrard (who works with
Danny and Shep), to a meeting in New York City with her and the
Elektra staff. There she laid out plans for the next album after the one
we were waiting to release. She had gone so far as to select songs and
match them to specific big-name producers. I left New York feeling
relieved, certain that the past months of uncertainty were just a fluke,
that everything was going to be all right.

Then, out of the blue, Danny called and told me that Sylvia had
informed him that Elektra was dropping my contract. *What?* I
couldn't believe what I was hearing. I mean, I heard the words, but
they didn't make sense. To say I was furious, heartbroken, devastated—well, maybe that covers about 10 percent of it. I was totally
crushed. I felt that Sylvia and I were partners—as much as an artist
and a label chief could be. I could almost have dealt with being
dropped if Sylvia had shown me the basic respect of calling me to explain the decision. I'm a big boy. I understand that business is business, that she may have been under pressure to move the label in a
new direction. But there's business and then there's trust. I'd opened
my heart to her, trusted her as a friend. That was my mistake. After
all these years in this business, I should have known better.

For many days afterward, I sat alone, depressed in a way I'd never been before, and considering everything I'd been through, that's saying something. For an artist, the canceling of a recording contract is like the canceling of his livelihood. To me, this wasn't just Sylvia Rhone saying she didn't want me at Elektra. It was the whole industry saying, "You've had your ride, Teddy, baby. Time's up! Move over and let somebody else in." And no matter what was said or what other possible excuses I ran through my mind, I couldn't stop thinking, *It's this damned wheelchair. They think I can't do it anymore.* I wasn't just depressed; I was in mourning for a career that I believed had died. Or, more accurately, had been murdered in cold blood.

Then what happened? My head was ready to give in, but my heart just wouldn't get with that program. One day, I snapped to and started thinking, *My time is not over! I'm not a has-been. I refuse to quit.* In times like these, anger can be a very constructive defense. I wrote Sylvia a letter telling her exactly what I thought of her. She called me to "explain," but there really wasn't anything to say. Instead of feeling sorry for myself, I decided I had two words for the Sylvia Rhones of the world, and they are not "happy birthday." I was heartened by the interest expressed by several competing labels, and I was pleased to find a new home, with another label.

I wanted to prove myself onstage; now the question was, How? My managers and I had been fielding all kinds of offers for everything from limited concert tours to roles in Broadway shows (including *Grease*). They were all attractive and, needless to say, challenging, but something always made me hold back. In late 1995, we were in the midst of planning a limited-engagement tour. I'd hired the band, made up my set list, worked out the staging (I had to pay particular attention to planning where I would take breaks to rest, how I would use the wheelchair onstage, and so on), and was on the verge of actually committing to some dates. Looking back, I can see that I was waiting for something. I just didn't know then what it was.

Then, Shep and Danny passed on to me the offer I could not refuse: a role in the twentieth-anniversary revival of Vinnette Carroll's legendary gospel musical *Your Arms Too Short to Box with God*. When I looked at everything this role offered me, there was no denying that this was a blessing in every sense. I felt as if He looked down and said, "Teddy, you think you're doing this, but I'll give you something better!" And He did. The story of Jesus' last week, his crucifixion, and his resurrection, *Your Arms Too Short* celebrated and honored the spirituality and the Spirit who'd saved me so many times. My good friend Stephanie Mills had already agreed to star in the show, and the prospect of returning to the stage with someone I felt so comfortable working with was another major, major plus. And toward the end of the tour, gospel star BeBe Winans was added to the cast. After I met with playwright Vinnette Carroll, she agreed to write a new role for me, that of an unnamed Spirit. The play would open with me alone singing "Truly Blessed." Perfect.

What could possibly stop me? In a word, logistics. The national tour, set to begin in Chicago in late February, would hit twenty more cities before ending in New York in late June. Reviewing the rigorous schedule—eight shows over six days a week (meaning two shows Saturdays and Sundays), one day a week for travel, five weeks on and one week off, and a few one-nighters and three- or four-day engagements thrown in with no full day for travel between them—I almost said, "Forget it." I'd never done anything like this, and I knew what a project traveling to do a single television appearance could be. But in the preliminary planning stages of my own tour, I'd already begun working through some of the details. To increase my stamina, I'd spent several months working out in a gym, so physically I was up to the challenge.

My staff and I had learned a lot about travel through trial and error, and the secret to success is to plan for disaster. We knew how to locate the special equipment and services I'd need in every city: hospital beds and medical equipment, specially equipped wheelchair-accessible vans, doctors I could call in an emergency, and medical supply companies that could immediately service my particular type of power chair, if necessary. My nurses and my friend Henry had to rearrange their own lives so that they would be free to travel with me. We made sure that every commercial flight I took was direct and that the airline knew how to handle me and my wheelchair. I traveled with two, and the one I didn't travel with had to be specially packed to travel via truck with the other equipment for the show. Everything was set.

I said good-bye to Karen on Valentine's Day, 1996, and left to begin rehearsals in Springfield, Massachusetts. I felt I had left with a lot of love. I had so many things to worry about—my performance, the "performance" of my wheelchair (which I once accidentally turned off without realizing it, complicating my "exit")—so, so much. I had to learn how to hit my marks onstage in the wheelchair and maneuver without having it detract from my performance. That could involve wheeling in reverse without looking back, for example. This gave the term *stage choreography* a whole new meaning. At one point during midsong, I had to execute a complicated maneuver in my wheelchair that—if all went smoothly—brought me within eight inches of the edge of the stage. Everywhere we played, a six- to eight-inch-tall lip was installed at the stage's edge just in case I overshot my mark. That possibility always crossed my mind, but a real performer can never allow something like that to interfere. Thank God, it never happened. I admit, in the back of my mind, I held on to the irrational belief that because this was a play about faith, He wouldn't let me roll off *this* stage.

But what weighed on me most heavily was the question, Will people accept me singing from a wheelchair? It was one thing to take that chance for a few minutes at Live Aid, but this was the real test. Sure, I could sing, but could I still cast that spell? Could I still transport my audience? In short, did I still have *it?*

After a few weeks of rehearsals and some previews, we opened in Chicago on February 27. The first time I rolled out and sang "Truly Blessed," it was more incredible than I ever could have imagined.

Though I was singing about the spirit rather than the flesh, I could see in the audience's faces the same passionate enthusiasm I'd seen before. It was twenty years later, and while there were many younger women there, I could spot the fans who had been with me from the start. They came out in more modest attire, perhaps with a husband and a kid or two in tow. But as I sang and heard and saw them respond to me, I thought, *I know these women.* I'd grown up, and they'd grown up with me. And though my song spoke for me, I felt that it spoke for everyone there. None of us gets through this life untouched by pain, disappointment, or tragedy. Every night, to me, was like the best welcome-home party anyone could ask for, a reunion. And I was home. So many of my friends came out to see me, but the night I performed in Cincinnati knowing my friend Johnnie Wilder was in the audience felt extra special. He still tours, and I see him whenever I can. Nobody else understands the experience like we do, that's for sure.

Of course, the tour was not without glitches, and we had to overcome everything from my wheelchair breaking down to a nurse quitting in midtour without notice. In several cities special dressing rooms had to be built for me just offstage, since the regular dressing-room areas could not be made wheelchair accessible. It could be nerve-racking at times, but every problem had a solution, and we kept right on going.

Probably my lowest moment on the tour came in Detroit, the second-to-last stop. I've always believed that celebrities are entitled to privacy, even when they're in public. Being in the wheelchair now, I sometimes feel "trapped," unable to escape unwanted attention. Once a few years earlier I was rolling through a mall near my home when an eager fan grabbed my arm while I was driving my chair, causing me to spin around and nearly tip over. That was a scare. But nothing before came close to what I experienced in Detroit.

It was a high time in the tour, and I was feeling so good. We'd just finished a week in Philadelphia at the Merriam Theater. Interestingly, the Merriam used to be called the Shubert, and it was the last stage I'd performed on before the accident. (Coincidentally, Stephanie had opened for me that night.) The response from my hometown was incredible, and although I have so much farther to go on my journey, one circle had been completed.

With only my nurse accompanying me, in Detroit I ventured out to a local mall. I was shopping, but when I was approached by several polite, considerate fans, I stopped to chat. The crowd around me kept growing, so I tried to keep the exchanges short and sweet. I was talking to someone when one particular woman said hi.

"Hi," I replied, then turned my attention back to the first person.

"Well, I've got my mother here with me, and I just wanted to—" the woman said loudly.

I stopped, looked up, and as nicely as I could, replied, "Excuse me. I can't talk to everyone at the same time, okay?"

The woman shot me a dirty look and marched off. I thought that was the end of it.

About an hour or so later, I was wheeling toward the exit when the woman suddenly ran up alongside my nurse and me. "So, you couldn't talk to *me!*" she shouted. "Or talk to my mother. You were *too busy* talking to some other—"

"Let's get out of here," I said to my nurse.

People were stopping and staring at me. I glanced around anxiously for a security guard, or anyone who could help, but I saw no one. I was trapped.

"*Well,* Mr. Teddy Pendergrass"—the woman was now screaming at the top of her lungs—"if it wasn't for people like me, you'd be nothin'! I bought your damn records! I made you!"

Hard as it was, I didn't respond. I just kept moving. This woman had attracted so much attention, the whole mall was frozen in an eerie silence. All I wanted to do was get away. I didn't even look in her direction, which only seemed to enrage her more. Then she said it:

"Why, you crippled motherfucker, you! Who the fuck do you think you are?"

I stopped, turned around in my chair, and stared at her. It was one of the most painful moments of my life. A security guard finally appeared and told the woman she was out of line, but it was too late. The damage was done; the cruel words had pierced my soul. If I could have gotten up out of that chair, I might have killed her. Instead I rode back to the hotel, wishing I could cry.

I know what you're thinking: *But, Teddy, it was just the ranting of some nutty fan. Celebrities endure this all the time.* Maybe. But sitting in my dressing room, I seriously considered not going on, not that night, maybe not ever. To be spoken to as if you're less than human is devastating. *This is why I didn't go out for so many months,* I thought to myself. *This is the reaction I struggled so hard to avoid. This is what I feared.* You hope that people won't act that way, but you know there will always be a few, and you never know who they are until it's too late. I'd like to forget that happened, but I know I never can.

There were times during the tour when I was so exhausted, I'd find myself wondering, *What the hell was I thinking?* But every night the love of the audience kept bringing me back, reminding me that I had a dream, a place to get to, a message to deliver. Every night, they applauded and called out my name. Every night, they told me that the wheelchair didn't matter. Every night, the part of me that seemed to be missing all these years, the part I feared I'd lost forever, shone. In their acceptance, the audience gave me a precious gift that will continue to inspire me until the day I die. They confirmed my dream, rewarded my faith, erased my doubts. Two little words hardly seem enough to say all that I feel about that tour, but I say them with all my heart: Thank you.

EPILOGUE

Often I wonder as I sit all alone,
Is there anything in life guaranteed?
I search for an answer or even a clue
That would satisfy my every need.
But through it all, I realize
There's so much to life than we see.
I'll sum it all up in one phrase:
I am truly blessed.

Yes, there are times when my road gets so long,
When I stumble alone, I stumble alone in the dark.
As I searched for the truth, see, it all became clear,
You see, the answer was not very far.
So I reached out my hand, and I called out His name,
And His spirit, His spirit filled me within
If I could sum it up in one phrase:
I am truly blessed.

I've been truly blessed.
There's nothing more precious than life.

I didn't realize at first, that it could have been worse.
I've been truly blessed.

Now that I know just what I must face
And I see exactly what life can put you through,
I go through life now with a smile on my face,
Because there's nothing, there's nothing, there's nothing
that I cannot do.
Now that I know that I'm not all alone,
He's there, and I know that He'll see me through.
I guess I'll sum it all up in one phrase:
I am truly blessed.

Just as sure as the sun lights up the days,
Just as sure as the moon lights up the night.
I've got me a light of my very own.
I know I've got to be strong, dealing with the situation,
I say it in my prayer and now I sing:
I've been truly blessed.
There's nothing more precious than life.
I want the world to see the light that shines in me.
                    — "Truly Blessed"

I had it. I lost it. I got it back.

Several years ago that could have been the title of this book, but
while it certainly rings true, it doesn't tell the whole story. Yes, I had
so much, and I lost so much. And although I haven't gotten all of it
back yet, I've discovered things about myself and about life I never
knew before.

When I began writing this book, it was the inspirational part of my
story I wanted to tell: the triumph over adversity. Growing up in

North Philadelphia, I'd learned to march through life with blinders on, always looking straight ahead, to the future. Whenever my collaborator tried to scratch below the surface of that, I stopped her. I didn't keep a diary, I protested. I couldn't tell anybody else in my situation how to cope; I wouldn't tell anybody who wasn't in my situation what it was like—any fool could figure it out. If pressed to explore my darker moments, I resisted, yet at the same time I could easily summon a low-burning rage *and* say I didn't want to show it to the world.

One afternoon, sitting behind the closed doors of my music room, weary of answering questions with words I didn't believe my collaborator was truly hearing, I ordered her to sit in a chair, close her eyes, and not move. And just imagine. When she truthfully replied that she couldn't, I snapped, "No, you can't do it!" then ran down the frustrations and indignities of my daily life. But I quickly added, "I don't think I need to tell the world that." Many months later, after we finished the manuscript, she told me she left my house that day crying. I admit I was rough on her that day, but I won't apologize for it. Words alone could never give her the understanding she needed to help me express what I wanted to say here.

It took a while before I could celebrate all that was good about my life without glossing over what was bad, though deep inside I knew that's what I wanted to express. Sometime after that unpleasant afternoon, the walls started coming down. It wasn't clean and neat, like an epiphany. The edges were ragged; it stopped and it started again. But finally I accepted that for me to change the way people look at disability and people who are physically challenged, I'd have to risk changing the way people looked at me. Framing my triumphs was a joy; hanging them on a wall of pain and loss was torture. And opening the door to that room—more than once, I seriously considered throwing away the key. But I didn't.

Come on in. Close the door.

———

God, grant me the serenity to accept the things I cannot change, the courage to change the things I can, and the wisdom to know the difference."

When I first heard the Serenity Prayer years ago, it struck a chord and has held a special meaning for me ever since. A copy of it sits on my desk. Patience and acceptance were never my strong suits, and I'll never be able to resist the challenge of changing everything that I can, and even some things I can't. And as for the all-important God-granted wisdom: I know He's always trying. That I don't always embrace it is my failing, not His.

From where I sit, "acceptance" is a word charged with meaning. The physically challenged hear a lot about learning to "accept" their circumstances, usually from well-meaning people who truly believe in what they're saying. Or, more likely, they can't handle the anger, depression, and pain that often keep our acceptance at bay. At the same time, we physically challenged people expend an incredible amount of energy trying to convince the rest of the world to "accept" us and to join us in building a society that allows us to live to our fullest potential. I've had plenty of time to think about why there's a wall between us, what it's made of, and how to tear it down.

While I live with my injury and have adapted to it, I will *never* fully accept it. Not an hour goes by without a reminder of how I used to be and what I used to do. I know that I will never fully accept the limitations my disability imposes on me or the demands it makes of me, *because fighting to overcome them is what keeps me alive.*

My personal struggles as a physically challenged person are inevitable and unavoidable. If the challenges of my situation began and ended with me, it would be one thing. But the real tragedy of disability lies in our society's outmoded, destructive ideas of what disability is and what constitutes an "acceptable" life for the physically challenged. The prevailing misconception is that physically challenged people are "different" and "rare." But think about it: The force that put me in this wheelchair didn't care who I was; it was an accident, something that happened to me. If you live long enough, you'll have to be extremely lucky not to experience some level of disability, from injury or illness, permanent or temporary.

We live in a world built by and for the able-bodied. It's heartening to see all the federally mandated access ramps and physical accommodations for the physically challenged, but they can't level the greatest barrier: the limitations society imposes out of ignorance. We all need to change the way we think about disability. My accident surely changed my life. But it didn't change who I am or what I want from life or what I need to feel good about myself. It changed only how I went about doing what I could do. It didn't dilute my ambition or dull my drive to succeed, and it was these things, along with the love and support of my family, that kept me from succumbing to hopelessness.

I am the same man, but I didn't have to look into too many faces before I saw how differently people saw me. When you're visibly physically challenged, you're subject to extremes in social responses. People either stare or deliberately avoid eye contact. They either treat you like you're totally helpless or carry on about how brave and strong you are. They often treat you like a child.

Worst of all is the presumption that because the physically challenged can't do *some* things, they can't do *any*thing. It's nice to applaud anyone's accomplishments, but when we make a big fuss over the physically challenged person who leads a "normal" life—say, by continuing a career, having a sexual relationship, going to school, raising children—what are we really saying? That he's so different from other people? That most physically challenged people don't want to lead productive, fulfilling lives? That this is a big deal because we don't expect anything from them? It reminds me of hearing people say that somebody is "smart for a black person." It's an ignorant, destructive prejudice.

Maybe you don't see legions of physically challenged people at your job, in your school, or on your streets. It isn't because they don't want to be there. All the physical accommodations in the world mean nothing if at the top of the ramp there isn't a place where you can make a contribution to society and be treated with the same respect as anyone else. When we're able-bodied, we take it on faith that productivity is a cornerstone of self-esteem. Is it such a leap to see that in the wake of disability, the need to be valued as an active participant in society is even greater?

The lack of opportunity to do meaningful, fulfilling work is the problem, not disability itself. We have the means to save the physically challenged from living their lives "warehoused" out of the mainstream. Now what we need is the will to put it to work. Like anyone else in my situation, I pray for a cure. But we can't put our lives and our dreams on hold waiting. That's why I recently formed the Teddy Pendergrass Education/Occupation Alliance for the Disabled, a national organization that helps people with spinal cord injury bridge the gap between potential and productivity. We serve as a conduit, making the resources of government, universities, and private industry more readily available to people who seek education, training, and employment. Learning new skills, setting new goals, and accomplishing things I never imagined I'd ever do are what keep my spirit alive. To feel and to be regarded by others as actively involved and productive is the best therapy in the world. I may be *dis*abled, but I'm not *un*abled.

I once heard a recently disabled friend say, "It gets better over time," and it's easy to feel that way in the first few years because it is better—better than being dead, better than being worse off than you are now. They say time heals, and it certainly does. But it also has the power to wound, and I've got the fresh scratches on the old scars to prove it. Still, you learn, you adapt, you move on. I can be euphoric in the presence of my grandchildren and would love to be able to swing them up on my shoulders. The fact that I cannot do that, however, doesn't ruin the moment for us. Children are brilliant; they come to this world blissfully ignorant of what's "normal" and what is not. Early on, my grandbabies figured out that if they wanted to get up there to kiss and hug me, they'd have to climb up there themselves. And they do. Nothing of the moment is lost, because it's all about what you get when you get there, not how you get there. I wish the rest of the world could be as wise.

I never fail to appreciate that every day I live in this wheelchair is a day I might easily never have seen. It's still a bitch, and it will probably always be a bitch, but I'm still here. I have learned to appreciate so much in life that I'd overlooked before. My life will always be filled with uncertainty, but I refuse to die. I have so much to live for.

I survived the depressions, the medical crises, the disappointments and hurts, but I didn't vanquish them. They'll be back. Before, I described living in a disabled body as being trapped in a carnival's haunted-house ride. I've been on it enough times now to have memorized the turns and dips, where the skeleton shakes and the werewolf howls. But the ride's still going and I'm still on it. Even God can't stop that. But I find faith in knowing that He didn't choose this path for me, and He is here beside me all the way.

So I *am* truly blessed. It may have taken me a few months to write the song, but the truth of it was written in my soul from the day I was born. I say it in my prayer, and I sing it. But most of all, I try to live it. There may be moments when I don't feel it, moments when I'm tempted to doubt it, but He has given me a heart that can never deny it. And among His many gifts, a light that shines in me and a way to see that the glass half empty is also the glass half full.

Again, and forever, I am truly blessed.

DISCOGRAPHY*

❧

SOLO

Teddy Pendergrass (Philadelphia International), 1977
"You Can't Hide from Yourself," "Somebody Told Me," "Be Sure,"
"And If I Had," "I Don't Love You Anymore," "The Whole Town's
Laughing at Me," "Easy, Easy, Got to Take It Easy," "The More I
Get, The More I Want"

Life Is a Song Worth Singing (Philadelphia International), 1978
"Life Is a Song Worth Singing," "Only You," "Cold, Cold World,"
"Get Up, Get Down, Get Funky, Get Loose," "Close the Door," "It
Don't Hurt Now," "When Somebody Loves You Back"

Teddy (Philadelphia International), 1979
"Come Go with Me," "Turn Off the Lights," "I'll Never See Heaven
Again," "All I Need Is You," "If You Know Like I Know," "Do Me,"
"Set Me Free," "Life Is a Circle"

★ This listing does not include foreign releases and early greatest-hits collections.

Teddy Live! Coast to Coast (Philadelphia International), 1979
"Life Is a Song Worth Singing," "Only You," Medley: "If You Don't Know Me by Now" / "The Love I Lost" / "Bad Luck" / "Wake Up Everybody," "When Somebody Loves You Back," "Get Up, Get Down, Get Funky, Get Loose," "Come Go with Me," "Close the Door," "Turn Off the Lights," "Do Me," "Where Did All the Lovin' Go," "It's You I Love," "Shout and Scream"

TP (Philadelphia International), 1980
"Is It Still Good to Ya," "Take Me in Your Arms Tonight" (with Stephanie Mills), "I Just Called to Say," "Can't We Try," "Feel the Fire" (with Stephanie Mills), "Girl You Know," "Love T.K.O.," "Let Me Love You"

It's Time for Love (Philadelphia International), 1981
"I Can't Leave Your Love Alone," "I Can't Live Without Your Love," "It's Time for Love," "Keep On Lovin' Me," "Nine Times Out of Ten," "She's Over Me," "You're My Latest, My Greatest Inspiration," "You Must Live On"

This One's for You (Philadelphia International), 1982
"This One's for You," "Don't Leave Me Out Along the Road," "I Can't Win for Losing," "It's Up to You (What You Do with Your Life)," "Loving You Was Good," "Now Tell Me That You Love Me," "Only to You," "This Gift of Life"

Heaven Only Knows (Philadelphia International), 1983
"Crazy About Your Love," "Judge for Yourself," "I Want My Baby Back," "Life Is for Living," "You and Me for Right Now," "Just Because You're Mine," "Heaven Only Knows," "Don't Ever Stop (Giving Your Love to Me)"

Love Language (Asylum), 1984
"In My Time," "So Sad the Song," "Hot Love," "Stay with Me,"

"Hold Me" (with Whitney Houston), "You're My Choice Tonight (Choose Me)," "Love," "This Time Is Ours"

Workin' It Back (Asylum), 1985
"Love 4/2," "One of Us Fell in Love," "Never Felt Like Dancin'," "Let Me Be Closer," "Lonely Color Blue," "Want You Back in My Life," "Workin' It Back," "Love Emergency"

Joy (Elektra), 1988
"Joy," "2 A.M.," "Good to You," "I'm Ready," "Love Is the Power," "This Is the Last Time," "Through the Falling Rain (Love Story)," "Can We Be Lovers"

Truly Blessed (Elektra), 1990
"She Knocks Me off My Feet," "It Should've Been You," "Don't You Ever Stop," "It's Over," "Glad to Be Alive" (with Lisa Fisher), "How Can You Mend a Broken Heart," "I Find Everything in You," "Spend the Night," "With You" (with Minnie Curry), "We Can't Keep Going On (Like This)," "Truly Blessed"

A Little More Magic (Elektra), 1993
"Believe in Love," "Slip Away," "I'm Always Thinking About You," "I Choose You," "Voodoo," "Tender," "Can't Help Nobody" (with Patti LaBelle), "A Little More Magic," "My Father's Child," "Say It," "No One Like You," "Reprise"

You and I (Surefire), 1997
"Don't Keep Wastin' My Time," "Let's Talk About It," "Without You," "You and I," "Can We Try," "One in a Million You," "Hurry Up," "Interlude," "Give It to Me," "Slow Ride to Heaven"

Greatest Hits (Philadelphia International), 1998
"I Don't Love You Anymore," "The Whole Town's Laughing at Me,"

"And If I Had," "The More I Get, The More I Want," "Close the Door," "Only You," "When Somebody Loves You Back," "Life Is a Song Worth Singing," "Turn Off the Lights," "Come Go with Me," "Shout and Scream," "Can't We Try," "Love T.K.O.," "Joy," "It Should've Been You"

WITH HAROLD MELVIN AND THE BLUE NOTES

Harold Melvin & the Blue Notes (Philadelphia International), 1972
"I Miss You (Part 1)," "Ebony Woman," "Yesterday I Had the Blues," "If You Don't Know Me by Now," "Be for Real," "Let Me Into Your World," "Let It Be You"

Black & Blue (Philadelphia International), 1973
"Cabaret," "The Love I Lost," "It All Depends on You," "Concentrate on Me," "Satisfaction Guaranteed (Or Take Your Love Back)," "Is There a Place for Me," "I'm Weak for You," "I'm Comin' Home To-morrow"

AS HAROLD MELVIN AND THE BLUE NOTES
FEATURING THEODORE PENDERGRASS

To Be True (Philadelphia International), 1975
"Where Are All My Friends," "To Be True," "Pretty Flower," "Hope That We Can Be Together Soon" (with Sharon Paige), "Nobody Could Take Your Place," "Somewhere Down the Line," "Bad Luck (Part 1)," "It's All Because of a Woman"

Wake Up Everybody (Philadelphia International), 1975
"Wake Up Everybody (Part 1)," "Keep On Lovin' You," "You Know How to Make Me Feel So Good," "Don't Leave Me This Way," "Tell the World How I Feel About 'Cha Baby," "To Be Free to Be Who We Are," "I'm Searching for a Love"

All Their Greatest Hits! (Philadelphia International), 1976
"The Love I Lost," "Bad Luck (Part 1)," "If You Don't Know Me by
Now," "Be for Real," "Wake Up Everybody (Part 1)," "Hope That
We Can Be Together Soon" (with Sharon Paige)," "Where Are All
My Friends," "I Miss You (Part 1)"